Turn Your Kitchen into a Gold Mine

Turn Your Kitchen into a GOLD MINE

Alice and Alfred Howard

Stellar Books

**Distributed by
Harper & Row, Publishers
New York**

Our love and thanks to our son,
Henry Lovett Howard, who assisted
in the preparation of this book.
His appreciation of women's
capabilities and his belief that
anything is possible, made the
writing of this book a joyous
experience.

"Stellar Books" is a division of Pantry Press, Inc.

ISBN 0-938542-00-1

81 82 83 84 85 10 9 8 7 6 5 4 3 2 1

Contents

Contents

v

CHAPTER 2

Earn Up to $19,500 a Year Selling
Six-Foot Party Sandwiches   19

The Original Six-Foot Party Sandwich • How to Get Started in
the Catering Business   •   How One Italian Grocery Store Is
Cashing In on This Product • How to Turn Your Kitchen Into
an Italian Grocery Store • What Do I Charge? • Is It a Good
Buy for the Hostess? • Is It Profitable for Me? • How Do I Get
Customers? • Advertising • Find a Willing Copywriter • What
Makes a Good Ad?   •   Chapter Summary

CHAPTER 3

Earn Up to $14,144 a Year Selling
Roast Turkey and All the Trimmings   31

One Thirty-Pound Turkey with Stuffing, Cranberry Sauce,
and Sweet Potatoes to Go, Please! • What to Charge • One
Stop Does It All • Where to Get Supplies • Why People Will
Order Turkey In • Economical for All Your Customers • Will
the Profits Add Up?   •   How to Expand Your Business
• Chapter Summary

CHAPTER 4

Earn More Than $23,000 a Year Selling
Delicious Homemade Baked Beans   39

The Miraculous Comeback of Baked Beans • Can You Make
'Em the Way They Used To?   •   The Secret of Captain Ken's
Firehouse Baked Beans • Start Small, Think Big! • Follow
These Steps • How to Get a Sales Force Without Hiring One
• How to Expand • How to Get People to Remember Your
Product   •   Remember to Personalize It   •   A Good Lawyer
Can Be Indispensable • What to Charge • Never Be Intimi-
dated • When Your Costs Go Up, Your Prices Should Go Up
• Chapter Summary

CHAPTER 5

Earn $12,500 a Year Selling
Hearty, Homemade Sausages   51

Sausages—the Old-Fashioned Kind People Really Love!
• Learn From the Success of John Slovacek • How to Make
Kielbasa • How to Make Swedish Potato Sausages • How to
Make Mildly Hot Italian Sausages   • How to Make French
Breakfast Sausages the Way French Farmers Make Them
• Why Sausages Are a No-Competition Item • An Amazing
Book About the Secrets of Sausage Making • Advertising Copy
That Gets People to Buy   • Chapter Summary

CHAPTER 6

Earn $25,000 a Year Catering
Low-Fat, Low-Salt, Low-Sugar
Gourmet Meals   61

How to Make Money and Help Save Lives Too • A Billion-
Dollar Market That Restaurants Are Neglecting • How to
Cash In on This Market Without Opening a Restaurant • The
Secret Is in Catering Low-Fat, Low-Sugar, Low-Salt Meals
• How to Make Special Tomato Garden Soup • How to Make
Special Split Pea Soup • How to Make Special Hot or Cold
Watercress Soup • How to Make Special Apple-Glazed Cornish
Hens • How to Make Special Old-Fashioned Sauerbraten
• How to Make Exotic Stuffed Roast Chicken • How to Make
Special Baked Turkey Hash • How to Make a Delicious, Low-
Calorie Ratatouille • How to Make a No-Salt, No-Sugar Chick
Pea Salad • How to Make a Tasty Low-Calorie Cole
Slaw • How to Bake Low-Salt, Surprise Cookies • Chapter
Summary

CHAPTER 7

Earn Hundreds of Dollars a Week
Selling Jams and Preserves
Through the Mail   73

Hundreds of Dollars Every Week in Your Mailbox! • Every-body Has a Sweet Tooth • The $78,000 Mail Order Product • What Sells Through the Mails? • Don't Be Afraid of Competition • Make the Best Jam Anyone's Ever Tasted • How to Make Lifelong Friends Through the Mail • The Most Important Person You'll Need to Know • How to Pack Your Product for Shipping • The Best Times of the Year to Make Money • Using Mail Order to Cash In on the New Shopping Trend • Who Your Best Customers Are • The Secret of Reaching People • Renting Mailing Lists • How to Avoid Mistakes • Advertising • Testing Is the Key to Success • Compare Costs • That All-Important Message • Don't Go Overboard! • Telling Your Story in a Classified Ad • A Word About the Crocks • Getting Your Mail Out on Time • Your Address vs. a Post Office Box Number: Which Is Best? • How the Space Sales-person Can Help You • Lobsters by Mail • Remember the Packaging • 1949 Prices vs. Today (Read 'Em and Weep) • Others Who Have Discovered the Secret to Mail Order Success • Chapter Summary

CHAPTER 8

Earn $14,000 a Year Selling
Delicious "Nut House" Brownies   101

Jobless and Widowed, with 3 Children to Care For • Susan Grant Comes Up with a Winner! • Putting Pride Aside • An Encounter with a Potential Customer • The Phone Call That Changed Katherine's Life • How the Name "Nut House" Brownies Was Born • Getting Down to Business • Katherine Was Smart Enough to Be Honest • How Katherine Earned $162 a Week—Just from One Store • Katherine Thought She Could Double Her Money • A Word of Caution • How Kather-ine Was Able to Expand Her Baking Capacity • The Real Se-

Foolproof Way of Selling Soups That People Really Want
• Breads—The Amazing Extra Money Maker You Shouldn't
Pass Up • Favorite Breads People Love to Sink Their Teeth
Into • How to Expand Your Menu So You Can Expand Your
Profits • What to Charge • Whom to Hire • A Day in the Life of
a Soup Kitchen • What It Takes to Become Successful • The
Secret to Hiring Dedicated Employees • The Two Profession-
als You Must Seek Out for Advice • Your Overall Expenses
• The All-Important First 30 Days • A Review of Your Total
Investment • $50,000—Your Take-Home Pay!

CHAPTER 11

Everything You've Always Wanted to Know
About Cooking . . . But Were Afraid to Ask   153

Where to Get Cookbooks for Free • Learning About Other
Cookbooks for Just $1 • Where to Get the Finest Gourmet
Recipes for the Price of a Self-Addressed Envelope • An Amaz-
ing List Of Gourmet Cooking Schools Throughout the Country

CHAPTER 12

Want to Earn $10,000 a Week?
Meet a Woman Who Really Did   223

The Most Amazing Kitchen Lady Success Story We've Ever
Heard • Imagine—$75,000 Earned in Her First Six Weeks of
Business • A Husband Walking Out on You Doesn't Mean the
End of the World • How Nadine Got the Idea to Go Into Busi-
ness • How to Create the Perfect Atmosphere • What to Make
and What to Charge • Sometimes You Have to Make a Person-
al Sacrifice • People Will Pay $13.75 a Pound for Gourmet
Food • Nadine Was in Such Demand That They Sent for Her
by Private Plane • The Two Factors for Success in a Gourmet
Take-Out Store

CHAPTER 13

How Good Will You Be in Business?
Test Yourself!   229

How Well Do You Know Yourself? • Getting to Know Yourself
• Who Are You? • Why Do You Want to Go Into Business?
• What Makes You Think You Can Succeed? • When Did You
Decide to Go Into Business? • Report Card Time • Are You a
Self-Starter? • How Do You Feel About Other People? • Can
You Lead Others? • Can You Take Responsibility? • How
Good an Organizer Are You? • How Good a Worker Are You?
• Can You Make Decisions? • Can People Trust What You
Say? Can You Stick With It? • How Good Is Your Health?
• Score Your Answers Honestly • Don't Be Discouraged—Just
Make Improvements

CHAPTER 14

The U.S. Government
Will Help You Financially—
Here's How to Get Your Share   237

Women and the U.S. Small Business Administration • Publications • Business Loan Programs • Venture Capital • Disaster
Loans • Management Assistance • Pre-Business Workshops
• Minority Small Business and Capital Ownership Development Program • Advocacy • National Women's Business Ownership Campaign • How to Apply for a Loan • Wherever You
Live, There's a Small Business Administration Office There to
Help You • Small Marketers' Aids • Small Business Bibliogra-
phies • Free Management Assistance Publications

CHAPTER 15

Need Money From Banks?
Here's How to Talk a Banker's Language   255

Why You Should Never Walk In Off the Street to Open a
Bank Account • If You Can't Deal with the Manager, Don't
Deal with the Bank at All • Banking Terms You Should Know
• Why You Shouldn't Open an Account with a Big Bank • How
to Get Banks to Trust You • Study These Banking Questions
and You'll Get the Loan You Need   •   Is Your Firm Credit-
Worthy? • What Kind of Money: Short Term? Term? Equity
Capital? • How Much Money? • What Kind of Collateral?
• What Are the Lender's Rules? • What Kind of Limitations?
•   Never Be Intimidated!

CHAPTER 16

Now That You're in Business, Learn How to
Be Your Own Bookkeeper   269

You're Already Better Trained to Be a Bookkeeper Than You
Realize! • The Very First Thing You'll Need to Go Into Busi-
ness • Who Keeps the Books? • The Secret to Preparing a
Financial Statement • Drawing the Picture • Small Business
Financial Status Review—How to Account for Every Penny,
Every Month!

CHAPTER 17

Preparing Yourself for That Day—
April 15: Income Tax Time   277

April 15—Income Tax Day • No Set Records Required • A
Simple System • Checkbook • Cash Receipts Journal • Cash
Disbursements Journal • Petty Cash Fund • Other Records
You Will Need • What to Do if You Become a Corporation or
Form a Partnership • Retaining Records • Plan with Records
•   Outside Help

Introduction

We're living in difficult times. Skyrocketing inflation is forcing many housewives to look for ways to bring in a second income because their husband's salary is no longer enough. In addition, more women are getting divorced than ever before, and *they* are in desperate need of a *first* income.

Most housewives find it very difficult to get a job. After years at home raising a family, they have rusty job skills and most employers prefer young women who are fresh out of business and secretarial schools.

What are these housewives supposed to do? We've heard and read about a *growing number* of them who are successfully selling food specialties that they prepare in their own kitchen! There's one woman in California who's selling and delivering roasted turkeys with all the trimmings. These catered meals are being bought year round for "Sunday dinners" by working mothers who have neither the time nor the talent to prepare turkeys the old-fashioned way.

Another woman, working out of a tiny kitchen in her New York City apartment, is baking as many chocolate brownies as she can and selling them to gourmet food stores.

And there are many other women, some of whom are selling cheesecakes to fine family restaurants and other housewives who are selling jams and preserves nationwide through the mail.

The success of these women and many others like them should put to rest forever the idea that *women who have no job skills have no future.* Quite to the contrary, women who have acquired their skills in the kitchen, patiently and slowly over the years, can now use their knowledge to make more money than they ever dreamed possible.

We wondered if there was a name we could give to this group of enterprising women. We wanted to write about them, and we wanted to dignify their effort by giving them a collective name. We created one: THE KITCHEN LADIES OF AMERICA.

Kitchen Ladies are special people. The outside job market was closed off to them, so they started one of their own. They learned from scratch what it takes to get a business off the ground. They learned how to get help from the government, and how to get loans from banks. They learned how to "keep the books" day by day, and how to show a profit at the end of the year.

The more we discovered about what they were doing, the more we became convinced that this was an untapped gold mine. Countless women across the country would benefit greatly if they, too, could become Kitchen Ladies. So we decided to publish a book that would teach women how to do just that.

We urge you to read this book carefully, from cover to cover. We don't mean to compare our book with the greatest book ever written—the Bible—but like the Bible, the more you study it, the richer you'll become.

In our book, we've spelled out ten different ways for you to make money; each of them can start right from your own kitchen. Feel free to use any one of them. Or, after reading this book, make your own list of food specialties that you've won praise for over the years. Only *you* know what you do best in the kitchen; but in this book we tell you how to make it pay off.

The truth of the matter is, you've probably been a Kitchen Lady all your life. The only difference is that now you're going to get paid for it.

May 1, 1981

Chapter 1

How to Earn Up to $16,000 a Year Selling Monster-Size Chocolate Chip Cookies

Cash In on the Cookie Craze

The Commerce Department estimated that cookie-craving Americans will buy *$6 billion* worth of the goodies annually by 1985. America is going crazy over cookies. In metropolitan areas, it's the #1 impulse purchase. Stores are opening up that sell *only* cookies and they can't stock them fast enough. Cookies were always considered "kid stuff," but not anymore. Millions of adults seem to want to return to the sweet, buttery treat of their childhoods, and enterprising bakers are meeting their needs.

1

The Original Toll House Cookie

The woman who is credited with creating the original chocolate chip cookie didn't even call it that. Back in the early
1930s, Ruth Wakefield owned The Toll House restaurant in
Massachusetts. She featured extremely good American dishes
such as lobster, fish, and the traditional specialties of New England. Her restaurant was praised by food critics and people
traveling in New England.

It seems that about that time, chocolate chips first came
out. Ruth, who was a very creative cook, played around with
them and originated the Toll House cookie, with a goodly
amount of chocolate bits, enhanced by nuts and sometimes
raisins.

The cookie was an instant success in the restaurant. In fact,
it gained such a following that within a few years, Ruth sold
the rights and the name to the company that had introduced
the chocolate bits. The popularity of the cookie grew steadily;
finally it was put out as a mix with chocolate chips.

Famous Amos

Then about six years ago, a man in southern California had
the bright idea of merchandising the "Famous Amos Chocolate Chip Cookie," from which he made a fortune—far more
than Ruth Wakefield ever got from her invention. Famous
Amos inspired others to get into this cookie business, and now
you'll find chocolate chip (other flavors as well) cookie shops
everywhere—in shopping malls and in downtown areas as well.

How <u>You</u> Can Get Started

We *don't* want you to go out and open up a store! Absolutely
not. It's too big an investment; you would have to make long-
term commitments such as rent, utilities, phones, etc. Then
you have to pray that the store has enough pedestrian traffic

going by, and, even if it does, you have to hope that it will stay that way. You often see a shopping mall lose out in popularity to another one that opens up only a few miles away. On top of that, you always have to worry about the *gasoline problem.* The price of gasoline seems to go only one way: *up!* There's clear evidence that people are using their cars *less* and that means retail stores everywhere are likely to suffer.

The Secret to Success: Cookies-on-Wheels

Go where the people are! Take the cookies to them! *Cookies-on-Wheels!* It's amazingly profitable. And *you* don't have to go out and sell the cookies. You can hire a youngster to do it. (We'll get into all the details in a short while.)

Give the People Something Different

But before you can even think of baking and selling cookies for profit you have to decide that you are a good enough baker. Throughout the book, we're going to give you many lucrative ideas on how to profit by becoming a Kitchen Lady, but *you*—and only you—can decide on which specialty to make and sell. You have to be happy with your choice. Right now, ask yourself if you have that certain "touch" when it comes to baking. It's no big mystery to bake delicious chocolate chip— and other—cookies, but you have to *want* to! We only suggest, *you* have to decide. Whatever specialty you decide to go into business with, it must have that "something extra" in order to become a really big success. With a chocolate chip cookie, there can't be any question that the ones you bake taste better than ones which can be bought in the supermarket.

People Love Monster-Size Cookies

The cookies we want you to bake will be much bigger than the commercial type. We want you to bake cookies that are *five inches* round. That's right. Monster-size cookies, bigger than anything that can be bought in a supermarket. We want you to experiment with different flavors: chocolate chip, oatmeal raisin, peanut butter chip, butterscotch chip, and others. We'll give you a recipe for five-inch cookies sent in by a Long Island housewife. Feel free to use this one, or come up with your own recipe, one that has *your* personal touch. If you're a "newcomer" to baking and want to experiment, there are lots of choices. There are enough "commercial" recipes already printed in cookbooks and on packages containing chocolate bits for you to get started with. On top of that, we ask you to let your imagination take over. Bake a dozen or so five-inch-round cookies of different types, and let family and friends be the judge. You'll know when you have one or two winners. Here's the recipe (and what it costs) plus directions on baking nine five-inch cookies. Always remember: cost of ingredients will vary in different parts of the country *and* will increase with inflation.

Monster-Size Chocolate Chip Cookies

The ingredients and what they cost. The time: April, 1981; the place: New York City.

1 cup flour	.10
½ teaspoon baking soda	.01
½ teaspoon salt	.01
½ cup margarine (1 stick)	.12
¾ cup sugar (brown and white combined)	.10
½ teaspoon vanilla extract	.03
1 egg	.07
6 ounces semi-sweet chocolate bits	1.29
	$1.73

Preheat oven to 375 degrees. In a small bowl, combine flour, soda, and salt and set aside. In a larger bowl, cream margarine and add sugar and vanilla. Beat in the egg. Gradually add flour mixture. Mix well. Stir in chocolate bits. Use two table-spoons of batter (or an ice cream scoop full) and place the batter on an ungreased cookie sheet. Use a large cookie sheet that will hold 6 large cookies. Be sure to lightly flatten the batter so it spreads evenly, and leave about 3 inches between the cookies. Use one cookie sheet at a time. Bake for about 10 minutes or until lightly browned. Makes nine 5-inch cookies.

You will be selling these cookies direct to customers for *60¢* each. How many you should expect to bake each week and the precise method of selling will be discussed shortly.

Where to Find Your Customers

As we've said, cookie stores have already become successful in shopping malls. For the reasons outlined, however, we don't want you to get involved with that expensive and uncertain future of being a cookie store owner. Instead, make your delicious cookies available to people at bustling street corners near department stores and office buildings and by shopping centers. What you're doing is simply becoming a street vendor; you're bringing your products to *where the people are.* (And as we've said previously, you don't have to be there; you'll be hiring young people to do it.)

How to Bring Your Cookies to Them

There is a company in New York City that, for *$20,000,* will sell you a small, motorized, antique-looking car. The car attractively holds hundreds of cookies, and you simply drive to a busy street corner, park, and you're in business. But $20,000 is a lot of cash to come up with to go into the cookie business! Do you know how many cookies you would have to sell to make back the $20,000? TOO MANY! We'll show you how to get into business for a *fraction* of that cost—$400, $500, tops! And if you don't have even that much to spend, you could put cookies-on-wheels for less than $100!

How Much to Charge

First, let's discuss how much Kitchen Ladies are charging for their five-inch cookies and how much it's costing them to bake them. We're all in this business to make a profit. Whether it's going to be cookies or any of the other ideas we give you—or an idea *you* have that you've always wanted to go into business with—you must make an *excellent* profit. There's no point to it otherwise!

To arrive at what each cookie costs you, bake five-inch cookies, adding up the cost of *all the ingredients*. Leave nothing out. Add up the costs of whatever ingredients you are using. Once you know the price of the "whole," then you figure out the cost of the "part" you're using. For example, if a dozen eggs cost 84¢, then one egg costs 7¢ (84¢ divided by 12). Do the same when you buy a 5-pound bag of sugar. Estimate how many ounces you use at any given time and determine the cost of that "portion" based on the price of the "whole" (5-pound bag). The recipe we gave you produced *nine 5″* cookies. One of your own recipes might produce more or less. Experience in baking these will guide you on the size of your recipe. And of course, to arrive at the cost of each cookie, divide the cost of your recipe by the number of cookies produced. We came out to *20¢* per 5″ cookie. You should come out close to that.

If it costs you 20¢, we suggest you charge *60¢* per cookie. That's *triple* your cost, and that's a decent markup. You don't often get such high markups, but you can when the item will be cookies. That's because you're selling a *high-volume*, low-cost item, and you're selling retail (direct to consumers). This won't always be the case. Some specialty items we will be recommending *won't* be a high-volume item; in other instances, you'll be selling mostly to stores and restaurants (wholesale). But we will deal with each situation separately, and we'll go over all costs carefully and discuss our reasons for all suggested selling prices. On all of them, you can be sure that you'll be making a fine profit. After all, that's what you're going into this business for. Your job is to make sure that the specialty you decide to go into business with is truly *delicious;* we'll make sure you'll make money with it.

How to Make More Profit

The way to keep your profits up is to keep your costs *down.* Two very important words in this business: SHOP AROUND! Yes, shop the various supermarkets and look for the best buys, keep an eye out for the "specials," on flour, or sugar, on *whatever* ingredients you're using. The less you pay to bake, the more profit you'll make! Also, as you start to *increase* your baking capacity, the cost per cookie will drop. (This will be discussed shortly.)

How Your Children Can Cash In on This

You'll be doing the baking. Who's going to go out and do the selling? Most Kitchen Ladies hire youngsters at a commission of 10¢ a cookie. That's your *selling* expense. So, the baking cost per cookie at the beginning is 20¢, the selling expense is 10¢, you're selling each cookie for 60¢, so your profit is 30¢. If you have one or two youngsters in your family (they should be at least 16 years old), then they might go out and sell for you. Why not keep the money in the family?

We want to refer once more to the New York cookie company. Some of the youngsters they hire are selling 400 cookies a day. At 10¢ commission each, they are pocketing—on the average—$40.00 a day; working five days a week, they are grossing $200. Not bad at all.

The More You Bake, the More You'll Make

We *fully realize* that since you're getting into this business by working out of your own kitchen, you can hardly be expected to bake 400 five-inch round cookies each day. What we want you to do is to start each day and bake as many as you can and build up your inventory for sale on the weekend. What we all know is that these cookies have an excellent "shelf life"; that is, they stay fresh four to six weeks. You don't have to hold them for that long, but consider the idea of baking up a batch during the week and selling them on the weekend. Here's the story of the way one Kitchen Lady started out, and how she multiplied her profits very quickly.

Profit from the Success of Corinne Taylor

Corinne Taylor is divorced and has two kids. Michael is 18, Kim is 17. She's always been an excellent baker—like many of us, her brownies, cookies, and pies have won praise from friends and family alike. Like all of us who needed the extra money, she started out her Kitchen Lady career by trying to bake and sell the cookies we've discussed in this chapter. She bakes a terrific chocolate chip cookie and an equally delicious peanut butter/oatmeal cookie. Each is five inches round, as we've suggested, and sells for 60¢. She's developed to the point where she's selling 800 cookies a week at a profit of 40¢ per cookie—that's *$320 a week!*

For the first few months, she set a goal of baking 100 cookies per day, five days a week. She baked Monday through Friday, and on Saturday, Michael and Kim sold all 500 just at one location. This happened to be the entrance to a park close to their home. Corinne estimates her baking cost per giant cookie to be 20¢, so she is making 40¢ per cookie. The children know that the money is really *needed* at home, so they don't ask for any of it.

In those early months, Corinne was making a 40¢-per-cookie profit on 500 cookies a week, for a total of $200. The markup in that situation was as suggested—*triple!* There were some car expenses but they were minimal, as the family only drove three miles to reach the park entrance where they sold their cookies. Still, Corinne added up these gas and oil expenses at the end of the week, and deducted that from her gross profit in order to arrive at her net profit. (There will be a special chapter on bookkeeping that will teach you how to "keep the books" on your business.)

It should be mentioned that turning out 100 cookies each day, from Monday through Friday, was work; there's no denying that. And Corinne did have a double oven in her house, which was vital. Still, she estimated that the five to six hours she spent each day in the kitchen to bake the cookies were far better than an eight-hour day she would have to spend at some downtown office. Then she would also have to fight the commuter traffic back and forth each day. There's none of that when you work at home!

After a few months of turning out 100 cookies a day, or 500 over five days, she was looking for a way to increase her baking capacity. She asked her neighbor, who went to business every day, if *her* double oven could be used as well for the same purpose. Corinne knew what her utility bills were running, and she assured her neighbor that she would gladly pay the increased cost of her bill. Corinne also promised that she and Kim would make her neighbor's kitchen spotless after each day's use. The neighbor was pleased to give Corinne the use of her kitchen. Now that there were two double ovens to work with, Corinne became determined to nearly double her baking capacity. She did it in the following way.

Working with two double ovens, Corinne and Kim were able to bake two hundred cookies per day. They did that for four days, Monday through Thursday. Kim and Michael then were able to sell the 800 cookies on Friday and Saturday of each week. They sold the first batch of 400 at a busy downtown corner each Friday; they sold the second batch of 400 on Saturday, at a nearby park where thousands of adults and youngsters would come on a typical weekend afternoon. Corinne was operating on the same profit per cookie. It cost about 20¢ to bake each one, and it was sold for 60¢; with Michael and Kim refusing to take any commission, that left a neat 40¢ per cookie profit. That times 800 cookies for the week meant an income of $320. They're now in the business of doing this fifty weeks a year. That adds up to an income of $16,000. And they're even having *fun* doing it!

Make Your Product Appealing!

We want to spell out some tricks of the trade which are very important for you to follow in order to succeed at this "street vendor" game. The first thing to realize is that it's nothing to be ashamed of. Some folks, when they first start selling, feel that street vendors are not very respectable people. Nonsense! There are all kinds, just as there are all kinds of retail shops. You've seen both beautiful shops and stores so awful-looking that there's no way you would ever walk into them. It's the same with street vending. You must make certain that your cookie stand looks appealing and appetizing. Remember: you're selling something people *eat,* so it's very important that the "atmosphere" surrounding your cookies have real appeal. We'll tell you what steps to take.

The easiest thing in the world would be to spend the $20,000 we've mentioned before so you could buy one of those small "Cookie Cars." They are very attractive-looking of course, but who wants to invest that kind of money? You have a lot of alternatives available to you. One way is to invest in a beat-up jalopy. Check some of the used car dealers in your area. They have more cars on hand than they know what to do with. Perhaps for a few hundred dollars they'd sell you an old car that could be spruced up and made to look absolutely adorable. It's amazing what a little imagination can do. A new paint job, perhaps a bright firehouse red. Put some cute cafe curtains on the windows; add coach lights, one on each side of the car. Perhaps a tiny vase on the outside that would hold some artificial flowers. See if you can find such a jalopy, *cheap,* and see if you can get someone—in your family or among friends—to find one of those quaint, old-fashioned horns that have that special "AARRRUUUUGGHA" sound. Why not? Always have a "trademark" to your business whenever you can. Let the people *know* you're coming. Since you'll be baking delicious cookies, folks will really have something to look forward to.

The Cookie Monster

We have several names for you to consider. Remember in any business it's important to know how to *merchandise* your wares. Everyone has to have a flair for this in order to succeed. Whether you're SEARS, REVLON, or just plain "Mary Jones," you have to create an atmosphere for your product. If you can put together a spruced-up jalopy, why not call it *The Cookie Monster?* Yes, have that painted right on the car, in an old-fashioned lettering style. What about rich blue lettering with a gold outline. Fill up that funny little Tin Lizzie with delicious chocolate chip cookies and drive it down the block with its horn cranking out, "ARRRUGGGGGHA, ARRRUGGGHA," and you'll draw more customers than you can handle.

If you cannot afford even *this* investment to get into business, don't despair. You can still succeed. Use your own car just for transportation to the selling site, and then be prepared to set up an attractive "booth" right at that location. This could be a table or a booth with your cookies set out attractively under lucite covers to protect your product. Have the table or booth covered in an attractive chocolate-brown cloth, used either as a tablecloth (for the table) or pinned up over the booth.

What About a Name?

We have a wonderful and memorable name for you to consider. What you're selling are *big* cookies. We'd like to suggest that you call them "Frisbees." The entire name which should be clearly seen on your booth or table is, *"Original Chocolate Chip Frisbees."* Believe us, this has terrific appeal. Always use your own name—we offer "Emma Fairchild" as an example—and follow that with "the Original Chocolate Chip Frisbees." The word "Original" has that nice old-fashioned feeling to it, and we believe that *we* invented the idea of associating the well-known term "Frisbee" with jumbo-sized chocolate chip cookies. Since folks love to eat cookies, they'll flip over the idea of eating these chocolate chip *Frisbees.* It's simply a merchandising twist that we are pleased to pass along to you. Everyone knows what Frisbees are. Now you can be the first one in your own area to introduce "Chocolate Chip Frisbees." We are only suggesting this name to women who want to become Kitchen Ladies and want to sell cookies in particular. But please understand, if someone else comes along before you do and calls her cookies "Frisbees," we can't stop her. So, if you like the name, get moving and be the first Kitchen Lady in your area to use it. You could also use *The Cookie Monster* as an overall name and not use the Frisbee expression. You have those and other options: *Emma's Chocolate Chip Flying Saucers* is another possibility. You decide.

Learn from the Success of McDonald's

There is one more merchandising appeal that we want you to associate with your product: a *uniform* for your salesman (or salesgirl). You have a special product; it's important that the person selling your product look special as well. An inexpensive uniform is all that it takes. Look at the youngsters who work at McDonald's. Each must wear a uniform provided by the company. A uniform provides an *"identity,"* and customers like to see that. People want to *trust* what they are buying. Something as simple as having the salesman (salesgirl) in a uniform adds that dimension of trust. You wouldn't like it if a fellow was serving you food and he was dressed in shabby street clothes. Somehow you wouldn't trust him, and that would affect your opinion of the food being served.

Call a few *Uniform Supply* houses; you can find several in the Yellow Pages of your phone book. It's not expensive to have two or three uniforms: three sets of cap, jacket, and pants, each in a size that can be worn by the average teenager (boy or girl). Ask someone to stitch on the uniform the name of your product, i.e., *"Emma's Original Chocolate Chip Frisbee."* You will now have a *total* package: the display booth or table, the youngster selling, and the jumbo-sized cookies—all with that "merchandising" touch designed to enhance the sale of your product. That means more profit for you, and that, naturally, is what you are striving for.

Keep an Eye on Your Costs

Always remember what it's costing you to do business. In addition to the cost of the ingredients you'll need to bake five-inch cookies, there is the cost of your "point of sale." That includes the booth or table you might be setting up. Also, the cost of any artwork or signs that would go on display must be considered. There's the cost of uniforms and having them cleaned every few days. (They must always look spotless.) Every penny you spend must be written down in order to know how much is going out and how much is coming in.

How to Expand

The more jumbo cookies you can bake, the more you could sell. You might currently have only a single oven and not be able to use a neighbor's oven. As a result, your output would be curtailed. If you can only bake a few hundred cookies a week and you want to work that up to a thousand or more a week, you need to consider *leasing* an existing commercial oven. We're not suggesting that you go out and rent store space and then buy a large commercial oven to bake your cookies. (But, mind you, your business might grow to such an extent that it would be very profitable for you to get to that point.) Since the cookie business is a *$6 billion* annual business, it stands to reason that your own delicious cookies can enjoy a small but rewarding share of the market.

Look at it this way: if you were able to use, in another location, a commercial oven and turn out 3,000 large cookies a week, you could well reduce your per-cookie cost to about 12¢. You would thus have a profit of 48¢ to the retail cost of 60¢. Forty-eight cents a cookie times 3,000 cookies comes to $1,440.00 per week. Even deduct 10¢ a cookie as commission if you're using a youngster (or two). That's a deduction of $300, which leaves you with $1,140.00. Say you are leasing a commercial oven at a cost of $100 a week; that leaves you with a net profit of $1,040.00 a week. Even if you hire a part-time baker to "moonlight" for you and work to help you out, you'd still come out way ahead. You might pay the baker $200 a week to work the extra shifts you would need to produce a bigger volume. Deduct that $200 and you still have a profit of $840.00 a *week*. Turning out that volume every week is a big job, of course, but it can be done. Suppose you made $840.00 a week and chose *not* to do this all year round. Let's say you did this work only forty weeks a year, allowing a twelve-week consecutive period away from the baking. All you need to do is to multiply $840.00 a week times forty weeks and you get a total of $33,600.00. Even throw in an energy cost you didn't figure on; as high as $100 a week for the forty weeks—that's an extra $4,000.00 in expenses. You'd still clear *$29,600.00!*

Where can you find a commercial oven to lease if you want to produce the bigger volume? There are several places to look. The first thing to do is to look in the Yellow Pages of your phone book under "Restaurant Supplies." Call as *many* of these companies as there are listed. Tell them you want to lease an oven. Whom would they suggest you call? They would know, because they sell their equipment to various establishments. Among these might be: (1) a local cooking school. They might be delighted to have the extra income of renting their oven to you when their classes are not in session; (b) restaurants. Many will often rent oven space at early morning hours before they open; (c) schools, camps, and resort kitchens that would be available to you during the months they are closed.

When your baking business grows to the point when you really need to set up your *own* commercial kitchen, then the first person to contact is a real estate agent in your area. He or she may know of an existing kitchen, the owners of which went out of business for one reason or another. You could take over that lease on a very favorable basis. If the real estate agent has no existing space of that kind, then look at empty space, but be sure it is zoned for manufacture. You'll also need a license, but that is only a routine matter to acquire. Simply keep clean work habits and you'll meet the standards of the health authorities.

It's all a matter of how much you want to grow, and how capable you are of meeting that growth. Having the desire to make money is one thing. Being able to fulfill promises is another thing entirely. The jumbo-sized cookie business is a proven money-maker. If you can bake 'em, we're giving you the know-how to sell them. You'll make a fine profit, and this cookie business will never fall apart. People will never lose their craving for sweets, and cookies are a simple way to cash in on this business. As we will tell you throughout this book, growing takes time. Don't rush it.

Chapter Summary

At the end of certain chapters, we will highlight their features. This will help you remember some of the key points.

1. Experiment with various chocolate chip cookie recipes. Bake the five-inch-round cookies and give samples to family and friends. All have to agree that they are superior to any cookie sold in supermarkets. Though chocolate chip cookies

are the most preferred, bake other types as well. Oatmeal/raisin, peanut butter, butterscotch chip, etc., are also popular choices.

2. Charge 60¢ a cookie. This selling price should be about three times your costs of baking them. But remember this: your costs can only *increase,* so be sure to raise *your* price. Who knows where prices are heading? You might soon have to charge *75¢* for a five-inch cookie. *Even $1, or more!*

3. It's important that everything have eye appeal to your customers. Four points to remember: (a) Wherever you set up your location, be sure that the cookies are under lucite/plexiglass covers. (b) A uniform is a *must* for the youngster selling the cookies. (c) If the cookies are displayed on a table or in a booth-like setting, be sure to use tablecloths or material pinned to the booth (preferably chocolate-brown in color). (d) Have artwork on signs announcing who you are: *Emma Fairchild's Original Chocolate Chip Frisbees.* Another possibility is *The Cookie Monster.* Still another is *Mary's Chocolate Chip Flying Saucers.* (Be sure to use your *own* name!)

4. If you're able to afford a jalopy, paint it to look quaint and cute—even a bit outlandish. You can call it the "Cookie Car." The idea is to get people to *remember* you. Much less expensive than a jalopy is a two-seater bike to pull a "cookie trailer" holding all your goodies. Add all the cute frills to give it that old-fashioned look. Or have a local mechanic take a chain-driven motor (such as those used in lawn mowers) and on top of that build a small vehicle big enough to be driven by one person. The type of conveyance you use will depend on the distance you have to travel in order to get to where the bulk of your customers are.

Whatever you end up using, it must stand out. Pick out places to "set up shop" such as downtown department stores and office buildings, shopping malls, sporting events, conventions, grand opening celebrations, fund raising events, flea markets, swap meets, church socials, county and state fairs, and local parks. Go where the crowds are!

5. When you've outgrown your own kitchen and you need much more oven space, look under *Restaurant Supplies* in the phone book. Speak to as many of these suppliers as you can and ask them to provide you with names of restaurants, schools, camps—any kind of establishment where you could rent, on a part-time basis, their oven for your baking. Contact the owners and look for the most reasonable cost you can find. Also ask the restaurant supplier to send you brochures on ovens that would be best for you, in case you eventually need to lease a store and install your own oven.

6. When you are considering this, look for a real estate agent to help you find space. (It would be ideal to find a small restaurant or coffee shop that went out of business. You could take over their equipment at a cheap price.) If you're going to lease an empty store, only look in a low-rent area. You are *not* going to attempt to build up a big retail business, so you don't need an expensive location.

7. Everybody needs to make extra money these days. When you see that you could make *more money* if you were able to bake and distribute *more cookies,* then get more help. Get a part-time baker and hire teenagers for selling. There's never a problem finding extra help. Your object is to keep your "Cookie Car" out on the streets selling cookies. Let all your decisions revolve around that. Remember, you've got several options: (a) go outside your kitchen and make other arrangements to rent or lease an oven with a much bigger capacity; (b) hire a baker to do your work on a freelance basis; (c) hire teenagers to do your selling, during the week as well as on weekends. The multibillion dollar airline industry realizes that they make no money when their airplanes sit in hangars. Each plane is scheduled for maximum flying time, getting passengers to and from their destinations. Learn your lesson from them. The more your little vehicle is in operation, the more money you'll make.

8. If you don't have a car, or cannot afford to buy a cheap second-hand one, you can still make money in this "mobile

cookie" business. A simple but neat cookie-cabinet-on-a-carriage will do just fine. We're talking about taking a four-wheel carriage and mounting an attractive cabinet on top and storing your cookies in that. Customers see your delicious cookies through the glass windows and feel secure that they are kept free of dirt. Always, it's a good idea not to *touch* a cookie when serving it to a customer. Use prongs and simply put each cookie into its own napkin.

Your cookie carriage is, of course, inconvenient if you have to go a great distance to reach large groups of people. However, if you live in a large populated area and clusters of people are within walking distance, this is the most *inexpensive* way to start into business. We still advise you to invest in a uniform. Every respectable establishment that sells food to the public has its employees wearing uniforms. It's a sign that you care.

9. Most of all, you must remember to maintain *quality*. Eventually, you could work your way up to selling thousands of cookies a week, owning several vehicles and employing a group of youngsters, but be sure that *each and every* cookie is super-delicious. Your cookies must taste better than anything available in a supermarket. Keep the quality up and you keep the profits up. Let it slip and your sales will slip. It's as simple as that. So do your best. It pays!

Chapter 2

How to Earn Up to $19,500 a Year Selling Six-Foot Party Sandwiches

The Original Six-Foot Party Sandwich

Here's a way to make money without cooking or baking a thing! You're going to get six-foot loaves of bread from one place, the ingredients that make up the filling from another place, and you're going to put both of them together and sell party sandwiches at a handsome year-round profit to you!

How to Get Started in the Catering Business

Before we tell you exactly how to do all this, let's discuss the *catering* business. That's what you'll be going into.

Catering involves preparing food for someone else. Sometimes a caterer prepares everything in his own kitchen and delivers it to the customer; at other times, the caterer comes and cooks it all in the customer's home. Many caterers also provide the help to prepare and serve the food in the home. Bartenders come to serve drinks, and waiters arrive to serve food. Everything from cutlery to candelabra is brought into the home, and the next day it's all picked up and gone. What took place is perhaps a successful party, but certainly an *expensive* one!

We're in the 1980's now and although people will always love to give parties, they're all looking for ways to do it for less money! Everybody today is watching the buck, and here's your chance to cash in. You probably have never seen a pizza parlor with a sign reading "We Do Catering," but it might come to that. With these days of staggering inflation, it wouldn't surprise us that people might decide to have the local pizza parlor cater their next party. It's simple and cheap. Just invite your friends over. Tell them the party is being catered, and order up half-a-dozen large pies with extra cheese. Make sure the pizza delivery man arrives after the guests and introduce him as your caterer.

We're just trying to make a point. To be successful in any business, you have to be aware of the trend of the times. What do people want? How is the economy affecting them? As a Kitchen Lady, what could I produce to capitalize on this trend? The *six-foot party sandwich* is a perfect idea!

How One Italian Grocery Store Is Cashing In on This Product

Manganero's, an Italian grocery store in New York City, seems to be the originator of this idea and they do a booming business, catering to parties all over town. And in these times, they're also getting calls from folks living in $3,000-a-month apartments on Park Avenue and Fifth Avenue. The caterers whose businesses are suffering are the ones who feature the fancy catered parties. Almost everyone is cutting down on their entertainment expenses. The great feature of the six-foot party sandwich is that it's a real crowd-pleaser. This giant sandwich is *fun* to look at, *delicious* to eat, and *economical* to serve. You can't beat that combination. If this idea appeals to you, here are the steps to take.

How to Turn Your Kitchen Into an Italian Grocery Store

Chances are you've never baked an Italian loaf of bread before (sometimes called French bread), and certainly your oven can't handle a six-foot long loaf. No matter. Someone else will do it for you. Look in the yellow pages of your phone book and make some calls to a number of bakeries—not the giant ones who bake and distribute to supermarkets, but the small local bakers. Most likely, some of them already bake the small "hero" loaves (in some parts of the country called "subs"). These run in sizes from six inches up to the full French bread length of about 18 inches. Just ask the bakers if they're willing to "think big" and produce six-foot loaves. You're sure to run across at least one who will agree to do it. Advise them that you're starting out and that you'll only need a few loaves at a time, but assure them that your business is going to grow fast. If they'll be low on their costs now, you'll give them all your business later. Place calls to many of them; try to sense who is reliable and who offers the best deal. The most important thing to do is to go to their premises and see their baking facilities with your own eyes. It must be clean and up-to-date. After you have one or two local bakers picked out, you're ready to take the next step.

Your first stop is an Italian grocer. Are there any in your area? Again, go to your phone book. If you can locate one, what you want from him are the following ingredients: Swiss cheese, ham, mortadella, capocollo, pimiento, giardiniera, cooked salami, prosciutto, provolone, and lettuce. These are the exact ingredients that fill up the original six-foot party sandwich. If the grocer you contact doesn't have these exact ingredients, get his advice on what could be substituted without sacrificing the overall appeal and taste. Always speak to as many Italian grocers as you can. One might not have one or two of the ingredients you need, but another might be able to supply just what's missing. Tell all of them to go *easy* with their per-pound price at the beginning. Those who give you a break at the beginning deserve your business when you expand. If you like what you hear on the phone then go and visit their stores. Their stores must be clean and their meats and cheeses must look appetizing. *You* must be satisfied before your customers can be satisfied.

What Do I Charge?

The six-foot party sandwich with the ingredients we just listed can be sold for $89.00. And this monster sandwich is delivered on a cutting board that runs the length of the sandwich. You must also provide a sharp knife. The $89 does not include tax or delivery charge. Be sure it's all wrapped in tinfoil when you deliver. (People want to see food wrapped to ensure that it stays clean during delivery.)

Regarding the "cutting board": It's the only time a Kitchen Lady has to do business with a lumber yard! Call a few of them and get prices on their standard cuts of wood about 6 feet long, about 5-6 inches wide, and 1 inch deep. Also check some *cardboard* manufacturers. Today they make very heavy corrugated cardboard strips that would give adequate support for the sandwiches. The last supplier you need is a wholesaler of cutting knives. Nothing fancy that's imported from England or Germany; just cheap but sharp knives.

Is It a Good Buy for the Hostess?

At $89, the six-foot party sandwich is a *great* buy for the hostess. Here's why: this monster sandwich serves an average of *five people per foot*. Each person gets slightly more than a two-inch-thick slice and that's plenty delicious and filling. The hostess could invite as many as 30 people to the party, and that's a cost to the hostess of *$2.96 per person*. If she added soda, beer, pretzels, and potato chips, it would still be cheap enough for entertaining a whole party in these times. Once people hear about your unique party sandwiches, you'll be getting all the business you can handle.

Is It Profitable for Me?

Yes, despite the fact that you cannot get anywhere near *three times* what it costs you. On this item, you cannot even get *double* your costs. The reason is, you're not actually *making* anything. You're buying *everything* on the outside already prepared and you're putting it together in your kitchen and then selling it. But it can still be very profitable for you. Here's an entire breakdown of costs, selling price, and profit to you.

First of all, you're selling the six-foot sandwich for $89. Go to a local baker and offer him no more than $2 a foot for his six-foot loaf. This Italian-style loaf is 72 inches long and about 6 inches wide, soft and chewy in the middle but with a firm, crispy crust outside. The baker may want as much as $3 a foot, but promise him all your business and urge him to keep the price to $2 a foot.

(A)	$89	(Your sale price)
	−12	(baker's price)
	$77	

Your biggest cost will be the filling—the meats, cheeses, and other Italian specialties listed previously. For the five people-per-foot scale of eating this sandwich (or thirty in all for the six-foot sandwich) you will need about 12 pounds of ingredients. You will need to strike a special agreement with the Italian grocer that you pay no more than $4 a pound, or $48 total.

(B)	$77	
	−48	(Italian grocer's price)
	$29	

The remaining costs to you are small. They include the board or heavy corrugated cardboard strip for support in transporting the six-foot sandwich; the knife to supply for cutting; and the tinfoil to wrap the entire sandwich. (This means cleanliness to the customer.) Allow $4 to approximate the costs of these elements. Again, when you are ready to buy any of these in quantity, then your costs will start to come down.

$$(C) \quad \begin{array}{r} \$29 \\ -4 \\ \hline \$25 \end{array} \quad \text{(Three minor items)}$$

That's a profit to you of $25 on each sale of a six-foot party sandwich. That's approximately a 40% markup on your costs. The 40% is *below* the Kitchen Lady "rule of thumb," which is to charge at least 100%, 200%, 300% or more over your expenses. In this instance, however, it must be remembered that *nothing* is originating in your own kitchen. You're bringing everything in from the outside and assembling it all to sell. A $25 clear profit per six-foot sandwich is not bad at all. When the news starts to get around of your terrific six-foot sandwiches, it will soon become easy for you to pick up ten to fifteen party orders per week. At ten orders a week—at $25 profit per order—that's $250 of clear profit to you. If you're selling 15 monster sandwiches a week, you're now clearing $375. If you can make this a year-round business, you'll be taking in an impressive $19,500—and every cent of it earned right from your own kitchen! Be sure to charge extra for delivery, and don't forget to add any sales tax that might apply. Delivery would be $3 by car if it's a reasonably short distance of a few miles.

You will also want to be flexible about the length of the sandwiches. Since an average of about five people consume a foot of this sandwich, a hostess might have only twenty-five coming to her party. Thus she might request a five-foot party sandwich. Another time your services might be required for a party of twenty people, which would only require a four-foot sandwich.

For the five-foot party sandwich, charge $79 (this time $10 to the baker, $40 to the grocer, and the same $4 for the incidentals). Total: $54. Add your profit of $25 and it comes to $79.

For the four-foot party sandwich, your price should be $69. (The baker now gets $8, the grocer $32—eight pounds of filling for twenty people—plus the same $4 for incidentals.) Total: $44. Add your profit of $25 for the total of $69.

At first glance, the prices we've been suggesting you charge may seem a bit high. You may wonder if you'll be able to convince someone to pay that much for your sandwich. However, just make the hostess aware of the cost per person for her party, and she'll see how economical it is over serving other dishes. Let's say you tell her it'll cost her $3 a person to enjoy this unique treat. Suppose she has thirty people coming to the party, and she'll need the original six-foot party sandwich as discussed first. That's $89. Obviously, she'll be serving other things at her party, so her *total* costs will be more than $89. But the main entrée at the party—indeed the high point of it—will be this unique sandwich! And where else in these inflationary times can you entertain guests at a cost to the hostess of only $3 per person? Even with extras, which may bring the cost to $5 per person, it's still a great bargain!

Most Kitchen Ladies who are selling these party sandwiches are getting the $3 per person and $89 for the six-foot sandwich. (Of course, you keep the same ratio of costs and profits as you go down in size to the five-foot and four-foot party sandwich.) The prices are flexible, but you *must* know what your costs are all the time in order to stay ahead and earn a respectable profit. Before we get into telling you how you can create a demand for the party sandwich, we urge you not to give up on this idea even if you find there's *no* Italian grocer in your area. Most likely there's one within convenient distance to you. Usually, the local pizza parlor man will know a good Italian grocer—not necessarily so if your local pizza parlor is simply part of a national chain. (There might not be a single Italian working there!)

However, even if you can't locate an Italian grocer, you can create your *own* fillings of meats and cheeses, and buy peppers and olives from the supermarket to round it all out. There are usually some types of Italian meats and cheeses sold in most supermarkets anyway. The unique feature of what you're offering is the monster size of the sandwich itself. This six-foot giant is really something to see—it's the "life of the party." That is a *must* to have, so be sure to find a baker who will make the six-foot loaves for you. If you can get the Italian ingredients to fill them with, fine; if not, all is not lost—you'll still get customers. If you're going to do the filling, experiment with different combinations to get the most delicious taste before you search for customers.

How Do I Get Customers?

Let's say you are capable of turning out six-foot-long Italian party sandwiches which, when filled with meats, cheeses, etc., will sell for \$89. How are you going to get people to find out what you have? You know it's a winner at parties. You have our word on that; as we mentioned earlier, this item is very successful in Manhattan and doing a booming business with New York party givers.

Advertising

The cheapest form of advertising is *no* advertising. It's called word-of-mouth, and it's free. One person tells another who in turn tells another, and so on. While you're waiting for that to build up, you should consider the cheapest form of *paid* advertising: classified advertising. Call up the local newspaper and find out about their rates. Tell them what your product is and ask them to help you by suggesting what days are best to put your ad in their paper. Remind them that you don't have a lot of money to spend and if they can sincerely help you then you'll repeat the ads in their paper. And you really will. When advertising works, the smart advertiser just keeps doing the same thing.

Find a Willing Copywriter

Before you go to the newspaper, you'll want someone to write a small classified ad. If you feel that you don't have the talent, then hire a young copywriter on a free-lance basis. The newspaper itself might get you a young man or woman who works in the advertising department. These young copywriters often have experience in knowing what makes a good classified ad. They would be happy to write you an ad for an extra $25 in their pocket. If the ad is not effective, they are usually inclined to help you again at no extra cost. Hiring a person who works for the newspaper has the extra advantage of insuring that your classified ad gets the best possible position in the classified column. If the newspaper can't provide a copywriter for you, then your best bet is to call any local department store. They always have a copywriter on staff.

What Makes a Good Ad?

Whoever writes the ad—you or a professional copywriter— should know that a good advertisement has these four points working for it. It's the AIDA formula:

> (A) Attention
> (I) Interest
> (D) Desire
> (A) Action

The headline in the ad—or the first sentence of a classified ad—must immediately attract people's *attention,* and the next words written must hold their *interest.* Next, you must create a *desire* for what you have to sell, and finally, you must make it clear what *action* they must take to complete the sale. This AIDA formula never varies. It's simple but basic. Just for your interest, when you see ads in the paper or on TV, study them to see which ones really grab your *attention,* hold your *interest* and create a *desire.* Most of them don't accomplish this; those that do earn tremendous sums of money for the advertisers who stand behind them. It's important you study these ads; you're about to become an advertiser yourself!

We'll write a piece of sample copy that could well become your classified ad for your party sandwich. (We're not necessarily suggesting that this is the ad you should use; you should still get a local copywriter and see what he can come up with.)

> *Serve what they've never seen before!* The biggest party sandwich in the world. *Six feet long* and filled with delicious Italian-style meats, cheeses, peppers, and pimientos. Nothing could be more delicious or economical. Thirty hungry people will enjoy this monster sandwich at a cost to you of only $89. The perfect party sensation for everyone from six to sixty! Call XXX-XXXX. We deliver.

The ad accomplishes four things: (a) it attracts people's attention in the first sentence by talking to those who are in the market for giving a party: "Serve what they've never seen before!"; (b) it holds their interest by the description of this unusual six-foot-long sandwich; (c) it establishes desire, by talking of the delicious Italian meats and cheeses inside the sandwich; (d) finally, it demonstrates action by spelling out how economical it all is, how many people can be fed, and how a hostess can purchase the sandwich. (The ad is followed up by your phone number.) Whether you choose to use this small advertisement or another one, the AIDA formula is the one to follow for the most effectiveness.

Chapter Summary

1. Look in the directory section of your phone book and call a number of local bakers. They probably already bake the small "hero" loaves (also known as "subs"), which range in size from six inches to the full French bread length of about a

foot and a half. Just ask the bakers if they're willing to "think big" and bake six-foot loaves. When you find a few willing bakers, go and discuss your needs with them. Assure them that your business will grow rapidly, and if they'll be low on their costs now, you'll make it up in volume later. Before you make any arrangement, be sure you visit their premises *personally;* their facilities must be clean and modern.

2. Visit several Italian grocers and inspect the meats, cheeses, and other ingredients you'll need for the sandwiches. Try not to pay over $4 a pound for the grocer's products. Look at it this way: if you have orders for ten six-foot sandwiches, you'll need twelve pounds of ingredients for each sandwich— that's 120 pounds in all! That's a very sizable order, so the grocer should cooperate with you on the price.

3. Go to a lumber yard or a corrugated cardboard manufacturer for a board or strip that would provide adequate support for the sandwich.

4. Go to a wholesale cutlery house to purchase your knives. These don't have to be expensive imports, just cheap and sharp knives.

5. Tinfoil can be found at supermarkets, of course, but check a few restaurant supply houses for a cheaper price.

6. You should be able to get $89 for your six-foot sandwich. Remember to also offer a five-foot sandwich for $79, and a four-foot sandwich for $69. With each order you must provide the same three additional items: support board, knife, and tinfoil wrapping.

7. No matter which sandwich size you'll be selling, try to clear $25 on each order.

8. If there's no Italian grocer in your area, go to a supermarket that stocks Italian-style meats and cheeses. Also purchase olives, pimientos, and peppers to round it out. If you can't get the *real* Italian ingredients, don't worry—you'll still get plenty of customers. It's the *monster size* of the sandwich that will attract business, but make sure it *tastes delicious* as well!

9. The least-expensive way to start advertising is in the clas-

sified column of your local newspaper. Call the paper to learn the procedure: cost for each line of copy and best days to advertise.

10. If you can't write an effective ad yourself, hire a young copywriter on a free-lance basis. The newspaper could recommend one, or you can find one at a local department store.

11. A good advertisement embraces the four-point AIDA formula: *A*ttention, *I*nterest, *D*esire, *A*ction.

12. In addition to classified advertising, consider using *Direct Mail.* This means writing long copy plus showing a picture of your unique party sandwich. This goes on a sales letter, which is sent *direct* to various social clubs and organizations. This alerts them to the availability of your party sandwich for their various functions. In this sales letter, it's a good idea to include testimonials from satisfied customers. (See a later chapter in the book for a *thorough* explanation of this advertising technique.)

Chapter 3

How to Earn Up to $14,144 a Year Selling Roast Turkey and All the Trimmings

One 30-Pound Turkey with Stuffing, Cranberry Sauce and Sweet Potatoes to Go, Please!

There are several ways to make money. One way is to introduce a new idea; another is to take an old idea and use it in a new way.

Every family loves to sit down to a delicious roast turkey dinner on Thanksgiving Day. For the mother or grandmother of the house, it's the most gratifying day of the year—her family is together. Just about everyone loves turkey and all the trimmings that go with it.

We tell you this: if you know how to make a delicious oven-roasted stuffed turkey with all the trimmings, you've got one profitable year-round business! You start to run classified ads like this:

SARAH'S SUNDAY TURKEY

A stuffed, roasted, butterball turkey, dripping with giblet gravy and complete with sweet potatoes and cranberry sauce, delivered when you want it. Now you can make every Sunday Thanksgiving Day, but you don't have to do the work! You'll love it. Reasonably priced according to weight, and ready to eat. Call Sarah, XXX-XXXX.

Thanksgiving doesn't have to come only once a year. People would really love to eat turkey throughout the year, but preparing it is a lot of work! That's what you have to be prepared for, but we promise it'll pay off. If you can cook truly delicious roast turkeys, you'll get more orders than you can handle. What's more, there's a lot of profit in it for you.

What to Charge

A roast turkey is *not* a high-volume, low-cost specialty, so there's no way you can get *three* times your cost. But you must charge at least double (100% markup)—sometimes more—in order to make a decent profit. It's all a matter of what the "traffic will bear." Chances are, you'll be the first in your area to be offering this. Even if a local butcher does sell prepared roast turkeys (and it's highly unlikely), people will want to buy from you—for that homemade taste. The majority of people feel that a specialty made in the store can't compete with one that's made in the home.

As this book is being written in the spring of 1981, we buy turkeys for about 79¢ a pound where we live. Sometimes a dime more or less, but that's about the current supermarket price. At that rate, a 30-pound turkey will cost you $23.70. We suggest you charge $69 to deliver—with all the fixings—a stuffed and roasted 30-pound turkey right to someone's doorstep. Your other costs will be: tinfoil containers to hold the various fixings—the stuffing, the gravy and the sweet potatoes, and a plastic container for the cranberry sauce. All the fixings and the containers to hold them should cost you about $10 per order, and so you have an overall cost of about $34 and your selling price is $69, which gives you a 100% markup.

One Stop Does It All

You must make one trip. Bring the turkey, the fixings, pick up your money, and that's it. Your turkey should be completely covered in tinfoil and set in a tinfoil roasting pan. To reheat, the housewife simply pops everything into her oven. The tinfoil roasting pan and containers are simply thrown away when she's about to serve. But make sure you have your name and phone number imprinted on labels. They get *affixed* to the plastic containers holding the cranberry sauce. She'll keep *that* container, so your "advertising" stays in the house after you've left.

Where to Get Supplies

Look in the phone book (yellow pages) and look up several packaging and container manufacturers. You'll soon want to be able to buy in *volume* the tinfoil roasting pans and containers and rolls of tinfoil itself. Shop around and get the best price. Always tell the manufacturer—and it's true—that you're starting out small now, but your business will grow and you want the best *wholesale* price for your pans and containers. It's too expensive to get these from the supermarket. You have to deal with the packaging and container manufacturers. You'll get cooperation; a smart manufacturer is always on the lookout for new business.

Why Will People Order Turkey In?

Years ago, housewives would have considered themselves failures if they had to resort to bringing in meals already prepared outside the home. A woman would have been upset if she had to resort to having someone else prepare turkey for her family. Well, that's changed. Over half the women in the United States today are out working to bring in an extra salary—sometimes the only salary! These women are the half you're going to sell your ready-to-eat turkeys to. These women still want to do the best for their families. They still want to serve them delicious meals, but once in a while on a Sunday, they feel they *deserve* to have someone else do the cooking.

And do you want to know something surprising? You'd think that a woman would tell her family that *she* made the turkey; she would try to hide the fact that someone else prepared it. Well, some women would, but many others have no qualms about admitting that it was ordered in. The family knows that the wife or mother works hard enough all week, and as McDonald's TV commercials have said, "You deserve a break today." The amazing thing is, her family likes it better that way. Instead of Mom slaving in the kitchen all day and having no time to talk to the family, she can now be right in the living room with everyone else.

In addition, there are many housewives, generally married only a few years, who just don't have the know-how to prepare a delicious turkey. They grew up in a generation to whom ordering in meals once or twice a week was common practice. So they represent another source of customers for you. These young housewives often don't try to "kid" their husbands that they're going to try their hand at making a roast turkey dinner. They and their husbands belong to that younger generation to whom it's just no crime to order in. Both of them will smack their lips right along with their children and invited friends. These friends are likely to say, "Gosh, this turkey is delicious. C'mon, give us the name of the person who prepared it, so we can order it ourselves."

Believe us, "Sarah's Sunday Turkey" can become a profitable business for you. (Always use your own name, please!) During the spring and fall, when the husbands are watching sports on TV, it's a great treat for the whole family to sit down afterwards to a turkey dinner.

Economical for All Your Customers

Examine the fact that on a Sunday, when a family most often goes out for dinner, it's about $60 spent right there. With skyrocketing gasoline prices and an average cost of $12 per person spent on dinner at a fine family restaurant, it's not hard for a family of four to spend $60 or more to enjoy a good dinner away from home. How much more satisfying it would be to stay home and enjoy a delicious turkey—with all the fixings—that is all prepared and brought in. No traffic to fight, no crowded restaurant, and Mom still doesn't have to do the cooking for everyone to enjoy. It's much easier and cheaper, and there's more of a feeling of togetherness.

There's an additional savings for the family that orders your 30-pound, $69 delivered roast turkey: there's probably going to be enough meat left over for one or two more sliced turkey dinners or turkey salads. And that means another evening or two that a grateful housewife won't have to prepare a meal from scratch.

Always remember, make your delivered turkey a one-stop affair. Deliver everything, collect your money, and go. Your tinfoil containers are all disposable—the housewife will be grateful for that—and the plastic container (holding the cranberry sauce) has your name and phone number affixed to it. Since you leave your "advertising" with your housewife, you stand an excellent chance of getting other orders from that family or their friends.

Always check over your costs: turkey, trimmings, and containers. With this specialty, you should be able to charge *double* your costs. As we get further into the 1980s and your expenses go up, remember to pass them on. We never suggest that you price yourself out of business, but you are offering a *specialty*—a unique, delicious one, and you have to make a good profit on it. You're doing a lot of hard work, so be well paid for it!

Will the Profits Add Up?

By selling each prepared turkey and trimmings for $69, you should be making a profit of about $34 on each order. Once you become known, you should have no problem getting four orders on any given Sunday, so that's a profit of $136 for the day. You should easily be able to work your way up to getting Saturday orders as well, thus doubling your profit intake to *$272 for the weekend!* On a 52-week basis, that comes to $14,144. For these eight weekend orders, you'll be cooking on Friday for Saturday deliveries and cooking on Saturday for Sunday deliveries.

How to Expand Your Business

To handle this volume, you'll certainly need another oven. Perhaps you're good friends with a neighbor who would be willing to help out for a small share of the profits. This way, you have at least two ovens available—and if there'a a double oven in your neighbor's home, then you're really cooking! When your business expands to a volume of ten to fifteen orders a week, it's time you consider getting another cooking premises entirely to handle all the preparing. Look to *lease* inexpensive space in a commercial area. For example, a vacant store that was once a restaurant or coffee shop might be ideal for your purposes. (It'll be no problem to hook up an oven in that space.) Incidentally, since you won't be a retail operation—which would entail bringing customers into your store—you don't have to be located in a fancy area. You'll be preparing roast turkeys for outside delivery, so look to lease inexpensive space in an out-of-the-way area. What your space *must* be is clean and capable of meeting all health requirements. We'll talk more about legal requirements further on in the book.

We also advise you to *lease* the equipment you'll be using. Don't buy a new large oven until you have the cash to invest. You're in this business to make as much money as you can and that can only be accomplished by keeping your expenses to a minimum. Look in the yellow pages of your phone book under "Restaurant Supplies." Shop around and get the best leasing price on available ovens. In the long run, buying and owning equipment is more economical than renting it. In the early stages of a business, however, that kind of cash outlay is too risky.

Chapter Summary

1. It should be safe to charge $69 for delivering to someone's house a 30-pound roast turkey with all the trimmings. The $69 should represent a 100% markup over your total cost of approximately $34. Since we are living in inflationary times, you must remember to pass along any cost increases to your customers.

2. Some customers might prefer a smaller roasted turkey, so scale down your prices accordingly. (But always urge them to order the larger turkey. It's more profitable for you and really more economical for them as there will be plenty left over for additional meals.)

3. Be sure you deliver the turkey, the stuffing, the gravy, and the sweet potatoes in their own disposable tinfoil containers. Your customer merely needs to heat everything in her oven, then transfer to her dishes for serving.

4. The container you leave that she will *keep* will be the plastic container holding the cranberry sauce. Be sure you have your name and phone number printed on a label which will be affixed to that container. This technique makes it easy for housewives to reorder from you or to recommend your services to others.

5. When you start to get really busy with orders, think about getting another cooking premises entirely. Remember to rent a store in an inexpensive location. Also remember to lease—not

purchase—the equipment at first; don't buy until you can accumulate enough profits to warrant the investment.

6. The success of catering roast turkeys depends greatly on
the income level of people in your area. To put it bluntly, people living in an impoverished area won't be able to afford this
specialty. But those in a middle-income bracket or above represent prime customers for your product. So, always be sure
your advertising reaches the people who have the dollars to
spend on something unique and delicious. A roast turkey,
which most people only have on Thanksgiving, is a treat they
would dearly love at any time of the year.

Chapter 4

How to Earn More Than $23,000 a Year Selling Delicious Homemade Baked Beans

The Miraculous Comeback of Baked Beans

Housewives are looking at every possible means to save a dollar these days and baked beans are a perfect answer. They're not that expensive, and they're filling. A few generations ago, they were very popular; but as income levels grew, baked beans retained a certain "poor man's dish" image. Then in recent years, everyone began to talk about losing weight, and a lot of folks decided to drop baked beans from their meals. It was popular to believe that they were too fattening. However, new studies show that beans, as complex carbohydrates, are less fattening than many meat and dairy products. As a matter of fact, this point of view has been most recently expressed by the United States government in its revised nutritional guidelines. But a debate on calories is not our concern.

Now baked beans are staging a dramatic comeback, and *economy* is a major reason. The problem is that, like most foods found in the supermarket, today's baked beans don't taste very good. It doesn't make much difference which brand you buy, because none have that old-fashioned homemade taste. Nothing mass-produced can. That's where the Kitchen Ladies come in!

Can You Make 'Em the Way They Used To?

Can you make a specialty out of baked beans? Remember how they used to taste? Remember that zesty homemade flavor? Can you recall when a big pot of beans came out of the oven tasting of bacon, molasses, minced onion, celery, green pepper, a dollop of catsup, a dash of Tabasco or grains of red pepper? Some cooks preferred Boston-style, using dried Navy beans and adding diced salt pork, some dry mustard, and a little Worcestershire sauce. After cooking, it all went into a greased baking dish and was decorated with sliced pork strips or bacon. Then it was browned for a while. Do you want to make this specialty? You have to be the judge. Right now, we'll tell you the story of a man who made this dish his specialty and cashed in on it handsomely. But never forget: this is a big country, and there's room for everyone!

Captain Ken's Firehouse Baked Beans

Ken Freiberg* proved that there's room for Kitchen Men in this business as well as Kitchen Ladies. His success story is

*Actual name.

fascinating. Before we get into it, we ask you to recall that we're always telling you to give your own name to your specialty. It personalizes your product, and makes it distinctive and memorable. Captain Ken did just that, and it paid off! Now we'll tell you his story, which we read about in a newspaper.

Ken was a fireman from St. Paul, Minnesota. Today he's a millionaire! How did he do it? He had the knack of making delicious baked beans. That's all he sells—baked beans, frozen in aluminum foil boxes. He sells them to supermarkets, restaurants, and schools, and it seems that he can't make enough of them.

He retired as Captain Ken from the fire department to start his own frozen food business. He decided to turn professional chef after years of cooking his baked beans for his fellow firemen. Lots of firemen do their own cooking, and Captain Ken had a terrific recipe for baked beans. You know how the advice goes: "Wow, if you could package that, you'd make a million." Well, Captain Ken did just that.

He first introduced his baked beans, which he called "Firehouse Baked Beans," to the people at the Minnesota State Fair. The fair ran for ten days, and Ken netted a handsome $6,000 profit. With that kind of acceptance, he branched out to try to sell his product to stores. He determined that frozen baked beans was the way to go, and at first he used only his freezer at home. It soon became clear that the little freezer in his refrigerator couldn't begin to hold the amount of baked beans that was demanded of him. He then expanded by setting up a second kitchen space and renting a vacant store. In this new space he put an oven, two upright home freezers, and one chest freezer. He was afraid to spend the money to buy them new, so he purchased them second-hand. Today, he has an immense frozen food facility, and orders come in without let-up. Just imagine: one of his customers is Kentucky Fried Chicken! Captain Ken's company packs frozen baked beans in packages of one pound, and as high up as 30-pound containers.

All in all, his sales total about 10,000 pounds of frozen baked beans each day!

Start Small, Think Big!

All of this comes from a delicious recipe for baked beans. The whole idea is perfect and, more than ever, the timing is right. People love baked beans, and since it's a great way for folks to economize, it's a sure winner today. Experiment with various baked bean recipes. Every day add a different "touch" and give samples to friends and family. Get their comments. If you want to get involved with this particular specialty dish, we're sure you can make it taste delicious.

Be prepared, first in a small way, to sell it frozen. The frozen food business does over *$1 billion* a year in sales. It's dominated by the big companies, but you can compete with them if you have a unique and delicious product. It doesn't matter that women are buying the Heinz or Campbell's baked beans; those brands are mass-produced, and their flavor can't begin to compare with the unbeatable homemade taste you will offer. Believe us, it's only a matter of time before one woman will tell another about your wonderful dish.

Follow These Steps

Start small, just like Captain Ken. After everyone is saying, "Wow, they're delicious! I haven't tasted baked beans like that in years," you're ready to sell them. Use your own refrigerator to store your first batches and, when orders justify expansion, then either lease new equipment or buy second-hand equipment. Soon you might well be using a 6-foot by 10-foot walk-in freezer that's capable of freezing one thousand pounds of baked beans a day. That type of freezer might cost over $5,000 new, but you'll be able to buy a second-hand one for much less. Another alternative is to buy one on time payments or even lease (rent) it as mentioned above.

How to Get a Sales Force Without Hiring One

Once you're ready to introduce your product to the public, consider hiring a *food broker*. Look in the yellow pages of your phone book and speak to several such brokers. Their job is to pave the way for you. A food broker employs salesmen who call on food stores, caterers, restaurants, schools, and other institutions and get orders for you. Be sure to give away free samples of your delicious baked beans for the salesmen to give to the store owners. Always remember: one taste is worth a thousand words! The broker gives you all the orders his salesmen get. All you do is turn out the product, put it into suitable containers, and deliver it to your customers. For his effort, the broker earns 5% of your sales. We think that 5% is worth it, as you don't have to call on the stores to get the initial sales. He (the broker) has done it for you, and you simply deliver the product.

How to Expand

You will be ready for a vacant store at this point. You'll need a stove or oven (or several), some big pots, maybe an electric mixer, work tables, various utensils, a supply of aluminum foil boxes, and a small area to handle the labels needed. When you are first starting out, the boxes can be packed by hand.

Remember to Personalize It

As we have said throughout the book, give your product that personal touch—give it a name, an identity. Captain Ken properly called his specialty "Firehouse Baked Beans." The expression "Firehouse" had a wonderful feeling to it. The image was right: firemen would seem to *know* what delicious baked beans tasted like. They'd want a hearty dish, for they are men who work under great pressure and often in extremely cold weather. The name seems to suggest that if firemen would eat these baked beans, then it must surely be great-tasting to the average person. Yes, the name "Firehouse" was an absolute inspiration.

Take a lesson from Captain Ken! When you choose a name for your specialty, try to combine a personal touch with an additional image. If you—and others—feel that your own name is not right for the product, then dream up another one. (If it's not your own name, have a lawyer do a "search" to be sure that the name you select is free for you to use. A search might cost $50—it shouldn't be more—but it's worth it. If you used a name without checking on it—only to find out later that it has already been in use—then you'll have wasted a great deal of money printing that name on bills, business cards, letterheads, etc.) Getting the proper name for the product isn't an easy matter, and it is extremely important for the success of your specialty.

How to Use an Advertising Agency Without Hiring One

Let us go back to a previous suggestion: think of hiring a freelance copywriter. This young man or woman would take your assignment to create a name for your product. Offer $25, with a maximum of $50, and have this bright copywriter give you a dozen names to choose from. Stipulate that you'll pay only if you use one of his suggestions. Then try out a name or two on your family and friends, and on several of the food brokers you will be in contact with. Also have that copywriter suggest an art director to design a label for you. That might cost an additional $25, but then you will have it all: a perfect, appetizing sounding name that fits your product to a "T." Plus, the name will be set on a label that is just as appetizing in terms of color, design, and overall visual appeal.

A Good Lawyer Can Be Indispensable

In a later chapter we'll be discussing the role of a lawyer in any specialty you'll be selling, but it's appropriate to mention the specific help he'll be giving you in this situation. You'll be needing a food license to comply with the health regulations. In addition, if your baked beans contain meat, you must conform to the rules of the U.S. Department of Agriculture. Have your lawyer speak to the Health Department, and ask him to tell you exactly what kind of equipment you'll need to conform to the legal requirements. The equipment, the boxes, and the wording on your labels must all be approved.

If you don't have the funds to hire a lawyer, you can do this yourself. It's no big deal, and the Health Department officials go out of their way to assist you. Go ahead, give them a taste of your fabulous baked beans. It's not a bribe; it's a great way of getting them to realize that you're really worth helping. (Besides: just realize that they're working for the government—the biggest business in the country. They'd find it refreshing to help someone starting out in business for herself—especially when they appreciate what she makes!)

What to Charge

Our rule-of-thumb is generally to charge three times the cost of your ingredients. Sometimes you can have a higher markup, and sometimes it will be lower. In the case of frozen baked beans, you can get a 100% markup on your costs. We'd like to point out that Captain Ken charges double his costs, but since he works on such a large *volume*, his profits really mount up.

Examine his psychology for a moment. He fully realizes that the stores and restaurants he sells to would just as easily use the mass-produced (and cheaper) baked beans, if his price was too high. So he has to stay within reason. Remember, it's the law of supply and demand. If you have something that's one-of-a-kind, then you can get triple, perhaps even quadruple, your costs (some specialty cooks do get as much as a 300% to 400% markup). But when your product is competing with what's mass-produced, don't set your price too high. (Consult your food broker on this important point; he knows "what the market will bear.")

Here's how Captain Ken figured out his costs with his baked beans: he estimated that his beans cost him 25¢ for a one-pound package (this was a few years ago, so the prices have gone up). To this he adds the broker's 5% commission, which is based on the amount paid by the store or restaurant. Captain Ken's price to the store is 55¢, which is slightly more than 100% above his cost. This is the average markup, and is sufficient to cover the costs of rent, salaries, and insurance expenditures, while still leaving a fine profit.

The figure of doubling the cost will do just fine, because baked beans are a high-volume business. You need only a few cents profit per pound in order to make a lot of money. For example, let's say that your net profit is only 9¢ a pound after all expenses have been accounted for. If you sell an average of 1,000 pounds a day (and you'll need a commercial operation to turn out that much), your net profit is a respectable $90 a day. Once your product takes on real volume, you could make ten times that amount: a net profit of *$900 a day*—and that's after everyone and everything has been paid! By the time you reach that stage, you'll have made a heavy investment in equipment and personnel to help you produce and distribute the huge volume demanded of you. That's the price of growth—but it's well worth anticipating!

Never Be Intimidated!

Don't be frightened by the frozen food business. You won't need the giant refrigerated trucks that the big companies use to distribute their foods. They need those trucks because great distances must be covered, and the companies can't risk food spoilage. Your own car will do fine. The rule-of-thumb is that your specialty food should not exceed 30 to 45 minutes in travel time from your freezer to the store. There are usually enough restaurants and stores within that distance to make it worthwhile for you.

When Your Costs Go Up, Your Prices Should Go Up

Another important point is not to be afraid—once your product has the stores calling for more—of gradually increasing your price. Your costs are sure to go up, so don't be ashamed to ask for more money. By that time, the word-of-mouth that has been spreading about your delicious baked beans will inspire the stores and restaurants to keep stocking your specialty.

The large commercial companies are raising *their* prices all the time, and their products can't hold a candle to yours! Your baked beans are deliciously homemade and *natural,* as opposed to the chemicals and inferior ingredients in mass-produced products.

Don't price yourself out of business, but be aware that your product deserves to be more expensive than brand-name baked beans. It's been our experience that people are willing to pay extra for the pleasure of eating something that's a cut above the rest. That's been proven over and over again, and it's the very reason for the success of the Kitchen Ladies!

Just what *kind* of success can you have with this specialty? Selling baked beans for a net profit of $90 a day will earn you a handsome profit of $450 a week! On a 52-week basis, that comes to $23,400 a year. At that stage of the game, you'll be leasing oven and freezing facilities outside of your home, and working hard to maintain such a high income. But think of the rewards! If you have that certain "touch" needed to make baked beans the old-fashioned way, then by all means consider this specialty. It pays!

Chapter Summary

1. Sell your baked beans frozen. Start cooking small amounts at first; use your own freezer to store your initial batches of beans, and when you start to expand, either lease new equipment or buy second-hand.

2. Think of hiring a food broker. He employs salesmen who get orders for you. The broker gives you all the orders his salesmen get, and you cook the beans, pack them in aluminum foil pans, and deliver them. For his work, the broker collects 5% of your sales.

3. Always remember to personalize your specialty. If you feel that your own name isn't suitable for the product, hire a lawyer to do a "search" to be sure that the name you do select is legal for you to use.

4. If you need to, hire an advertising copywriter to create a name for your product and an art director to design a label. Pay a minimum one-time fee for their services.

5. Hire a lawyer to speak to the Health Department; he'll tell you what steps you must take to meet all legal requirements. If you don't have the money, consult with the Health Department directly.

6. With a specialty of baked beans, doubling the cost of your ingredients will be sufficient to make a good profit, because baked beans are a high-volume business. You need only a few cents profit per pound to make a very fine living.

7. You'll need a large supply of aluminum foil pans—in various sizes—to hold your frozen baked beans. These may be obtained from several companies. The biggest company in the field is the Ekco Company in Wheeling, Ill. It's also a good idea to keep up-to-date with what's happening in the frozen food business. A good trade journal to read is *Canner/Packer*.

If you can't find the magazine in the library, write them at: 3460 John Hancock Center, Chicago, Ill. 60611.

8. Never be afraid of gradually raising your price. If your costs increase—as they almost certainly will—don't be shy about passing them on to your customers.

Chapter 5

How to Earn $12,500 a Year Selling Hearty, Homemade Sausages

Sausages—the Old-Fashioned Kind People Really Love!

Biting into a plump sausage is one of the most richly satisfying taste treats that can be experienced in a lifetime of eating. The wonderful butcher shops that once sold sausages seem to have disappeared, and in their place are the sterile supermarkets with all their meats wrapped in plastic. Many people have turned away from sausages because they can't even pronounce all the chemicals printed on the package labels! As a friend once said, after studying the ingredients on a package of sausages, "If I can't pronounce 'em, I'm not gonna eat 'em!" The taste seems to have gone out of all store-bought sausages—no matter which brand you buy. Today, manufacturers seem to be more interested in how long a product can *last,* not how good it tastes. As a result, all kinds of chemicals and preservatives are pumped into nearly every product we see on the supermarket shelf.

But never forget that people still yearn for food the way it *used* to taste—rich, pure, and satisfying. And, as we always say in our book, you as a Kitchen Lady can answer that need and make a fine profit because people are willing to pay more for delicious foods. Do you think you can make sausages? It helps if you're of European extraction. We came across an interesting newspaper article we'd like to pass on.

Learn from the Success of John Slovacek

If you want some inspiration, we'll tell you about John Slovacek*of Texas. He operates a sausage-making plant in Austin, Texas, but he started out the way we all begin—right from his own kitchen. He made his first batch of sausage—35 pounds— one Saturday night in 1953. He sold every ounce of it the next morning to the few neighborhood grocery stores that were open on Sunday. He now has six helpers, and makes 650 thousand pounds of sausage a year. He sells about 90% of it wholesale to markets and restaurants within a 100-mile radius of the plant and the remainder in a retail shop at the plant itself.

The success of his business is built along the same principle that applies to all of us in this business—it's homemade! John Slovacek says he's producing sausages "like my father and mother made when we butchered hogs at home—no newfangled equipment, no ingredients you can't pronounce in the sausage." Naturally, he became a big success.

To start into this business, you'll need information about sources for sausage-making ingredients and supplies. For a free catalogue listing everything you'll need, write to:

*Actual name.

Richard S. Kutas Company
1067 Grant Street
Buffalo, New York 14207

His catalogue lists all the supplies he carries in his immaculately clean, impressively stocked small warehouse in Buffalo. Everything you'll need for sausage production in the home is itemized in this catalogue. Supplies such as meat grinders, sausage stuffers, casings, numerous pre-mixed sausage seasonings and so on are but a few examples.

Here are the recipes for various sausages that people really love. Each is very popular in different parts of the country, and none of them can be found in any conventional supermarket.

Kielbasa

(Smoked Polish Sausage)

10 **pounds boneless pork butts**
 6 **tablespoons salt**
 1 **teaspoon sugar**
½ **teaspoon Prague Powder (see page 56)**
 1 **tablespoon ground black pepper**
 2 **large bulbs (clusters) fresh garlic, peeled and finely chopped**
 2 **teaspoons dried marjoram**
 2 **cups nonfat dry milk or soy protein concentrate**
 4 **cups water**

Trim off and discard any blood clots, sinews, etc., in the pork butts. Cut off all fat and place it in one pile. Cube the lean meat and place it in another pile.

Grind the lean meat using a grinder blade with holes ¼ inch in diameter. Grind the fat using a grinder blade with ⅛-inch holes. Combine the lean meat and the fat in a bowl.

Add remaining ingredients and blend well.

Stuff the meat into large-size hog casings (40 to 42 millimeters). Tie the sausages at each end into 16-inch lengths. Tie the ends of each sausage to make rings. Hang the rings at intervals on a stick and let the sausages dry in a smoker preheated to 130° Fahrenheit. Leave the dampers open.

When the casings are dry, increase the temperature to 160–165°, keeping the dampers open about ¼ inch. Using heavy smoke, let sausage heat to an internal temperature of 152°. Remove the sausages and run under cold water until the internal temperature is reduced to 110°. Let hang at room temperature about 30 minutes. Let stand at between 28–40° overnight.

YIELD: *12 pounds of sausage*

Swedish Potato Sausages

1½ **pounds lean boneless beef**
 1 **pound lean boneless pork**
 6 **pounds potatoes, peeled and cut into 1-inch cubes (6 cups)**
 2 **cups coarsely chopped onion**
 1 **tablespoon salt**
1½ **teaspoons ground black pepper**
 1 **teaspoon allspice**

Put the beef, pork, potatoes, and onion through a grinder blade with ⅜-inch holes.

Put the ground mixture into a mixing bowl. Add the remaining ingredients and mix well. Put the mixture through the grinder again.

Stuff the mixture into hog casings (38–40 millimeters in diameter). Tie the sausages at each end into 16-inch lengths.

YIELD: *5 pounds of sausage*

Note: This sausage is highly perishable. It may be fried,

baked, or boiled. When kept in the refrigerator, it should be covered in cold water. It freezes well.

Mildly Hot Italian Sausages

10 pounds boneless pork butts
1 tablespoon crushed fennel seeds
1 tablespoon crushed hot red pepper flakes
1 teaspoon caraway seeds
1 tablespoon coriander seeds
1 tablespoon sugar
6 tablespoons salt
2 cups ice water

Trim off and discard any blood clots, sinews, etc., in the pork butts. Cut the pork into 1-inch cubes.

Grind the pork using a grinder blade with ¼-inch holes.

Put the meat in a bowl and add the remaining ingredients, blending thoroughly.

Stuff the meat into medium-sized hog casings (32–35 millimeters in diameter). Tie the sausages at each end into 6-inch lengths. Hang on sticks to dry in a cool place. Refrigerate. Do not keep sausages at room temperature longer than necessary.

YIELD: *10 pounds of sausage*

French Breakfast Sausages

8 pounds lean pork, cut into cubes
2 pounds pork fat, cut into cubes
½ cup salt
1 tablespoon ground white pepper
2 tablespoons rubbed sage
1 teaspoon ground ginger
1 tablespoon freshly grated nutmeg
1 tablespoon dried thyme

1 **tablespoon ground hot red pepper flakes (optional)**
2 **cups ice water**

Chill the meat and fat and grind it, preferably using a grinder blade with 3/16-inch holes.

Put the meat in a bowl and add the remaining ingredients, blending thoroughly.

Stuff the sausage mixture into hog casings (28–30 millimeters in diameter) or lamb casings (20–22 millimeters in diameter). Tie the sausages in 4- or 5-inch lengths at each end.

Let the sausages chill and dry in a very cool place.

YIELD: *11 pounds of sausage*

Note: In the first recipe (Kielbasa—Smoked Polish Sausage) we mentioned the use of Prague Powder. This is the common curing agent in sausage making today. Prague Powder #1 is sodium nitrate; Prague Powder #2 is a blend of sodium nitrate and sodium nitrite. There has been controversy over the years as to whether they are cancer-causing agents. One or the other—nitrites or nitrates—are present in almost all meats sold for home consumption. Their good effect is that they inhibit the growth of the bacteria that causes botulism, a deadly food poisoning. It is used only sparingly in the preparation of these sausages, but Mr. Kutas in Buffalo does recommend its use. He has investigated all its pros and cons and feels that its benefits far outweigh any possible drawbacks.

Why Sausages Are a No-Competition Item

There are very few people—women or men—who have the ability to make any of the previous sausage preparations in their home. If you might have the knack for it, we strongly advise you to go ahead and do it. People just can't get enough of delicious-tasting, homemade sausages, and you'll find it a most profitable enterprise to get into. You'll have virtually no competition. That means an entire community to yourself. If you can turn out a first-rate sausage, you'll easily get more orders than you can handle.

An Amazing Book About the Secrets of Sausage Making

If you are serious about going ahead, you will of course need more information than is provided in this chapter. In addition to the free catalogue listing the supplies and ingredients you'll need, Mr. Kutas has also written a book covering all the details you'll need to profit in this business of sausage-making. The book costs $7.95 plus 80¢ postage charge. This extra investment is well worth it, as Mr. Kutas is acknowledged to be perhaps the country's finest expert in sausage making. His address is given earlier in this chapter.

If you go into the sausage-making business, you'll have start-up costs that you wouldn't ordinarily have—namely special equipment and supplies. These will most likely have to be purchased brand new, since second-hand equipment of this nature will be hard to find. You have to take these expenses into consideration, but your first priority is to feel comfortable with sausage making as a business. If you have a feeling for making sausages, then by all means buy Mr. Kutas' book for a start. It all comes down to your own particular ability in the kitchen. Only *you* know what you can do best! Once you know that, we can show you how to profit by it.

Advertising Copy That Gets People to Buy

The technique of selling sausages to folks in your area will be similar to methods previously outlined. You can combine selling wholesale and retail. That is, combining sales to restaurants, stores, schools, and institutions (selling wholesale) and selling direct to consumers (retail). As we have said, the latter is more profitable since it's *direct* selling—there's no middle man, so you'll be getting the top price per pound of sausage. John Slovacek, if you recall, sold 90% of his sausages wholesale, and only 10% retail. Some people prefer selling wholesale because, although the profits are lower, they are more consistent. The stores generally give you a set order each week. When you sell direct to consumers, you are often unable to predict the number of orders you will receive. A great deal depends on two things: (1) the type of product you make; and (2) the manner in which you prefer to sell it.

If you're thinking of selling direct to consumers, the following ad might be effective in your local newspaper or regional magazine:

> *French Breakfast Sausages* the same way French farmers make them. Chock full of country pork, they turn a Sunday breakfast into a feast. You'll never again settle for dry supermarket meats once you sink your teeth into these pink, plump, delicious country sausages. Call (your name and phone number).

This ad might interest readers. For another approach, hire a young copywriter as we have previously suggested.

With a specialty item such as sausages, you'll need to charge at least double the cost of your ingredients (100% markup). You might be able to charge triple the cost of your ingredients (200% markup). In this business, a bigger profit can be made when there's a real *scarcity* of your specialty! And in the case of delicious homemade sausages, it's fair to say that you can hardly find them anywhere. Besides, you have a business consideration to think about: if you go into sausage-making, you'll have heavy start-up costs for new equipment. You'll have to set a high price per pound of sausage in order to start paying off your investment. However, since homemade sausages are such a unique treat, you can be sure that people will *gladly* pay a high price for them! Once you build up a steady supply of customers, it should not be hard to earn up to $250 a week.

On a 50-week basis—allowing two weeks for vacation—that amounts to a tidy income of $12,500 a year!

Chapter Summary

1. For a free catalogue listing all the supplies and ingredients you'll need to enter the sausage-making business, write to:

> Richard S. Kutas Company
> 1067 Grant Street
> Buffalo, New York 14207

2. To obtain the book detailing everything you'll need to know about sausage-making, write to the above address.

3. You can sell your sausages wholesale or retail, or you can combine both methods.

4. You charge a *different* price selling wholesale (to restaurants and stores) than you do selling retail. Of course, you charge less to stores and restaurants because *they* have to make their profit on it when charging their customers. You must get at least *double* your costs when selling your sausages to restaurants and stores, and at least *triple* your costs when selling direct to consumers. But always try for more, even go for triple your costs when selling wholesale. Visit several fine restaurants and gourmet food stores and give out samples of your delicious sausages. Figure out your costs and arrive at your price *before* you go out to sell, and then stick to your guns. If your sausages are really "out-of-this-world," the store owner will most likely meet your price. If he resists it, you can always come down a bit. If he's trying to bargain too much, you always have the option of walking away and going to other stores. He's not the only place in town!

5. Before you set a price for selling retail, it's a good idea to check the price of sausages in supermarkets, just to see what people are paying for them. Of course, you'll have to get more for yours, but it's a good idea to learn what people are currently paying for sausages.

6. Advertise your product in a local newspaper or regional magazine. Start off with a small classified ad and run it several times to see the response you get.

7. It can prove to be a *great* idea to send several samples of your sausage to the food editor of your local newspaper. If she loves it enough to write about it, this type of publicity will do wonders for your business. And this mention in the newspaper doesn't cost you a red cent.

Chapter 6

How to Earn Up to $25,000 a Year Catering Low-Fat, Low-Salt, Low-Sugar Gourmet Meals

How to Make Money and Help Save Lives Too

Wherever you are in the country at this moment, you can be certain that there are thousands of people in your area alone who, because of health problems, have been strongly advised by their doctors to eat meals that are low in fat, low in sugar, and low in salt.

You'd be amazed at the amount of people who suffer from heart disease, diabetes, and high blood pressure. Some 7 million Americans are afflicted by heart disease, 5 million suffer from diabetes, and an additional 23 million people have been diagnosed as having high blood pressure. On top of that, more than 50 million are overweight and headed for trouble if they don't change their diet.

Some doctors say that reduced intake of fats, sugar and salt is a *must* for all these people. Other doctors feel that the link between nutrition and disease has not been clearly made. But the American Heart Association—perhaps the most respected medical organization in the country—has come out strongly in favor of diets restricting the amount of saturated fats, refined sugar, and salt. They argue that such diets will help not only those currently afflicted, but may actually aid in the prevention of heart disease, diabetes, high blood pressure, and obesity.

A Billion-Dollar Market
That Restaurants Are Neglecting

We have a situation where millions of people have been told that they *must* change their eating habits in order to live. The biggest problem they face is not knowing where to turn. For their health's sake these people must change their eating habits, but many of them can neither prepare the proper meals nor find restaurants that can cater to their needs. That's where you, as a Kitchen Lady, can help. We'll show you how to prepare meals for people who must watch their health. Most of these people would be delighted to pay for these meals, if they could be delivered to their home perhaps once, twice, or even three or more times a week. What they don't want are dull, tasteless "diet foods." What they *are* looking for are delicious gourmet meals low in fats, sugar, and salt.

How to Cash In on This Market
Without Opening a Restaurant

If you can make this your specialty you'll find that catering to people who must eat a certain way will have two important benefits: you'll make money, and you just might help save lives.

The Secret Is in Catering
Low-Fat, Low-Salt, Low-Sugar Meals

We will give you the recipes for an assortment of soups, entrées, and desserts. Each is delicious, satisfying and conforms
to each person's need for low-fat, low-sugar, low-salt meals. If
you have the talent to make these dishes, we're sure that you'll
start to develop your own delicious health specialties. It's a
good idea to ask your new-found customers what dishes *they*
like. You'll be able to make their favorites, using less fat, sugar, and salt—and it'll be so delicious that they'll never know
the difference.

Tomato Garden Soup

This soup is especially good for people who are on strict diets.
It is low in fat, salt, and sugar, and low in calories. It is also
economical and could easily be frozen. The proportions can be
doubled without any problems. This serves 6 to 8 people.

4–5 cups V-8 juice
**3–4 cups vegetables (cooked leftovers or fresh-
      chopped, including onions, corn, green beans, zuc-
      chini, carrots, squash, green peppers, celery, broc-
      coli florets and chopped stems, potatoes, etc.)**
2–3 tablespoons cider vinegar
      Tarragon, basil, and coriander to taste

Put V-8 juice and all the vegetables into a pot. Bring to a boil.
Reduce heat and simmer for 15–20 minutes.

Add vinegar and adjust seasonings.

Split Pea Soup

This soup is an old-fashioned favorite, but it is adapted for
people who have to watch their fat intake. It is also ideal for
people on low-salt and low-sugar diets. The recipe serves ap-

proximately 8 people, but the ingredients can be doubled for a larger quantity. It also freezes beautifully.

>   2 **quarts (8 cups) water**
>   2 **cups dried green split peas**
>   1 **large stalk celery, roughly chopped**
>   1 **large carrot, peeled and chopped**
>   1 **medium onion, chopped**
>   1 **dash cayenne**
>   1 **large bay leaf**
>   ¼ **teaspoon ground thyme (optional)**
>   **Black pepper to taste**
>   **Hearty dash cumin and curry powder**
>   **Pinch of marjoram**

Put all the ingredients into soup pot and bring to a boil.

Boil hard for 20 minutes, then slowly over a gentle flame until peas are tender. Stir occasionally.

Put half of soup (or more) in blender and blend, then reheat and adjust seasoning.

Hot or Cold Tomato Watercress Soup

When tomatoes are in season, this is a delicious and economical soup to serve. It is low in calories and low in cholesterol. If serving cold, whisk in ¼ cup low-fat yogurt. It thickens soup and makes it creamier. This recipe serves 6.

>   1 **tablespoon corn oil**
>   1 **onion, minced**
>   1 **clove garlic, minced fine**
>   1 **leek, white part only (washed and minced)**
>   1 **shallot, minced fine**
>   1 **teaspoon wine vinegar**
>   ½ **cup water**
>   3½ **cups chicken stock (or broth)**
>   3 **ripe, fresh tomatoes, skinned, cored and chopped**
>   1 **tablespoon tomato paste**
>   ½ **bunch watercress (leaves only, washed & chopped)**

4 **dashes of cayenne pepper**
   Bouquet garni (¼ teaspoon fennel seeds, ½ tea-
   spoon thyme, ¼ teaspoon basil leaves, tied together
   in cheesecloth)

Heat oil in heavy-bottomed saucepan. Saute onion, garlic, leek, and shallot until soft but not brown. Add vinegar, and cook 2 minutes longer.

Add water, chicken stock, tomatoes plus tomato paste, watercress, pepper, and bouquet garni. Cover partially and bring to simmering point. Simmer for 20 minutes. Remove bouquet garni. Let cool in covered saucepan. Pour into blender and purée for 1 minute, then pour through a fine sieve.

Can be reheated or served chilled, sprinkled with chopped watercress.

Apple-Glazed Cornish Hens

This delicious dish serves 8 people if the hens are halved, or 4 people if served whole. It is a low-fat, low-salt recipe, and it is also low in calories.

4 **Rock Cornish hens, about 1 pound each**
1 **cup undiluted frozen apple juice concentrate, thawed**
1 **tablespoon cornstarch**
1 **teaspoon ground cinnamon**
3 **slices lemon**

Wash and dry hens and put them in a roasting pan.

In a pot combine apple juice, cornstarch, and cinnamon, and mix until smooth. Add lemon slices. Cook over medium heat until mixture thickens. Brush glaze over hens.

In a 375-degree oven, roast hens for 1 hour or until tender, basting with additional glaze several times during cooking.

Serve either cut in half or whole. Can be garnished with thin lemon slices.

Old-Fashioned Sauerbraten

This dish is for people on salt-restricted diets. It is also low in calories. Serves 8.

> 2 cups water
> 2 cups vinegar
> 10 peppercorns
> 3 bay leaves
> 10 whole cloves
> 1 good-sized onion, sliced
> 4 pounds beef pot roast
> 2 tablespoons flour
> 2 tablespoons vegetable oil

In a pot combine water, vinegar, peppercorns, bay leaves, cloves, and sliced onions, and bring to a boil.

Place meat in a bowl and pour hot mixture over meat. Cover and marinate in refrigerator for two days, turning occasionally.

Remove meat, drain, and rub with flour. Brown on all sides in hot oil. Put into heavy pot, add marinade, cover, and bring to a boil. Reduce heat and simmer 2–3 hours, or until tender.

Note: This is nice served with small boiled onions, potatoes, and carrots.

Exotic Stuffed Roast Chicken

This recipe serves 6–8 people. It is low in fat, and contains no sugar and minimal salt. It is high in fiber, and very, very tasty.

> 1 5-pound roasting chicken
> 1 good-sized lemon
> 3 cups partially cooked bulgar
> 1 cup frozen tiny peas, uncooked
> 2 tablespoons blanched sunflower kernels
> ¼ cup raisins
> Pinch of salt

 1 cup low-fat yogurt
 1 tablespoon powdered ginger
 2 tablespoons grated onions

Rinse out cavity of chicken and rub outside of chicken with cut side of lemon, then sprinkle juice from lemon inside cavity of chicken.

Combine bulgar (cooked only about 12 minutes), peas, sunflower kernels, raisins, and salt to taste. Stuff chicken cavity loosely, as it will swell as bulgar continues to cook. Truss.

Brush outside of chicken with a mixture of yogurt, ginger, and grated onions. Put on rack in shallow roasting pan and bake in oven at 350 degrees for about 1 hour or until tender.

Baked Turkey Hash

This dish is good for those who are staying away from red meat. It's also economical because it utilizes leftover turkey. This recipe serves 8–10 people.

 3 cups cooked, chopped turkey
 1 cup turkey gravy
 2 cups shredded wheat, crumbled
 ½ cup diced celery
 2 eggs, slightly beaten
 1 pimiento, chopped
 1 tablespoon chopped fresh parsley
 1 tablespoon lemon juice and the grated rind of 1 small lemon
 3 tablespoons minced onion
 ⅔ cup skimmed milk

Combine all ingredients in large bowl and turn into lightly greased shallow baking pan (about 7 × 12 × 2 inches).

Put this pan into a larger roasting pan, to which water is then added to depth of ¼ inch. Put into moderate oven (350 degrees) and bake for 50–60 minutes.

Cut into generous squares to serve.

Note: This is a good dish to offer with French-style green beans and gingered carrots.

Ratatouille

This is a lovely side dish which can be made into a main dish by offering it with brown rice or kasha. It is perfect for vegetarians and anyone on a low-calorie, low-salt diet. This recipe makes 8 servings.

- 1 **cup sliced zucchini**
- 1 **large green pepper, cut into chunks**
- 1 **large onion, cut into chunks**
- ½ **of a large eggplant, peeled and cut into chunks**
- 2 **finely chopped shallots**
- 1 **clove garlic, minced**
- ⅛ **teaspoon pepper (or to taste)**
- 1 **tablespoon fresh parsley, minced**
- 2 **cups fresh tomatoes cut into chunks (or diced canned tomatoes)**

Put all ingredients, except tomatoes, into a nonstick skillet, cover, and cook over low heat for 20 minutes.

Remove cover and continue cooking 15 minutes more over moderate heat, stirring often to prevent scorching.

Add tomatoes, heating thoroughly—but do not permit tomatoes to become mushy.

Note: One could also add, according to taste, basil or oregano.

Chick Pea Salad

This is a tasty salad to offer those on a low-fat, no-salt and no-sugar diet. It keeps well in the refrigerator, and the ingredients can easily be doubled.

  2 cups canned or cooked chick peas
1-2 garlic cloves, peeled and crushed
  1 good-sized tomato, chopped
  3 scallions (chopped, white and green parts)
  ½ cup sweet red peppers, chopped
  ¼ cup minced parsley
  2 tablespoons vinegar (white or cider) or more if de-
     sired
     Black pepper, freshly ground

Combine all ingredients, mixing well. Marinate several hours
in refrigerator before serving.

Cole Slaw

This salad is simple to make, delicious to eat, low-caloried,
and low in salt. It serves 8 and the ingredients can easily be
doubled. It keeps well in the refrigerator in plastic containers.

  1 small head firm white cabbage
  4 dessert apples
  1 carrot (or more if desired)
  2 celery stalks
  1 green pepper, seeded and chopped
  3 tablespoons chopped parsley
  3 tablespoons chopped chives
  ¾ cup chopped walnuts
     Juice of 1 lemon
  1 cup dressing (or more if desired)

Apple Cider Vinegar Dressing

½ cup apple cider vinegar
½ cup cold water
½ teaspoon prepared mustard
2 tablespoons apple juice concentrate, undiluted
   Put into a glass jar and shake well. Taste and add
   more apple juice concentrate if needed.

Shred the cabbage fine, discarding stalk. Leave the skins on apples and core and chop them. Toss in lemon juice. Wash and chop celery and grate carrots.

Put all the ingredients into a large bowl and pour the apple cider vinegar dressing over all, tossing well.

Refrigerate.

Surprise Cookies

These cookies contain 2 milligrams sodium per cookie, and are 45 calories each. This recipe makes 6 dozen cookies.

> 1 **cup unsalted margarine**
> 1 **cup sugar**
> 1 **egg yolk**
> 2 **cups sifted all-purpose flour**
> ¼ **teaspoon mace**
> 3 **teaspoons cinnamon**
> 1 **egg white**
> **Ground walnuts**

Cream margarine and sugar together thoroughly. Beat in egg yolk. Add flour, mace, and cinnamon. Blend all ingredients well. Roll pieces of the dough into 1-inch balls between greased hands.

Place the balls about two inches apart on an ungreased cookie sheet. With a floured spatula, press each ball paper thin. Brush with egg white and sprinkle with ground nuts. Put into oven and bake at 350 degrees for 10–12 minutes, until edges brown.

Chapter Summary

1. We've just given you several tasty recipes for soups, entrées, side dishes, and desserts that are low in fat, low in sugar, and low in salt. Today, there are dozens of cookbooks that specialize in recipes for people who must watch what they eat. You can borrow these cookbooks from your public library, or

you may wish to purchase one or two from your local bookstore. It all comes down to how serious you are about getting into this phase of the business. We *know* that there's a huge market for Kitchen Ladies who are willing to specialize in dishes for people who are on doctor-recommended diets. Remember, there are tens of millions of people in the country in that position, so you can reasonably expect that there are thousands in your community alone.

2. Just look around you! We're willing to bet that you yourself know several men and women who have health problems, and who should be more conscious of what they eat. But you know what happens: people often don't do what's best for them. They'd be willing to eat the right meals if someone else prepared them and delivered them to their door. That's exactly where you come in.

3. As we have suggested in previous chapters, use local classified ads to announce your unique service. Write a simple piece of copy or hire—on a free-lance basis—a professional copywriter.

4. Regarding what to charge: you should have virtually no competition in this "cooking-for-health" area. You should be able to charge *three* times the cost of your ingredients—sometimes even *four* times as much. This is not at all outrageous! If a couple on this special food program were to go to a fine restaurant offering these dishes—if such a restaurant could even be found—they'd pay about $15 per person. And we're not even talking about the added expenses of a night out. *You're* offering *home* delivery of delicious meals that are tailored to these peoples' needs. So you deserve to make a very healthy profit. We expect that you will build up a loyal following of customers who will be ordering your meals at least once or twice a week on a year-round basis. It will not be difficult for you to earn $15,000 to $25,000 a year selling this specialty— *right from your own kitchen!*

5. You could even earn more, depending on how ambitious you are. (And think of all the good you're doing!)

Chapter 7

How to Earn Hundreds of Dollars a Week Selling Jams and Preserves Through the Mail

Hundreds of Dollars Every Week in Your Mailbox!

Everybody loves to receive something in the mail. It's unexpected—a pleasant surprise. The mail order business is a *60-billion-dollar-a-year* industry. There are over ten thousand firms in this business—some large, most of them small. Of the small ones, most of them are run by a single person or a couple. It all comes down to this: mail order can work for you if you have something different—something the customers can't get so easily.

Everybody Has a Sweet Tooth

When it comes to buying jams and preserves, the fact is that today people are buying doctored fruit glue which is being

passed off as jam. If *you* can make a truly delicious cherry or
strawberry jam, or perhaps orange marmalade, you can sell it
for 50¢ an ounce. You can sell a 16-ounce jar for $8.95. You'll
get customers through the mail, some of whom will order a set
of two for a combined price of $17.90 plus postage. How come?
Because there are a lot of folks around who have enough money to spend on something that's really special and can't be
found anywhere else. Before we get into the details on how to
go about getting started in the mail order business we want to
call your attention to an advertisement in a magazine called
The Gourmet Shoppe.

The $78,000 Mail Order Product

A LINCOLN CONTINENTAL GOLD STAR
CUSTOM LIMOUSINE!

Impeccably handcrafted elegance is yours with this noticeably
superior motorcar. Each is custom built to your specifications
and personally delivered to you by our uniformed chauffeur
anywhere in the continental United States.
$39,500; $78,000 for a Matched Set

This ad *really* appeared in the magazine we mentioned. And
believe us, the ad worked and orders were taken. Why? First,
there are people in this country—despite the times we're living in—who can afford to spend that kind of money on a car
(or the pair!). Secondly, there's a "snob appeal" to buying a
car through the mail—it makes a person feel *different.*
     We brought this ad to your attention because it's an exam-
ple of matching the product to the reader. That ad appeared
in *The Gourmet Shoppe,* a magazine that's mailed to people
in very high income brackets. Men earning very high salaries
have subscriptions to that particular magazine. It's exactly the

audience that car ad is trying to reach. We'll have more to say about this later on.

What Sells Through the Mails?

Now let's discuss more down-to-earth products—specifically, what's being sold through the mails and enjoying success. Meats, smoked hams, lobsters, cheeses, fruits, preserves, fruitcakes, candy, nuts, pastry, coffee, tea, and similar items are selling successfully by mail order. Naturally, there are hundreds of other products sold through the mail; we, however, are solely concerned with products that can be made in the kitchen.

Don't Be Afraid of Competition

Before you start to think of selling your product by mail, it's a good idea to inspect the competition. Look over all the mail order catalogues and see who your competition is. Sure, there are other folks selling jams and preserves, but don't let that stop you. If your product is delicious, there's room enough for you, too. There's more than one person selling pecans and country hams who lives in Georgia. And in California, lots of mail order sellers ship olives, nuts, and citrus fruits through the mail. In Wisconsin, there are dozens of companies selling cheeses by mail. Fruitcakes are being sold by many people in the mail order business. Then there are maple syrups and fruit preserves being actively sold through mail order in the Northeast.

Thus, it's always a good idea for you to look through as many mail order magazines and catalogues as you can. Of course there will be competition, but never take the attitude of, "Gosh, they're already in business. How could *I* stand a chance?" The truth is, you stand a very good chance—it's a big country.

Make the Best Jam
Anyone's Ever Tasted

The constant inspiration for you in this business is that your product tastes terrific—and other folks have told you so. If it's jams or preserves you have in mind, just make sure you make the best there is. (Be sure others think so, too.)

The success in this business is *repeat* business. The people who will be sending for your product are already jam lovers, and when you please them, they become loyal customers. Getting your jams in their mail is their first surprise, and loving the taste is the second. When that happens, you've got yourself a steady customer who, in turn, starts telling other folks about you.

How to Make Lifelong Friends
Through the Mail

It often happens that when people order and reorder your product, they'll include a personal note telling you how pleased they are—pleased enough to tell friends about your great jams and preserves. Do yourself a favor and answer them. In the mail order business you actually make new friends thousands of miles away. We've known some mail order producers who, after years of selling to a particular customer and exchanging letters, actually arrange some time to visit each other. Lifelong friendships are made that way!

The Most Important Person
You'll Need to Know

When you start out in the mail order business, there's one person you must make friends with—your local postmaster. It's one thing to take a homemade product and deliver it personally to a store or individual customer. It's an entirely different matter to send it through the mail. It's done all the time of course, but your postmaster is expert in these matters. Most often, he'll be happy to help.

How to Pack Your Product for Shipping

Your first real task, once you have your preserves made and put in jars, is to find the best way to pack them for shipping. What type of shipping container? Go to the yellow pages of your phone book. Look under "Containers/Packaging" and call various suppliers. Advise them of what you have to ship, and ask them to suggest a suitable shipping container. The art of packaging is so advanced today that you'll find strong yet lightweight boxes that are perfect for your needs. It's extremely important that your product arrive undamaged. There is nothing more unappetizing than opening a package and finding its contents spread out all over the inside.

Here's one way to guard against that happening to your product: after you've selected what you feel is the right type of shipping box, send a half-dozen of your preserves to friends or members or your family. Preferably send your product to relatives who have moved to different parts of the country. Simply put a note inside asking for their opinions as to what shape the preserves were in when they arrived.

You'll find out that there are various ways to ship your preserves. You might combine the use of the U.S. Mail with a delivery service such as United Parcel. Usually, the most economical way is to have a delivery service call for a once-a-week pickup or drop-off at its shipping station.

The Best Times of the Year to Make Money

In the mail order business, there's a rule that Christmas comes twice a year. The big order season for gifts through the mail is Christmas, but there are also the two months embracing

Mother's Day and Father's Day. Most of your mail order business takes place during those two periods. Don't spend your time wondering, "How much money could I make in that brief time?" You can make plenty! Since *billions* of dollars are earned through mail order every year, the volume and movement of goods during those two periods has to be fantastic.

Using Mail Order to Cash In on the New Shopping Trend

Depending on your product, you could get repeat business throughout the year. The trend is on your side. More and more, the general public wants homemade products year round, and they're willing to pay for it. Aside from that, people all over the country are cutting down their visits to supermarkets. They still go to shop for their staples, but they often look to mail order for something special. A recent—and staggering—statistic reveals that by 1990, *one out of two people* will no longer be shopping by conventional means. That's an amazing turn of events!

Who Your Best Customers Are

Your market is that enormous number of people now earning a very good salary and living in the major cities throughout the country. These folks were often raised in small towns and communities, and they remember what things used to taste like. There are lots of jam lovers among them and they're not about to be satisfied with what they find on the shelves in their local supermarket. These are the people you have to reach. They'll respond to an advertisement that tells them of a real homemade treat.

The Secret of Reaching People

You've got two choices: you can buy mailing lists and send out brochures with prices to people on the list; or you can advertise in a local newspaper or regional magazine.

Renting Mailing Lists

Regarding the first option, look in the Yellow Pages under "Mail Order." You'll find individuals who rent mailing lists to people who want direct contact with potential buyers of their products. What this means is that you, selling a home-packaged product, primarily want to reach men and women who have been *known* to purchase products by mail. That method of mail order is called "direct mail," and it is what it says: you are directly contacting people who are favorably disposed to purchasing your product. They enjoy buying by mail!

These mailing lists vary in price: sometimes the man leasing them rents his list at a cost to you of about $25-$45 per 1,000 names. Compare prices by calling several mail order firms. Never fail to tell them the list you're looking for: *men and women of above average income who buy food products through the mail.*

How to Avoid Mistakes

Be sure to specify that you want "fresh" names. In other words, make sure you get names of people who have been recently contacted for other products, who still live at those addresses, and who are still alive! Beware of mail order companies who have lists that are years old and not used. Otherwise, you'll be mailing your brochures to people who don't exist. You'll have some letters coming back to you from the post office, but they should amount to no more than 5% of the total number mailed out.

The best idea of all is to ask each mail order company for references. Ask for the names of others who have rented their lists, and call and ask for their comments; find out if the lists they rented were profitable to their business. If the company doesn't want to give you any references, then *don't* do any business with them. If they want your hard-earned money, they have to prove themselves to you.

Mail order people are also called "list brokers," and they rent their lists to those who want to use direct mail. Remember, direct mail is used to reach those specific people who represent a market for a particular product. In the beginning you might be renting these mailing lists, but in a few years, chances are that you'll start to build up your *own* from new customers who will buy your product. When that happens, you then own your own list and can rent it out to others at rates ranging from $25 to $45 per thousand names. And you can rent out your list over and over again. This represents a separate profit area for you. (Rental prices keep escalating, so adjust your prices accordingly.)

Advertising

Whether you will try direct mail to sell your product or buy small space ads in a newspaper or regional magazine, you still need something to tell your potential customers in order to get them to buy. You need that all-important advertising message that will convince them that your product is worth sending away for.

In the case of direct mail, type your words on a sheet of 8½×11 paper (if you can't type, write it out in longhand and a local printer will set it in type). For a magazine ad, you'll still need to write out your advertising copy. When you go to the office of the newspaper or regional magazine, someone there will show you what "space" in the paper or magazine your copy will fit into. They are talking about size, by which they mean an ad of 50 lines, 100 lines, 200 lines, even up to a full page. It all depends on how big a space you can afford. If even the cost of a small space ad is too expensive, you might try a classified ad consisting of just a few lines. The factors you take into consideration are how much space you need to deliver your message and how much you can afford to invest.

Testing Is the Key to Success

Always remember that in mail order, there are two basic elements that must be tested: (1) the advertising message itself; and (2) where you test it, e.g., direct mail vs. local newspaper vs. regional magazines. You try several methods, and weigh the responses you get from each. That way, you are never putting all your eggs in one basket. Always experiment with *what* you say and *where* you say it. When one way proves better than the others, you are no longer investing just *your* money to pay for the ads—you're using some of the money derived from sales.

One simple measurement of the success of any particular ad is that you're getting back in sales *more* than it cost you to run the ad. Some mail order producers feel they have to make a "killing" on each ad; that's childish! Just make sure that each ad throws off a profit. If it does, be sure to repeat it.

The smart advertiser just keeps doing the same thing. If you were to read several popular mail order magazines, you would see—month after month—the same advertisers repeating their ads. They only do this for one reason: they're making money.

Compare Costs

When starting out, compare the prices for direct mail and for space advertising. In direct mail, find out how much five thousand letters and envelopes will cost to print, all done in an inexpensive photo offset manner. The printer will also design a letterhead that will carry your name and address (which should also appear on the envelopes). To the printing cost, add the list rental fee and the expense of mailing. Compare this against the cost of a space ad.

Remember, you'll be able to say a lot more via direct mail—after all, you have two sides of a large sheet of paper to write out your message. That amount of space would be extremely expensive in a space ad. On the other hand, a space ad reaches a lot more people.

For the beginner, mail order is a complex business. It's *your* money that you'll be spending, so proceed with caution. If you can locate one or two mail order specialists in your area, it would be extremely helpful to seek out their advice. These specialists sell no products of their own; instead, they offer advice to people who have products to sell.

That All-Important Message

As we've suggested in previous chapters, when an advertising message is to be written, it's sometimes best to hire a free-lance copywriter. But if you want to try your own hand at it, our advice to you is to be natural; be yourself. Write the words as if you're talking about your jams and preserves to a friend.

For a few moments, let's put ourselves in a situation where we have a really delicious strawberry preserve and orange marmalade we want others to buy. We would write a long letter, right from the heart, and use it as a direct mail piece to send to potential customers. The following piece of copy that we offer is *only* an example of the feeling you should try to communicate. What you eventually end up writing should be your *own* words as you would speak them. That's always the best kind of message.

Dear Friend:

I wish I was as good in writing words as I am in making preserves. No matter how I try, I just don't have the knack to write down the words which have a certain ring to them—words that make people say, "I want that." Maybe I should have gone to college; I don't know. What I *do* know is that I sure make the best-tasting strawberry preserves and orange marmalade that ever came down the pike.

You see, I grew up in a time when folks really cared about what went into their product. They had to, because their name was on the label. In those days, you made sure you gave your customers everything they expected—and a little more—for the hard-earned money they were spending. That's how you kept customers for life.

Today it seems as if we've lost something along the way. People stopped caring about the quality of what they made. Except us. We still make our jams the way my folks made them and their folks before them.

We still grow plum-sized strawberries, each one with firm, meaty, almost white flesh that imparts a delicate aroma. I place alternate levels of my berries and sugar in large preserving kettles, and they stand from 3 to 10 hours before cooking. Then they're heated very slowly, with little stirring until the sugar is dissolved. This is followed by a brief boiling period, and before I take the berries from the stove, I add a little fresh lemon juice. After that, I pour my preserves into heated, sterilized crocks. Each crock is hand-sealed as tight as a drum. Nothing artificial is added. It would be a crime to do that, so we just don't do it.

If you want our orange marmalade, you can't go wrong either. We use only the plumpest, juiciest oranges and lemons. They're cut into thick slices (I've removed the seeds beforehand), and soaked in water for 24 hours. I drain the fruit, then cut it into small shreds and put it back into the water in which it was soaked. Boil for 1 hour and add sugar. Then into the sterilized, heated crocks. Every spoonful you get out of it is pure marmalade, and there are never any chemicals added.

There's nothing more to say. Each filled 16-ounce crock sells for $8.95. After you've finished the jam or marmalade, you'll want to keep these crocks on hand for a lot of years. You can find all sorts of uses for them.

Once you've tasted our jams and marmalades, we think you'll be hard put to go back to store-bought stuff. They just don't taste right anymore. We admit we're more expensive than they are, but there's an old expression which says: "You get what you pay for." We think we're selling the best there is—and we've been in this business for three generations. So a lot of folks must agree with us. If you don't think our strawberry preserve and orange marmalade is the best you've ever tasted, just write us and ask for your money back. You don't have to return a thing. Keep the crock (or both of them) as our gift to you. We'll send you a complete refund, no questions asked. We might add that in all the years we've been in this business, no one's asked for their money back yet.

Sincerely yours,

Mrs. _____

That piece of copy is good direct mail advertising copy. It's long, but since you're using an 8½ x 11 (sometimes 8½ x 14) sheet for your selling message, you'll have plenty of room for long copy. Always make your copy *truthful* to the way you make your product—be it jams, preserves, or something entirely different. In this age of mass production, people love reading all the details of something that's made the old-fashioned way. Always avoid using words such as "stupendous," "fantastic," "best in the world," "you haven't lived until you tasted this." Those are all Madison Avenue huckster words, and they sound phony. If you're going to write a letter and send it to prospective customers, just be yourself.

Don't Go Overboard!

When we speak of placing ads in magazines, we always mean local or regional magazines. It would be wonderful to take out an ad in *McCall's*. But a decent-sized ad in that magazine would cost thousands of dollars, and that's much too big a bite when you're first starting out. Besides, if you got a very big response from the ad—and *McCall's* has a readership of *millions* of women—there's no way you could make enough of your product to meet the demand. Sure, it's wonderful to think that ten thousand women are each going to send you a check or money order for $8.95—that's about $90,000. (And you could do even better than that when you advertise in a magazine that reaches some seven million women.) But you have to be prepared to meet the demand, and customers don't like to wait months after they've sent you their checks.

We've known other mail order producers in our business who fell into the trap of taking more orders than they could handle. They couldn't get out enough product to meet the demand, so their customers started to insist on refunds; others contacted the postal authorities to take action against the mail order company. We point this out as a warning: make sure you have the supply to meet the demand!

Telling Your Story
in a Classified Ad

A classified ad is the most inexpensive way of getting your feet wet. Almost all mail order companies, large and small, start out in this fashion. It is their way of *testing* a new product in the most economical way.

Put an insertion in a regional magazine and see what response you get. If you get enough response to cover the cost of the ad, you've made a profit and it's worth another insertion in the same magazine. Whereas in direct mail you have two full sides of a page to fill with copy, in a classified ad you generally have to confine yourself to only a few lines. (Some classified ads run only one or two lines, but they can be as long as eight to ten lines. It depends on your budget and the message you have to get across.) Here's an example of a classified ad that is fairly lengthy, but that could tempt people to buy your preserves:

For three generations the women in this house have made strawberry preserves the same way. Rich, ruby-red berries the size of plums, plus clear spring water, and pure brown sugar are all we use. Spoon some out on a chunk of good bread and you'll remember what jam used to taste like. Comes in a 16-ounce crock you keep for life. *$8.95. Money-back guarantee.* Check or money order to [NAME & ADDRESS].

If you cannot afford to run a classified ad of this size in a regional magazine, then consider placing this ad in your local newspaper. It'll be less costly. If even *this* proves too expensive for you, you still have alternatives. An especially effective one combines a "mini" classified ad with the power of direct mail. The way it might work is as follows:

Rich, ruby-red strawberries the size of plums used in a preserve made the way jams used to taste! Free details. [YOUR NAME & ADDRESS]

When potential customers write you for information, send

them the direct mail piece—filled with copy on both sides of the page—which you have prepared for this occasion. Include a coupon. The way to judge the success of this "free details plus follow-up" approach is simple: the income generated by this method *must* exceed the costs of both the classified ad and the direct mail follow-up.

A Word About the Crocks

Look in the Yellow Pages of your phone book under Pottery/ Earthenware to find a supply of crocks for your jams and preserves. Also look under "Crafts"; you might locate some men and women who have their own small pottery business. You could hire them to produce your crocks in their kilns.

We are obliged to point out that—although crocks are an attractive element of your sale—you might have to do without them, for the following two reasons: (1) it's quite possible there's no one in your area to make these crocks; and (2) even if someone can make them for you, their cost might be prohibitive.

We should point out at this time our rule of selling your product for double or triple your expenses. Add up the cost of your ingredients plus the expenses of advertising and mailing. Also add the price of the crocks. Your selling price must be at least double all incurred expenses. In the case of your jams and preserves, we're suggesting a retail price of $8.95 for a 16-ounce crock filled with either strawberry preserves or orange marmalade. If you find that the crock becomes too much of an expense, replace it with unbreakable jars and perhaps lower your price to about $6.95. You should still make a good profit on that basis.

(*Note:* All our prices are suggestions only. Prices vary in different parts of the country and are constantly affected by economic fluctuations. In the 1980s, prices can only go one way— UP! You must be ready to adjust with the market.)

Getting Your Mail Out on Time

If you're selling by direct mail, let your postmaster guide you. Tell him the dates you have to meet and he'll advise you when you must get your sales letters out. In other words, let's say you want your jams in the hands of customers by November 15th to the 20th in order to meet the Thanksgiving business. Your postmaster might tell you to "back up," by sending your initial letters in the first week of September. Allow ten days for the letter to reach your customers and ten to fourteen days for their response. By that time, it'll be the end of September. Start shipping out your product during the first and second week in October so they all get into your customers' homes by the 20th of November. Use this time guide to figure the Christmas business. This time, using the week of December 20th as a target date, back up your second batch of sales letters to include the same time ratio that you used to get your initial mailing out. Then follow up the orders you receive, and ship out your jams and preserves in time for them to arrive no later than December 22nd. The amount of time needed for packages to arrive at their destination is based on the amount of money spent in shipping them. (Obviously, you know that from your own experience.) You *must* discuss shipping rates with your local postmaster and a representative from United Parcel. Tell both of what you're sending, how much it weighs, and what your due dates are for arrival. Get all rates from them for each class of shipment. Only on that basis can you arrive at your shipping costs—and in the mail order business, that's a major factor as to the amount of profit you'll make.

Your Address vs.
a Post Office Box Number

Should you use your own address in doing business, or should people write to a post office box number when they are sending you checks and money orders? The opinion on this among the professionals in the mail order business is divided—some say use your home address, others say use a box number. Ask the postmaster for his opinion, particularly regarding the safety and convenience of receiving your checks and money orders. Much of this depends on where you live in the country. Note: This can be *tested*. Using the *same* copy in the *same* newspaper or magazine—alternate issues of course—place your home address in one and your post office box in another. See which ad pulls better. If you're using a direct mail letter to follow up a classified ad, be sure the address in the letter corresponds to the address in the ad.

Incidentally, give your postmaster—or the United Parcel man, if you're using him—a free sample of your jam or preserves. It's not a bribe. Your postmaster or UPS representative is simply human, like the rest of us. Once he's tasted what you're selling, he'll put a little extra into seeing that your packages get out on time and your checks and money orders come in safely.

How the Space Salesperson Can Help You

In running space ads (non-direct mail), ask the advertising representative of the magazine about his ideas of backdating in order to meet your seasonal demands (which include Thanksgiving, Christmas, and the May-June period). Understand that magazines—unlike newspapers—need a *big lead time*. In other words, to get into the October issue in order to meet the Thanksgiving business (November issue) you will have to have your copy in their hands by early September. Work all this out with the salesperson. Why not offer *him* (*her*) a sample of your delicious homemade product? We say there's nothing like getting other people involved in your success. It makes them want to give that extra little push to see that you get every advantage. It will only cost you a few jars of jam, but it will gain you some devoted followers. And who knows how many extra ways they can be helpful?

The mail order business is worth billions of dollars, and we'll tell you about a few people who got their share of the riches. They all have one thing in common: excellent products.

Lobsters by Mail

To begin with, we want to tell you about a man who started in this mail order business over thirty years ago, selling the most unlikely product imaginable: live lobsters. He started in business in 1949, with $753 in his bank account. He did only local selling, and built up his business slowly but surely. At the end of one year he was realizing enough sales to take the chance of buying a full page ad in the Sunday magazine section of *The New York Times*. Back then, that ad cost $2,252.50. He received over $10,000 in orders. A fine success. But examine the advertising closely:

THEY THOUGHT I WAS CRAZY TO SHIP LIVE MAINE LOBSTERS AS FAR AS 1,800 MILES FROM THE OCEAN!

But I Have Already Shipped 18,685 Of Them
And My Customers Are Delighted!

Old time lobstermen told me I was crazy. Whoever heard of selling live lobsters by mail. Well, here's how my crazy idea works: you write me and tell me the day you plan to have a lobster feast. I select your lobsters from the cold Maine waters. I pick the plump, solid ones about a pound and an eighth in weight—the best eating size, when the meat is at its tender, delicate best. I pack these choice lobsters between layers of rockweed in my Ready-To-Cook metal container. Then I put the container in a pine cask, pack it with ice and rush it to you by first class Railway Express, with re-icing en route if needed. Your lobsters arrive on schedule for the royal banquet. You have only to punch a few holes in the container lid, pour in a quart of salted water and put the container on the fire—all without even touching the lobsters. Wait till the steam starts, then cook for 15 minutes longer and take off the lid. There are your lobsters, done to a gorgeous scarlet, steamed-cooked to perfection in a real Down-East clambake style. Good? They're heavenly. You've never tasted better lobsters. The tang of the sea is in each luscious morsel. They're a gourmet's dream come true.

> Ed Davis
> Lobster Cove, Saltwater Farm
> Damariscotta, Maine

We don't know about you, but after reading that ad, Mr. Davis' lobsters sure appeal to us. It must have appealed to many people, because Mr. Davis was in business for quite some time. There was a classic example of a product people loved, spoken about with great warmth and sincerity. The man's dedication came through the ad. You *knew* he must ship delicious lobsters! If *you* can live up to this standard—no matter what your product is—then you'll also be a success in the mail order business.

Remember the Packaging

Ed Davis took great care to see that his package was perfect. He took it upon himself to ship his lobsters all over the country, so they had to arrive *live!* If they were dead, people had every right to feel that they weren't fresh; consequently, they wouldn't accept the lobsters. Ed Davis hardly ever had a single complaint. The lobsters always arrived alive and kicking. If Mr. Davis was able to solve such a complicated shipping problem thirty years ago, you should be able to overcome *any* shipping problem you might have today. As we've said, look in the yellow pages under "Containers/Packaging" and get the most reliable package for your product at the most reasonable price. When one of these suppliers does a good job for you, *stay* with him! He understands your needs.

1949 Prices vs. Today
(Read 'Em and Weep)

We'll tell you the price Ed Davis charged for his New England Shore Dinner in 1949, and we'll compare that to what a current mail order company is charging for a similar shipment. In 1949, Ed Davis shipped 8 lobsters—each weighing more than a pound—for $14.95. On top of that, he threw in half a peck of steamer clams. Today, there's a company who will ship you 8 lobsters, each a bit over a pound, for *$99.95!* Forget about the steamer clams. So, what cost $15 in 1949 costs $100 today— about a *650% increase* in price. It's hard to believe, but true. What's amazing is that people are *spending* the $100 to buy these lobsters, because we see this advertisement repeated in several mail order magazines each month. In this business, you repeat an ad when it's successful! (Always remember that rule.) Also remember that in mail order, a lot of folks aren't scared by high prices. They're willing to spend their money on what *really* appeals to them. Keep that in mind and you'll profit handsomely.

Others Who Have Discovered the Secret to Mail Order Success

We're going to give you the names of other people who are in the mail order business and doing well at it. We know they make a good deal of money, because they constantly advertise in the better magazines. But remember, all of them started out small! Most started off with one, or perhaps two, products, and then expanded—rapidly and consistently. You'll frequently see many mail order products that seem to duplicate each other; but as we've often stated, it doesn't matter. Each mail order producer is making his product the best way he (she) can, and each knows that there's room enough for everyone to prosper. They also know that the mail order market is *grow-*

ing; with the price of gasoline going up, more and more people are shopping by mail! What follows is a list of some of the largest mail order companies in the business. In some instances, we describe what they're selling.

The HOUSE OF ALMONDS in California. They do a huge nationwide mail order business, and they only started in 1966. In addition to almonds, they arrange gift packages to include cheeses, cakes, toffee, pistachio nuts, and various mixtures of sun-dried figs, prunes, peaches, pears, and apricots. They also have boxes of chocolate-covered dates, almond crunch, and carob crunch almond nut corn. They also have fruit-of-the-month gifts that allow folks to send a 3-month or 5-, 7-, or 12-month gift. The House of Almonds people say: "The gift that's ordered once to be delivered throughout the year and always appreciated." A very fine idea and they do a good business on it, offering apples at Christmas time, big California navel oranges in January, and other fruits and treats monthly throughout the year. And as we stated before, how people *love* to receive something in the mail! Something that's a treat, a surprise—something the whole family can share and enjoy!

We never met a person who didn't love a delicious fruitcake. This cake is the best-selling cake sold through the mails. It's chock full of everything people love to eat: pineapple chunks, cherries, almonds, pecans, walnuts, raisins, orange peel, lemon peel, figs, and it goes on and on, each baker having her own variation. People love fruitcake, because it's really more *candy* than cake!

There are two companies in Texas that do a huge Christmas business: MARY OF PUDDIN' HILL in Greenville and the COLLIN ST. BAKERY in Corsicana. A 2-pound cake in a gold foil gift box sells for $10, and they make a nice profit on it. You can count on that price going up year after year; why not? All the ingredients and the costs of shipping are going to keep rising. But we come down to the same old story in mail order. It's a good business because people *love* to get something in the mail. It makes for a better gift than if you would bring it to someone yourself. It seems that when you get something delicious in the mail, like a fruitcake, you don't have to wait to enjoy it. Everybody takes it out of the box and starts to dig in. If a friend brings one to the house, everyone makes all the appropriate "thank yous," and it doesn't seem proper to dig into the fruitcake, right then and there—which is what your family really *wants* to do!

Mail order has a certain psychology to it, and that's a big reason why it's so successful. It's mind-boggling to realize that Americans spend *$60 billion* annually buying products through the mail. Sure, only a part of that is for food products; but anyway you look at it, that's an awful lot of money. And if you look into the future, that figure will only go higher. But enough about economics; let's continue with the list of companies that are profiting from this business. And look how diverse they are!

In Salem, New York, there's the very successful MENACHAH FARMS SMOKEHOUSE. They started in 1975, and today throughout the nation they are shipping bacon, turkey, smoked meats, and have even added the delicacy of smoked duckling. They do a big Christmas business.

HARRY AND DAVID'S BEAR CREEK BAKERY in Medford, Oregon, is known for delicious baked goods and candy gifts. You'd wonder who would want desserts through the mail, but plenty of people do. Harry and David ship nationwide their delicious cheesecakes, fruit tortes, baklava, plum cakes, lemon cakes, chocolate cakes, and more. They have a big candy line including rum and mint truffles, plum creams, apricot dandies, and nut clusters. They sell what they call "Pecan Perfection," luscious pecans in a sweet-dough pastry shell baked till the pecans are caramelly and crunchy. They ship two of them, slightly over a pound each, out for $15.95, and they can't bake 'em fast enough for the holidays. And remember, it's $15.95 now but sure to go up. (And folks will keep buying them because they're delicious!)

You've probably seen mail order ads for FRANK LEWIS

SCHULTZ in Alamo, Texas. He sells only one item, his famous Ruby Red grapefruit. They're specially picked, and he calls them Royal Ruby Reds. He calls it "crazy" that one day he saw these red-meat grapefruits growing unexpectedly on a single branch in a grove in the Rio Grande Valley. Now people all over the nation enjoy them.

THE SWISS COLONY located in Monroe, Wisconsin, puts out a huge mail order gift catalogue. They have all types of cheeses in all shapes and sizes, sold in gift packs of many varieties. They also pack their soft cheeses in reusable crocks, glasses, holiday snifters, mugs—you name it. They have a great assortment of other gift packs, such as the Northwoods Brunch—a combination of bacon, ham roll, pork, pancake mix, maple syrup, marmalade, a jam and a jelly, all for $16.95. Send something like that to a friend or family member now living in a bustling city of a few million people, and you're going to get one happy phone call expressing appreciation. The Swiss Colony people sell all kinds of smoked meats in many varieties and a whole line of cakes and candies as well. They've been in business a long time and are doing very well at it, thank you. They intend to keep it that way.

When you hear about these big mail order companies, all doing so well, you might pause and say, "Where do I stand a chance?" Well, you stand a *great* chance. This business always has room for one more. Every one of the companies we've told you about started off with just a "Mom" or a "Mom & Pop" business. With a really fine product, and dedication, they grew and grew and grew. *One* product to start with is just fine. You don't need anything else.

SUGARDALE FOODS, INC. puts out a beautiful mail order catalogue filled with all types of gift assortments for sale. One that will catch the eye is their "Beauty Baked Ham—11–13 pounds for $35.95." They have a short, but effective piece of advertising copy to go with it:

Neatly scored on top, coated with a rich brown sugar glaze, and then baked with a mother's care to the peak of perfection. Shipped ready to eat. Guaranteed to arrive in perfect condition.

They do a nice business with their hams, yet one would think that the SMITHFIELD HAM PRODUCERS in Smithfield, Virginia, would scare anyone trying to get into that business. But that's not true; yes, the Smithfield country ham is about the best-known ham in the business, but there's always room for one more. As we have stated, the mail order business is *so* large that with a first-rate product, and making sure that your message reaches the people, you have a very good chance of not only getting off the ground, but of growing and prospering.

Incidentally, if you do have the money to invest in an ad in a local newspaper, *always* include a mail order coupon. Make sure it's large enough to be easily filled out. You'll recall the long piece of copy we suggested earlier in this chapter when we wrote about a strawberry preserve and an orange marmalade. Well, that ad *must* contain a coupon!

And send for the catalogues from these fine mail order houses:

Bachman Foods Inc.
8th and Reading Avenue
P.O. Box 898
Reading, PA 19603

Colonial Garden Kitchens
270 West Merrick Road
Valley Stream, NY 11582

Pepperidge Farm Mail Order Company
P.O. Box 119
Clinton, CT 06413

Win Schuler's
P.O. Box 104
Marshall, MI 49068

Country Store
Centerville
Cape Cod, MA 02632

Harry & Jane Wilson Sunnyland Farms, Inc.
Albany, GA 31702

The Epicures' Club
Union, NJ 07083

Mission Orchards
Box 224
Santa Clara, CA 95052

Pfaelzer Brothers
4501 West District Boulevard
Chicago, IL 60632

Chapter Summary

1. Make a thorough study of magazines and newspapers, and review the mail order ads appearing there over a period of time. Note ads that run consistently, month after month or several times a year. Answer ads that are particularly interesting. Carefully study the catalogues, sales letters, brochures, and sales literature received. Study particularly all follow-up mailings received. Learn from the promotion of the successful mail order firms. It's all one big competitive market, so learn well what the competition is doing.

2. Once you have decided on what food product you want to sell, it is time to promote sales. Sometimes you might sell your product directly from a space ad, or you might write a sales letter and solicit customers via direct mail. Another alternative is buying a classified ad; then, upon receiving inquiries, follow up with the direct mail approach. Only testing may reveal the most profitable way to sell any product. In general, the least expensive way to sell a product by mail is via classified advertising (newspapers and magazines), as opposed to using direct mail—which involves buying mailing lists at a cost of $25 to $45 per thousand names.

3. Advertising rates for magazines and newspapers and other media are shown in *Standard Rate & Data Service*, together

with closing dates (the deadline for your ad), circulation, and other data.

4. The service also includes the mechanical requirements of each publication. This refers to how you should *prepare* your ad for placement, i.e., layout, typesetting, etc. Most libraries have a copy of the *SRDS*.

5. Describe your product accurately, honestly, and in a way that will make it desirable to the reader. Bear in mind that exaggerated claims will be quickly detected and will do more to turn off prospective customers than anything else. In addition, Federal, State, and local government agencies, as well as the Better Business Bureau and consumer groups, constantly watch advertising and are quick to take action against unsubstantiated claims or infractions of any laws.

6. Use direct mail and media for advertising in accordance with your budget. In addition, keep careful records of the returns from ads and mailings. This will indicate which ads pull and which seasons or time of year produce better results than others. *Key* each of your ads—use an abbreviation of a newspaper or magazine with the order coupon—so you know which paper or magazine is doing a better job.

7. Classified advertising can be an excellent and inexpensive way of testing your product. In many respects, it is the mail order operator's best friend. For relatively small sums, several ads can be simultaneously tested to determine which are more effective before investing in large-scale advertising. Many people rely solely and successfully on classified advertising.

8. Despite increasing costs of postage, printing, paper and mailing operations, direct mail continues to be an effective and profitable means of selling. Mailing lists covering virtually every conceivable type of market and customer base are available from a great variety of sources.

9. If you have the ability to communicate clearly, effectively and persuasively, write your own copy. Many mail order people do and often attribute their success to their own particular style of writing that "brings in the orders." That, of course, is

the ultimate criterion. If writing copy is not your skill, hire a competent professional. Earlier in this chapter, we gave you examples of persuasive copy.

10. To succeed in mail order, pay close attention to details! However, don't get bogged down in them. Keeping accurate records, results of ads, advertising costs, printing, postage, cost-per-order, and other figures is important to the success of the business.

11. *Repeat business is your key to maximum profits.* Continuous profits come from continuous sales. If you're successfully selling one food item through the mail, consider selling others. There are many ways to stimulate repeat orders, and create new orders at minimal cost.

(A) Never forget the customer. The list of customers built up is a most valuable asset. Use it to send offers of merchandise at frequent intervals.

(B) Use package stuffers. A regular catalogue or a special offer rides "free" in outgoing orders. This means that while you're sending one order to a customer, you're telling him/her about another product you have for sale. Since postage and packing costs already are being paid to ship the merchandise, package enclosures can bring in new sales and profits.

(C) Everyone loves a bargain. A discount or a special price; a premium for an order over a given amount; similar incentives stimulate larger orders. For similar reasons, gift certificates are often used profitably too, especially during Christmas and other holiday seasons.

(D) Advertise on envelopes. If mailing in envelopes instead of catalogues or self-mailers, consider utilizing the envelope itself to feature one or more specially-selected offers. The additional printing cost could prove insignificant compared to the extra sales produced.

(E) Use the personal touch. Occasionally send the *personalized* letters or mailings to "best" customers. Make special offers such as presenting special prices, and introducing new products to them. Consumers generally respond favorably to recognition, attention, and interest in an increasingly impersonal world.

(F) The mail order business requires very little working space. A small room in the house or part of the basement is all the space you need to set up your own small shipping department and store your records. Your lending library will have several books on mail order. Take out a few to learn the finer points of the business. It costs you nothing.

(G) If you are a really gifted Kitchen Lady, you can succeed in the mail order business. If your products are delicious, there will always be a market for them. How much *profit* you will make in mail order is all a matter of trial and error. Start out slowly so your errors won't be too expensive! As your experience grows, so will your profits!

Chapter 8

How to Earn $14,000 a Year Selling Delicious "Nut House" Brownies

Jobless and Widowed, with 3 Children to Care For

Katherine Grant didn't become a Kitchen Lady because she needed a second income—she needed a *first* income! Her husband died, leaving only a small insurance policy worth $10,000. How far is that going to get anyone these days? There were still three school-aged children at home, so the need for money was critical. Katherine had some secretarial skills, but they were rusty. She also knew that it would be tough to compete with girls who were 19, 20, and 21 years old and just coming into the job market. As a matter of fact, she went on a number of job interviews but was told she was "overqualified." Katherine, at 41 years of age, soon came to realize that when a

101

prospective employer told her, "I'm afraid you're overquali-
fied," he really meant that she was too old and too experienced for what he wanted to pay. In the tight economy we're
living in, most employers are cutting down every way they can.
They'd rather hire an inexperienced 21-year-old secretary and
pay her less than employ a 41-year-old experienced secretary
and pay her more. One employer was brutally frank with
Katherine when he told her, "Why should I hire someone over
40 when I could get all the 20-year-old secretaries I want?"

Katherine was in a bind. She had no prospects for a job, and
she despised the whole thought of going on the public assistance program. Going on "welfare" was deeply against her
grain.

Susan Grant Comes Up with a Winner!

Susan, Katherine's 14-year-old daughter, piped up, "Let's go
out and sell your chocolate brownies. We love them, and everybody else who has ever tasted them feels the same way.
Maybe we can sell them. If you can make enough of them,
maybe we'd make a lot of money!" Katherine was shocked.
She'd made lots of brownies over the years and they were delicious. Never, though, had she entertained the idea of selling
them. When you bake, you bake for your family and friends. It
was true that every year she baked a pan of brownies for the
church bazaar, and whatever money was raised went to the
church. Her baking ambitions never went further than that.

Putting Pride Aside

Katherine at first didn't like the idea. She had never thought
of herself as a peddler; she didn't like the thought of going
door-to-door, asking people if they wanted to buy her brownies. It did occur to her that there was a smart-looking gourmet
food shop in the shopping mall that just might be interested in
buying her brownies. She'd visited the store before, and they

carried very nice gourmet foods. (She'd never purchased anything there because the prices were too steep.) She thought that maybe the store would be interested in carrying her delicious brownies. "Let's give it a try," she told her children.

An Encounter
with a Potential Customer

On Friday morning—when school happened to be closed for the day—she and the children drove to the mall with a dozen freshly baked brownies. They walked into the gourmet food store and patiently waited for the owner to finish with a customer. The owner at last turned to her and asked, "What can I do for you?" Katherine replied, "You can buy my brownies, that's what you can do!" Katherine had to summon her courage to get that out; it wasn't easy. The store owner, a pleasant-looking man about 50 years of age, wasn't expecting that answer, so he was taken aback. But he started to smile. "Are they good?" he asked. "I mean, *really* good? Are they the best-tasting brownies you've ever eaten?" Katherine's youngest daughter, Tracy, piped up and said, "Nobody in the whole world makes better brownies than my Mom."

The Phone Call
That Changed Katherine's Life

Katherine left a sample of a dozen brownies at no cost to the store owner. And she left her phone number. At about 8 o'clock that evening, she got a call.

"Hello . . . hello . . . this is Mr. Baker."

Katherine didn't know any Mr. Baker.

"Mr. Baker, at the store where you left your brownies," continued the man.

"Oh, I'm sorry, Mr. Baker, I just didn't recall your name," Katherine replied.

"It might be my fault. It occurred to me that I forgot to give you my name, and for that I owe you an apology," Mr. Baker responded. "I had to call to tell you that your brownies are terrific. I had one, and it was so good that I couldn't resist taking another. I sold the rest to my best customers and they loved them as well. We all feel that your brownies are very special, very chocolate-y, and *filled* with nuts. Really, nobody makes brownies like these anymore."

Katherine was delighted to hear about all this. "Thank you, thank you very much," she offered.

"I want to pay you for the dozen you left with me, and I think I can easily sell at least five dozen brownies a day," chimed Mr. Baker. "It could be profitable for the both of us," he added.

"That's great, but I must confess that I'm new when it comes to the business of what to charge for my brownies," Katherine replied.

"Look, don't worry about that—we'll work it out," Mr. Baker assured her. "Why don't you come by Monday about 11 A.M., and we'll see what's fair to the both of us." Mr. Baker paused for a moment, then added, "Meanwhile, over the weekend, why don't you think of a name for your brownies? See if you and your daughters can come up with something kind of catchy, something different that would appeal to the public."

"Sure," Katherine answered, "I'll talk it over with the girls and try to come up with some ideas. I really appreciate your phone call, and I'll be sure to come in Monday. Good night."

"Good night," Mr. Baker replied, before hanging up the phone.

How the Name "Nut House" Brownies Was Born

Katherine arrived at 11 o'clock sharp on Monday morning, and she was grinning from ear to ear. She and Mr. Baker exchanged greetings, and Katherine couldn't wait to tell him what she was so happy about.

"Anyone who's tasted my brownies over the years has always loved that real nutty, crunchy taste, they get," Katherine said. She paused, looking for confirmation of that.

"I agree," Mr. Baker said. "That nutty taste is the difference."

"So we came up with a name we love: Kate's Chocolate 'Nut House' Brownies," Katherine announced.

Mr. Baker seemed speechless. Then he slowly smiled and said, "Kate's Chocolate 'Nut House' Brownies. Wow, that'll really catch on!"

Getting Down to Business

Then they started to discuss the business end of it, and Mr. Baker felt that he could charge 75¢ for each brownie. It sounded expensive to Katherine, but Mr. Baker said that if she would bake brownies as good as the samples she left, he'd have no trouble getting 75¢ for each one. Besides, Mr. Baker felt that the people who came in to his gourmet food boutique expected superior foods and desserts, and were willing to pay a higher price for them.

"That is, all except *you*," Mr. Baker said, smiling. "You would only come to look." Katherine smiled to herself. She never thought he'd noticed her.

Katherine Was Smart Enough to Be Honest

Katherine was completely honest with him. She admitted that she had thought about it for the whole weekend, but still hadn't arrived at what price to ask for her brownies. This was the first time she was trying to sell them, and she simply was at a loss as to what to charge. Mr. Baker told her that since he would sell a brownie for 75¢ to the customer, he would pay her 45¢ per brownie. That would mean he would get only a 67% markup, or 30¢ per brownie.

(*Note:* This is a very *low* markup for a store. They usually get much higher, but it's obvious to us that Mr. Baker saw that Katherine really needed the money. Thus, he lowered his profit so *she* could make more.)

Mr. Baker then examined the costs Katherine incurred in the baking of her brownies. He went over the list of ingredients she used: chocolate, butter, eggs, flour, nuts—all the ingredients. In addition, she was informed that she would now have another expense: each brownie should be cellophane-wrapped, and each would require a printed label identifying Katherine's "Nut House" brownie. Mr. Baker made a few calls to label designers and printing shops, and started to do some homework on his calculator. He estimated that in the beginning stages, all of Katherine's costs would come to about 15¢ per brownie. That would allow her to get approximately *triple* her cost, as she would be receiving 45¢ per brownie. And that means a healthy profit!

How Katherine Earned $162 a Week— Just from One Store

Mr. Baker suggested that Katherine be prepared to supply him with five dozen brownies a day. He'd want them fresh each day for six days a week, amounting to a total of sixty brownies a day—or 360 a week. Since Mr. Baker would be paying Katherine 45¢ a brownie, Katherine would be taking in a gross income of $162 a week—and that would be just from *one store*. Mr. Baker told her that after a month or two went by and she could see her way clear to handle more orders, he would contact another gourmet food shop. He knew of one which was located in another shopping mall and not competitive to his store. He felt that the man who owned this other store would be equally delighted to carry Katherine's brownies. If Katherine produced the same amount of brownies for the other store, then her income *for the week* would come to *$324!* Moreover, she would be able to continue this week after week.

Katherine Thought She Could Double Her Money

Katherine was ecstatic. From no prospects of money just a few days ago, here she was with a chance to bring in $324 a week through doing business with just two stores. More importantly, she'd be working at home where she could be close to the children.

A Word of Caution

Mr. Baker cautioned her that the other store owner might insist on getting at least a 150% markup on the brownies. That man might not pay Katherine more than 30¢ a brownie, while he sold them for 75¢. The 45¢ per brownie would give him a markup of 150%. But still, for her second order of 360 brownies a week, at 30¢ a brownie, Katherine would make $108 for the week. She would earn a combined profit from the two stores of $270 a week—that's close to $15,000 a year. As a matter of fact, on a 52-week basis, that comes out to *$14,040 a year!*

How Katherine Was Able to Expand Her Baking Capacity

Katherine wondered whether she could hook up another oven in the basement of her house. That way, she could dramatically increase her baking capacity. Mr. Baker encouraged her to do so. His brother was a home builder, and Mr. Baker offered to send him over, at no charge to Katherine, to investigate the possibility of installing a second double oven.

The Real Secret of the Name "Nut House" Brownies

Mr. Baker insisted on knowing one thing: how did Katherine come up with the wonderful name of "Nut House" brownies? She confessed that she didn't; one of her children did. They said that when she baked her brownies, the place got so topsy-turvy that it looked like a nut house! It really had nothing to do with the fact that Katherine put so many nuts into her brownies. Mr. Baker loved her refreshing answer. As it stands now, Katherine is selling her brownies at the rate of ten dozen a day, sixty dozen a week. Her income averaged about $14,000 for her first year of business.

How Katherine Got the Local Banker on Her Side

Mr. Baker recently took Katherine to his local banker with the thought of helping to get a loan for possible expansion. His thought was for Katherine to rent a store nearby with a large commercial oven on the premises. His reason was that Katherine was being asked to bake more brownies than she could handle, even using the second double oven that was installed in her basement. She was even getting customers coming directly to her house and buying brownies, so she suddenly found herself in the retail business as well. To customers who came to her directly, she charged 60¢ a brownie. This obviously created a bigger profit than when she sold her brownies to the stores because on this basis, there was no "middle-man."

The banker granted Katherine her loan. He was very impressed with the profitability of her business, and he was confident of her ability to pay off the loan. In putting some figures down, the banker realized that Katherine, by selling her brownies both wholesale and retail, could earn as much as *$25,000 a year!*

How One Kitchen Lady Found Romance

Something else has developed that's turning out to be an unexpected bonus. It seems that Mr. Baker lost his wife two years ago, and now he and Katherine are going out with each other. They are quite serious about their relationship. Seems to us that there's a *double* blessing here: business and pleasure have been successfully combined!

Chapter 9

How to Earn
$15,000 a Year
Selling Cheesecakes
to Fine Restaurants

Emily Gaber always knew how to bake an "out-of-this world" cheesecake. Over the years, everyone who tasted it would smack his lips and acclaim, *"That's* great cheesecake!" Emily's reply would usually be, "It's not bad."

Emily's Dilemma

A year ago, the last of Emily's three children got married and moved out. Her husband, Jack, who was two years from retirement on his job, broke his hip and was forced into early retirement. If you think that the so-called Workers' Compen-

111

sation really provides enough money for an injured worker and his family, you'd better think again. The compensation payments have increased slightly, but nowhere near the rate of inflation.

They began getting into deep financial trouble. They were even starting to have problems making ends meet, but they just didn't want to go to any of their married children to ask for help.

There was no way that Emily could go out and find employment. At sixty years of age and with no previous job experience, what chance did she stand? So yet another Kitchen Lady was born. She felt that perhaps she could start selling her delicious cheesecakes. Like other good home bakers, she had heard throughout the years, "If you could sell that, you'd make a fortune." It had never interested her before to try, but now there was a real need. Here she was, at a stage in her life when she wanted to spend *less* time in the kitchen; but the need for more money took care of that.

Her First Business Decision

Emily's first business decision was the same faced by every new Kitchen Lady: how much to charge? The first step was to figure out exactly how much it cost her to produce one cheesecake. She had never really thought about it over the years. If you bake something, you bake something. When the family loves it, you don't stop to think exactly what it costs you. It costs what it costs; you're not buying it, you're making it.

How to Break Down the Cost of Ingredients

Emily sat down to calculate the cost of every ingredient—including the eggs, flour, sugar, sour cream, cream cheese, lemon juice, and the stick of butter used in every cake. Everything that went into her cheesecakes had to be figured in. In order to arrive at the total ingredient cost per cheesecake, Emily had to add up all her ingredient costs and divide that by the number of cheesecakes she would now be baking at one time. Then she had to add in the total energy expense used in that baking period. She arrived at that figure by dividing the number of cakes baked by the cost of the hours of baking time used. On this matter, her utility company gave her the rates to the penny. They knew the exact cost when she told them the heat level used and the total baking time.

Emily's Expenses Surprise Her

When Emily compiled these costs, she knew for the first time what it actually cost her to bake her delicious cheesecakes. It surprised her, as it came to more than she thought. For a fourteen-inch cheesecake, the cost of ingredients and the utility charge (this will vary in different parts of the country) came to about $3.50 a cake. When it came to selling her cheesecakes, Emily felt that selling to restaurants was her best bet. With her husband not able to get around too easily, Emily felt that it would be too difficult to go around and build up a direct-to-the-housewife business. As we've discussed earlier, higher prices can be charged by selling retail (direct to the consumer). But Emily decided that selling wholesale—to restaurants— was preferable. It might mean taking in less money for each cheesecake, but it would provide guaranteed weekly orders with minimum transportation time required.

What She Had to Charge
to Make a Profit

As Kitchen Ladies know, you must charge at least *double* the cost of your specialty in order to make a *minimum* profit. It's safer to go for *triple* your costs. But cheesecake is a low-volume item, and Emily chose to sell wholesale (to restaurants), which means a lesser selling price. But she didn't do bad at all.

The arithmetic worked out this way: each cheesecake cost her $3.50 and she sold it for $9.00. That's a profit per cake of $5.50—between *double and triple* her cost. Now you can be sure that the restaurant profits very nicely on their own. Here's how their arithmetic works out.

The Restaurant Owner Has to Get His Slice Too!

From Emily's rich, delicious cheesecakes, each of which was fourteen inches around, the restaurant owners got sixteen slices. One owner charged his customers $1.75 a slice, while another owner charged his customers $2.00 a slice. Both of these restaurants catered to a decent middle-class family crowd. For the first owner, his income per cake came to $28.00, to give him a markup of over 200%. The second owner did even better: his income per cake—at $2.00 a slice—came to $32.00, and that's about a 250% markup. Many restaurants nationwide charge more than this—so *you* could charge more, too!

Fine Cheesecakes Should Only Be Sold to Fine Restaurants

Should the reader decide to sell her specialty to restaurants, she should understand that there's always a little give-and-take in this business of pricing. The restaurant wants to pay out as little as it can and you want to take in as much as you can. We'd like to give you the following advice: sell your specialty to the more expensive restaurants. Don't bother to call on small coffee shops or diners; they can't afford you! Instead, seek out those restaurants that draw a more affluent crowd. Their customers are more discriminating and are willing to pay higher prices for truly fine meals.

As Always, Never Be Intimidated

Never be intimidated by any restaurant owner. Hold firm to your price. Don't accept the owner's warning that "we can get other cheesecakes for a lot less than you're charging us!" If he says that, you reply, "Fine, then get them. I'm here because I always felt that this is a very fine restaurant whose customers are willing to pay more for really delicious food!" What we're saying is that this type of give-and-take will always go on, so learn how to play the game.

The Secret to Repeat Business

One thing is certain: once that owner has been getting raves from his customers about your cheesecake, then you know he's not going to stop ordering from you. His customers expect your cake and they're willing to pay extra for it, so he'll never have any complaints, as long as he gets his price. Once in a while, you'll find the tricky owner who "pleads poverty" all the time. If that were really the case, he'd close up. But as long as he stays open and does a thriving business, you make sure you get your prices all the time. In addition, as your costs go up—as they surely will—you pass it along to him. After all, he's passing his increased costs along to his customers all the time.

How Emily Increased Her Profits

Let's return to Emily; you ought to know that she's doing just fine. She's selling to three restaurants on a six-day-a-week basis, baking twelve cheesecakes a day for a total of seventy-two cakes a week. (A neighbor is letting her use her own double oven, as she's out working all day.) Between the three restaurants, all twelve cheesecakes are gone in one evening, and she's back the next day with another twelve. On a daily basis of twelve cakes, she is making a profit of $66.00 per day. By doing this six days a week, she is realizing a profit of *$396.00!* She deducts $37.00 a week for car expenses incurred in the delivery of her cheesecakes. In addition, she subtracts $25.00 for the increased energy costs. Even with this added $62.00 a week in expenses, she is still making a weekly profit of $334.00. She's working forty-five weeks a year, allowing herself six weeks off. Her yearly profit, after all expenses have been paid, comes to *$15,030.00.* Emily is a Kitchen Lady we're particularly proud of. At sixty years of age, with an urgent need for money and no possibility of employment, she turned to her kitchen to achieve this success!

The Secret to Keeping Profits High

After two years in business, each of Emily's cheesecakes is just as super-rich and delicious as the first one she made. There's never a let-up in quality. If for a moment her cheesecakes start to taste like those prepared by commercial bakers, then Emily could no longer command her premium price. In this business, you have to have that special homemade touch, and it must never slip even the least bit. The moment it does, you'll have a problem maintaining your customers. As long as a restaurant owner is getting raves about your cheesecake (or any other specialty you sell him), then he'll keep meeting your price. But his customers are very discerning people—if it's a truly fine restaurant. They expect the same high quality every time. If there are some occasions when a few customers start to complain, "Hey, what's happened to the cheesecake?" then you have to re-examine what you're doing. Some slippage could have occurred that you weren't even aware of!

Should Emily Expand Her Business?

Emily is now outgrowing both her own and her neighbor's kitchen, so she's looking around to lease a store with, or capable of holding, several large ovens. What becomes a distinct possibility at this point is that, although Emily continues to sell her cheesecakes to the restaurants, she—by having her own store—could start selling *retail,* direct to customers who come into her store. This is a bigger investment for her since she'll now have rent obligations to meet, and she'll have to fix up the store to make it attractive for customers to come in. There are many increased costs to face whenever you decide to get into the retail business, but again: if you have a product that people want, it can be a most profitable way of expanding the selling of your specialty.

Emily Has a Big Decision to Make

At this writing, Emily isn't certain that this is the wisest decision to make. She's very wary—and rightly so—of opening a retail bakery. She would then be obliged to produce a whole range of baked goods, because a bakery cannot exist on just one item.

Our Advice to Emily

We advised her, "Don't open a bakery; just specialize in your delicious cheesecakes. At this stage in your life, you can't start worrying about many different kinds of cakes, pies, pastries, cookies, breads and the like. You're making a very fine living at what you're doing, so why jeopardize it?" Emily will have to make up her own mind, but we think what we gave her is sound advice.

Do *you* know how to make moist and delicious cheesecakes? If you do, and there's a fancy restaurant in your area, chances are you'll be able to cash in on this specialty. Good cheesecake will never go out of style.

Chapter 10

How to Earn $50,000 a Year— Open the Restaurant of the Future: The Soup Kitchen

The Soup Kitchen

Another specialty that we ask you to seriously consider selling is soup and bread. To make the maximum profit in this business, you'll need to open a restaurant. This will require a substantial investment, and it's something we've never recommended before. In fact, if you'll refer back to the "Cookie" chapter, you'll notice we advised against opening a store. That's because with selling cookies you have an option. You can open a store, or you can also sell cookies successfully by "taking them out to the people." (Refer back to Chapter 1 to review how this can be done.)

Whereas cookies are an impulse purchase and are frequently

bought from a street vendor, soups are a *meal* purchase, requiring a sit-down restaurant.

How You Can Cash In on Economic Hard Times

The best reason to open a soup kitchen is because it's perfect for the times we live in. You can call your restaurant "Soup Kitchen," "Soup's On," "Soup Bowl," or any other name that catches your fancy. What matters is that the 1980s will be a period of economic hard times. People are watching what they're spending and they're cutting down on expensive meals. They still have to eat, of course, so what they are looking for are fast, filling, and inexpensive meals. The fast-food franchises have been cashing in on this, but you can enter this business another way. Everybody loves good homemade soup and freshly baked bread. You're also going to appeal to adults who are watching their waistlines as well as their wallets—and today, that's nearly everybody! Soups are an inexpensive and low-calorie alternative to the fattening hamburgers, French fries, and pizzas offered by the fast-food franchises. If you can make the investment to open a soup kitchen (and we'll get into the details shortly), you'll make *more money* from this specialty than any other specialty in this book!

Realize Fantastic Profits by Pushing Items Most Restaurants Neglect

Soup Kitchens are realizing fantastic profits by pushing two very basic restaurant items: *soup* and *salad*. These popular features are inexpensive to prepare and require no skill to serve cafeteria-style. You'll only need to hire—for a minimum wage—youngsters such as you see at the fast-food franchises. And, best of all, here's what you can charge: $1.79 for a mug of soup and a roll, 99¢ for a salad, and 79¢ for a glass of wine. A new soup kitchen restaurant seating 100 customers can take in as much as *$500,000* a year. Some are actually doing that. But let's take a more conservative figure—$350,000 a year. From a business of that size, you personally should have no trouble taking home *$50,000 a year.* After several years of experience in this field, there's no reason why you won't be able to expand to other locations. We know of *one owner* who has four Soup Kitchens. He and his wife expect the four restaurants to gross $2.2 million for the year. Imagine the take-home pay of this couple! They've been so successful that they are merely supervising the operation of their Soup Kitchens, and only visit the restaurants twice a week to make sure things are running smoothly.

A Good Location
Is Your Key to Success

You don't have to be a genius to make these restaurants successful. A restaurant consultant was once asked, "What are the three factors most likely to insure success?" His reply was, "(1) location, (2) location, and (3) location." In other words, where you locate is of crucial importance. Most of your business will come at lunch time, usually between the hours of 11:30 A.M. and 2:30 P.M. This means that your restaurant must be convenient to the working crowd. Your best location is the downtown area of your city. Try to be situated near large office buildings and big department stores. This will enable you to attract both office workers and shoppers. Both groups are looking for quick, nourishing, inexpensive lunches.

Establishing yourself near a college campus or close to a residential district will considerably enhance your potential for a dinner crowd, as well. If several movie houses are in the neighborhood, you'll attract even more customers in the evening.

Before you select any location, keep in mind these factors:

Vehicular traffic—How many people drive by in cars and is there available parking near your store?

Public transportation—Do buses pass your store and, better yet, is there a bus stop nearby?

Pedestrian traffic—analyze the foot traffic. Where is there a greater flow—the sunny or shady side of the street? Also, which side has the most popular shopping?

How to Duplicate the Success of Big Companies

Once you've selected a possible location, some of the passersby should be interviewed about the origin of their trip, their destination, and the approximate times in which they are in that vicinity. Because your Soup Kitchen is a from "lunch on" business, you're not interested in an early morning pedestrian count. Rather, you want to record and interview the number of people who are in the vicinity from 11:30 A.M. on. You are likely to find the lunch-time crowd to be mostly female, predominantly students and office workers. In the early afternoon, you will very likely find women who are taking a break from their shopping. At dinner, your customers will generally be couples—single and married—who are on their way to an evening of entertainment or late shopping.

In addition to your personal checking of potential traffic, it is advisable to talk to nearby store owners. Ask them what they think of the area. What trends do they foresee? Do they think that the crowd is increasing or decreasing? Tell them about your proposed idea for a soup kitchen. What's their opinion? Talk to men and women passing by. Would they like to see a soup kitchen? Tell them what you intend to serve and what you'll charge.

Before you go out to interview, conduct yourself the way professional pollsters do. Have a list with all your questions put down in advance. Check off every response and total them on a separate sheet at the end of each day's interviewing. Big companies spend millions on these surveys. You can get the same results on your own!

Don't be hesitant about locating near other restaurants; nearby restaurants mean there is a heavy traffic flow in that area. The only type of restaurant to be concerned about is one that features soups and salads as the main bill of fare—but it's highly unlikely that such a restaurant exists in your area.

Pre-existing information concerning traffic counts (both vehicular and pedestrian), population trends, and other useful data can be obtained from your local Chamber of Commerce.

However, you may need to modify this information to suit your special needs. For example, you should supplement data relating to total count of vehicles passing the site with actual observation. This should be done in order to evaluate such influences on traffic as commercial vehicles, changing of shifts at nearby factories, highway traffic, and increased flow caused by special events or activities.

What You Need to Know About Opening in a Shopping Center

A shopping center can be an effective site for a convenience restaurant such as a soup kitchen, but the rent is likely to be very high and you'll have to pay a share of your gross sales to the owner-developer of the shopping center. If the shopping mall steadily draws an excellent crowd, don't be put off by these negatives. It can still be very lucrative for you. Besides, you might be living in an area where there isn't any attractive downtown business district. Your *only* choice to open a Soup Kitchen is in a shopping mall. If you do locate in a shopping center, make sure that your site provides drivers with a clear view of your restaurant.

There are three main factors involved in establishing your Soup Kitchen in a shopping center:

Your space—Determine where your space will be. Your location in the shopping center is important. Do you need to be in the main flow of customers as they pass between the stores with the greatest "customer pull"? Who will be your neighbors? What will be their effect on your sales?

How much space is also important. You should plan enough space for about one hundred customers. That will require about 2,500 square feet. Most of that space will be taken up by customer seating. The remaining space is for the counter area and the serving line. You should also provide for male and female restrooms. About 500 square feet is all that's needed for a kitchen, storage, and work area.

Total rent—Most shopping center leases are negotiated. "Rental" expense may begin with a minimum "guarantee" that is equal to a percentage of gross sales. Typically, while this is between 5 and 7% of gross sales, it varies by type of business and other factors.

But this guarantee is not the end. In addition, you may have to pay dues to the center's merchant association. You may have to pay for maintenance of common areas. Consider your rent, then, in terms of "total rent."

Finishing out—Generally, the owner furnishes the bare space. You do the "finishing out" at your own expense. In completing your store to suit your needs, you pay for light fixtures, counters, shelves, painting, and floor coverings. In addition, you may have to install your own heating and cooling units (your lease should be long enough to pay out your "finishing out" expense).

An innovation is the "tenant allowance." By this system, landlords provide a cost allowance towards completion of space. It is for store fronts, ceiling treatment, and wall coverings. The allowance is a percentage of their cost and is spelled out in a dollar amount in the lease.

Some developers help tenants plan store fronts, exterior signs, and interior color schemes. They provide this service to insure that they get store fronts that *add* to the center's image rather than subtract from it.

Types of Shopping Centers

The *neighborhood center* generally serves 7,500 to 20,000 people living within a 6–10 minute drive from the center. The major store—and the prime traffic generator—in the center is a supermarket. The other stores in the center, which may include a drug store, hardware store, bakery, and beauty shop, offer convenience goods and services. The best location for a food specialty store in the center is adjacent to the supermarket. Other stores should be grouped by the compatibility of their merchandise.

The *community center* usually serves 20,000 to 100,000 people living within a 10–20 minute drive. The dominant store is generally a junior department store or a large variety store. The majority of the stores carry shopping goods such as wearing apparel and appliances. However, a number of the stores also offer convenience items. Since your store will depend on a rapid turnover of traffic in the center, be sure that you are located where there's always available parking.

The *regional center* serves 100,000 to 200,000 people within a 20–40 minute drive from the center. One or more department stores are its major tenants. Frequently, the center is an enclosed mall with a department store at each end. This type of center emphasizes shopping goods. These numerous shopping goods stores usually locate between the two major stores in order to take advantage of the traffic flow. Stores handling convenience goods generally locate at the edge of the center or near an entry to the mall where there is easily accessible parking.

Why the Shopping Center Owner Will Welcome Your Soup Kitchen

If you wish to locate in a shopping center, you must make the owner-developer of the center aware that you are *not* a junk food restaurant that might attract a rowdy group of youngsters. Instead, you are a very clean food operation specializing in homemade soups and home-baked breads, and the majority of your customers will be economy-minded working men and women. Also remind the owner that a first-class Soup Kitchen can earn several hundred thousand a year. Since he shares in the percentage of gross income, he'll regard you with high respect!

Once you've selected the proper location—whether it's in the downtown business district or in a shopping mall—be sure you get all the necessary permits you'll need from the zoning and health departments. This is particularly important if you plan to lease a space which was *not* previously a restaurant. Don't sign a lease until you are certain that you can establish a restaurant on those premises.

It would be *ideal* to take over the lease of a coffee shop or small restaurant that is going out of business. It's a good idea for two reasons: (1) you already know that the zoning permits a restaurant in that location; and (2) much of the equipment you'll need is already on the premises. You'll probably be able to purchase this equipment from the departing owner for a fraction of its original price.

The Image of Your Soup Kitchen

How your restaurant looks on the outside will play an important role in getting customers inside! We recommend the "Early Americana" look, as it creates a feeling of warmth and coziness. It also recalls an era when foods were natural, hearty, and satisfying. This image is a wonderful contrast to the fast-food restaurants, all of which look plastic and sterile.

We'll give you several decorating ideas, but you can get many others from *House Beautiful* and *Better Homes and Gardens*. Also check your local library for books on the early American period in our nation's history. We also suggest you speak to an interior decorator in your area. Tell him (her) the image you're trying to create for your restaurant, but caution him that you have very little money to spend. Look for a decorator who hasn't yet built a big reputation, since he's more likely to be reasonable with his prices.

We want to add that if you can't afford an interior decorator, you can accomplish this "Early Americana" look using your own ingenuity. Some of the touches you can feature outside the restaurant include a hanging, antique-looking sign, with the name of the restaurant inscribed. Think of using names such as "The Soup Kitchen," "Soup's On," "The Soup Kettle," or "The Soup Bowl." Outside decorations can include simulated wooden beams and brick facings in red or white.

In continuing this "Early Americana" look on the inside, be sure to include spice racks, copper pots on the walls, a copper hood, and perhaps an imitation brick fireplace. Shop around flea markets and swap meets to pick up posters and reproductions of early American art. If you can find any memorabilia of the early American household, include that in the interior of your restaurant. Have these artifacts *fixed* to the wall so that admiring customers can't walk off with them.

The look you're trying to create need not be expensive. The "antiques" we're talking about will merely be accents in your restaurant, and they'll only be reproductions, anyway. All you'll basically need is inexpensive wood veneer wall paneling and a linoleum floor covering, both of which reflect the "Early Americana" look. For the seating arrangement, you'll need about forty old-fashioned-looking tables with one hundred chairs to match. Most of these tables will seat four people, while the remainder will seat two.

A Layout for a Fast Turnover

Your restaurant will be a cafeteria, through which customers will pass on an average of 25 to 30 minutes each. Your lunch crowd will range between 300 and 500 people, arriving between 11:30 A.M. and 2:30 P.M. Organize the restaurant so that customers may pass through the entrance, along the serving line, up to the cash register, and to the seating area with maximum speed. One of the reasons people will be coming into your restaurant is because they don't like delays in being served. In addition, the food is filling, nutritious, and inexpensive. A cafeteria-style restaurant is advantageous to both the owner/operator and the customers. The owner doesn't have to employ waitresses and patrons don't have to worry about tipping. It's ideal from everyone's point of view.

The Equipment You'll Need to Make Soups at Home Before You Open a Restaurant

On one hand, we heartily recommend that you consider cashing in on the Soup Kitchen restaurant boom, but on the other hand, we know it's an expensive business to get into. Shortly, we'll spell out all of the equipment you'll need to open up the restaurant; but even before that, we want you to buy some equipment for your *own* kitchen. This allows you to familiarize yourself with the business. In a sense, it lets you get a "feeling" of the Soup Kitchen operation. Use this equipment at home for several months before proceeding to make the big investment you'll need for the restaurant equipment.

As we have suggested in other chapters in the book, look in the yellow pages of your phone book. In this instance, look under "Restaurant Supplies" for the various suppliers of this equipment. Shop around for the best prices on each:

Food Processor. There are several on the market, both European and American made. Shop the various appliance and discount stores for the best price. They are indispensable, and are designed for mincing, slicing, shredding, and chopping large amounts of herbs and vegetables or grating cheeses for soups. Be sure to buy one that has interchangeable discs and blades.

Electric Blender. You might already have one; if not, there are many good domestic models available. They are very effective in making fine purées, the basis of many cream soups.

Stainless-Steel Chinois & Tinned Steel Food Mill. These can produce coarser purées than ones which can be made in a blender. To arrive at a thicker purée, press food through the holes of a chinois, or select one of three textures and crank the food through a mill. Some types of food mills attach conveniently to any size bowl or pan.

Stainless-Steel Stockpot. Purchase one with a heavy bottom and strong handles. This kind is ideal for the long, slow simmering of bones, meat, and vegetables required to make broth.

Stainless-Steel Utensils. These consist of large, strong tools with long handles. They are constantly needed for ladling, stirring, and lifting solids from soups and broths.

How to Get Fantastic Savings on Your Soup Kitchen Equipment

Again, the equipment just listed is excellent to get started making fine soups at home. It'll also be good "back-up" equipment even after you open your Soup Kitchen. But now let's progress to the type of equipment you'll need to open up a first class Soup, Salad & Bread restaurant, one capable of serving hundreds of eager customers every day. Make *every* attempt to buy all of this equipment *used*. This can give you savings of 50% off its original price. If you can buy all this equipment at a foreclosure auction, better yet; you might get savings of 75% off all original prices.

Initial Equipment

Cafeteria serving line (12 to 15 feet)
Walk-in refrigerator (7 feet by 8 feet)
40- to 50-gallon stainless-steel kettles (2)
Exhaust hood and fan

Ice maker—250-pound capacity
Microwave oven
Stainless-steel sink with drainboards
Sink sprayer unit
Vegetable slicer with attachments
Shelving, dry storage
Prep tables (2)
Tables (40)
Chairs (100)
Coffeemaking equipment
Soft-drink equipment
Iced tea, hot chocolate equipment
Cash register

If you can get all of this at a *big discount*—50% to 75% off original prices—your total expense for this basic equipment in the restaurant should be about $12,000. In addition, there is optional equipment you'll be needing. This is primarily for baking in the store; we think it's important because baking is a profitable added feature to a Soup Kitchen.

Optional Equipment

Stove
Revolving bakers' oven
Freezer (frozen bread dough)
Tree rack with pans
Dough mixer (50 quarts)
Bowls, dollies, beater, etc.

This optional equipment for baking purposes will run about $7,500. We will be giving you some recipes for homemade breads. With this equipment, you can bake breads on the premises, both homemade and frozen bread loaves in the restaurant as well. (A very appealing feature to your customers.)

There is the additional expense of all the smallware and miscellaneous supplies that you will need. All the soup bowls, soup mugs, glasses, trays, paper products, knives, spoons, salt and pepper shakers, etc. Everything down to the mop, broom, and dustpan. A restaurant supply house can give this entire list. Estimate that it will cost you about $2,000. But before you get into all this expense, you must first find out how good you are at making soup! We want you to try these.

Good Soup Stocks Are the Secret to Delicious Soups

If you're in the business of making soups, you must have at least three basic stocks: meat, vegetable, and chicken. Here are the recipes for each one.

Beef Stock

   3 pounds lean brisket
   3 pounds beef bones, cracked
   2 carrots, peeled and thickly sliced
   1 large onion cut into quarters
   3 cloves garlic, minced
   1 large shallot, minced
   6 whole cloves
   6 large fresh mushrooms, washed,
       trimmed and coarsely chopped (optional)
   ½ cup yellow turnip, peeled and diced
   2 ribs celery, cut into 4 pieces
   2 to 2½ quarts water, enough to cover
       Salt to taste
       Bouquet garni

Trim fat from meat and bones and place in large kettle. Add water to cover and bring to boil. Then reduce heat.

Add balance of ingredients. Cover partially, and simmer for 3 hours, periodically removing scum that rises to top.

Remove meat and bones from kettle with slotted spoon. Discard bones and reserve meat for leftovers.

Strain stock through a fine sieve, placing bowl underneath, and pressing to remove all stock.

Transfer stock to freezer-safe containers. Cover loosely with waxed paper, and cool at room temperature.

Cover tightly and refrigerate overnight, then cut away and discard hardened fat from top of stock.

Refrigerate some of the stock for use within a few days, covering tightly. Freeze the balance.

YIELD: *about 2 quarts*

Vegetable Stock

1 medium onion, sliced
2 carrots, cut in half
2 celery stalks, chopped
½ cup dried lima beans
¼ cup dried green split peas
2 quarts water
   A few sprigs of fresh parsley
1 bay leaf
   A few pinches of dried thyme and rosemary
3 whole cloves
⅛ teaspoon mace
   Salt to taste

Put all the ingredients into soup kettle and bring to a boil.

Reduce heat, cover loosely, and simmer slowly for 3–4 hours.

Strain and discard vegetables, which should be mushy at this point. Makes 2 quarts.

Note: This stock also freezes well.

Chicken Stock

1 fat chicken, whole or cut into parts
1 large carrot, scraped and quartered
1 large stalk of celery, chopped
1 onion, peeled and left whole
   A few sprigs of parsley
   Enough water to cover chicken
   Salt to taste

Wash chicken thoroughly and put into kettle with remaining ingredients.

Bring to a boil, then reduce heat and cook slowly until chicken begins to fall apart. This should take about 1½ hours. Taste and add salt to suit.

Remove chicken and bones from pot and strain vegetables from broth.

Put the broth into a clean container and refrigerate. When the fat has risen to the top and congealed, remove as much of the fat as possible with a large spoon, and strain broth through cheesecloth to remove any remaining fat.

Note: Part of this stock can be refrigerated and the rest frozen to be used as needed.

Before we give you several of our soup recipes, we want to mention that if you don't have the time to make your *own* stock, there are a number of canned, clear chicken or beef broths, or bouillon which can be substituted. We have found these commercial preparations to be rather salty and occasionally a bit overseasoned, so try various commercial brands to see which you prefer. For best results, we go back to what Kitchen Ladies stand for: there's nothing better than home-made!

Hearty Meat, Bean, and Barley Soup

This soup is an all-time favorite, hearty and filling, a meal in itself. It can sit in the refrigerator for days and easily serves 6–8 people.

> 2 cups dried lima beans
> 3 pounds flanken (lean short ribs)
> 2–3 small marrow bones
> 3½ quarts water
> 1 carrot (scraped and roughly chopped)
> 1 celery stalk roughly chopped
> 2 chopped onions
> 1 handful chopped parsley
> 2 crushed cloves garlic
> ½ cup pearl barley
> Freshly ground pepper and salt to taste

Soak the lima beans overnight. Next morning, drain them and put into large soup kettle.

Add the meat, bones, and water and bring to a boil.

Skim off the scum that forms on top and reduce the heat. Simmer for one hour.

Add the carrot, celery, onions, parsley, garlic, and barley. Cook for two hours and add the pepper and salt to taste. Continue cooking until meat is tender.

Remove the meat and bones from soup. While soup is still cooking, cut the meat into bite-sized chunks and return to pot. Discard bones. Turn off heat.

Refrigerate overnight, and next day remove the fat that forms on top of the soup.

Reheat slowly and adjust seasonings.

Split Pea Soup

This is an economical soup to make, because you can utilize a leftover ham bone, a bit of salt pork, or even a turkey carcass. This recipe makes two quarts or more and can stand for days in the refrigerator. It can also be frozen.

    2 cups split peas
    3 quarts water or vegetable stock
      Ham bone or 2-inch cube of salt pork
    ½ cup chopped carrots
    1 cup chopped onions
    1 cup chopped celery (with leaves)
    1 bay leaf
    ½ teaspoon thyme
      Salt to taste
      Dash of cayenne
      Dash of cumin
      Dash of black pepper to taste
    2 tablespoons butter
    2 tablespoons flour

Put the peas and water (or stock) into a large soup kettle. Add the ham bone or salt pork. Cover and simmer for 3½ hours.

Add the carrots, onions, and celery. Cover and simmer for ½ hour longer.

Add bay leaf, thyme, salt, cayenne, and cumin. Simmer a little while longer, taste, and adjust seasonings. You may want to add the pepper at this point.

Put part of the soup into a blender, purée, and return to soup pot.

Melt the butter and add to it 2 tablespoons of flour. Stir until blended. Add a little of the soup mixture slowly. Cook and stir until it boils, then add to the rest of soup. Adjust seasonings again.

Spicy Meatball Soup

This recipe serves approximately 6 people. It's a hearty soup and can really be sold as a meal in itself.

        6 cups beef stock
        3 sprigs parsley
        2 stalks celery, roughly chopped
        1 bay leaf
        1 pound ground lean chuck
        1 small grated onion
        1 teaspoon salt
        1 cup dried bread crumbs
        1 teaspoon chili powder
        ⅓ cup cooked rice
        1 egg, beaten
        ¼ cup dry sherry

Put the stock in a saucepan, and add parsley, celery, and bay leaf.

Bring the stock to a boil, then reduce heat and simmer covered for 15 minutes.

Prepare the meatballs. Mix together the chuck, onion, salt, bread crumbs, chili powder, rice, and egg. Shape the mixture into 1-inch balls.

Strain the stock into a large pot and bring to a boil. As the stock continues to boil, add the meatballs a few at a time. Reduce the heat and simmer 20 minutes, covered. Add sherry and let simmer briefly.

Gazpacho

This is a highly popular summer soup to sell. It is a vegetable soup with fresh herbs, well chilled. It is sometimes known as "Spanish Soup." The ingredients in this recipe, which makes 6 cups, can easily be doubled.

> 2 large ripe tomatoes, peeled and seeded
> 1 large sweet pepper
> 1 clove garlic, minced
> 1 cup of the following fresh mixed herbs:
>   chives, basil, parsley, chervil, tarragon
> ½ cup olive oil
> 3 tablespoons lemon juice
> 3 cups chilled water or vegetable stock
> 1 mild onion, peeled and thin sliced
> 1 cup peeled, seeded, and diced cucumber
> 1½ teaspoons salt (or to taste)
> ½ teaspoon paprika

Place tomatoes, pepper, garlic, and fresh herbs into a chopping bowl, and chop them well. Gradually stir in olive oil, lemon juice, and chilled water or stock. Add onion, cucumber, salt, and paprika.

Chill the soup 4 hours or longer.

Note: When this is served, it may be sprinkled with dry bread crumbs.

How You Can Get the Recipes for Three Fabulous Soups

These are some of our favorite soups, and they might well be some of yours. In different parts of the country, some soups sell better than others. What we want to do at this time is to give the names of several excellent cooks who have their own personal soups. You might want to feature some of these additional soups in your "Soup Kitchen." It's possible that if you send them your name plus a self-addressed envelope, they'll send you their famous recipes. Here are a few you might want to write away for:

Minestrone Primavera (Spring Garden Vegetable Soup)

Write to: Nicola Zanghi
　　　　　Restaurant Zanghi
　　　　　Glen Cove, NY

French Onion Soup

Write to: Carol Cutler
         The Washington Post
         Washington, D.C.

Coach House Black Bean Soup

Write to: Coach House Restaurant
         Waverly Place
         New York City, NY

Important

The previous recipes given—and all other recipes you might send for—are for *home* use. You have to expand *all* the ingredients to accommodate the large Soup Kitchen operation. Plan on serving about 80 gallons a day to some 500 people.

How the Seasons Will Affect Your Menu

The seasons will affect what types of soups you serve. Good fall and winter soups include meat, bean and barley soup, split pea soup, black bean soup, French onion soup, and clam chowder. Good summer soups to serve are gazpacho, borscht, and vichyssoise.

The Foolproof Way of Selling Soups That People Really Want

Earlier in the chapter we advised you to interview potential customers on the desirability of having a soup kitchen in the area. It would also be to your advantage during the same interview to find out what *their* favorite soups are. We couldn't begin to list the favorite soups of people all around the country; each region seems to have its own likes and dislikes. Your survey will determine customer tastes. This is extremely important, as it will save you from the expense and labor of preparing what customers *don't* want. This doesn't mean you shouldn't introduce anything *new!* You might have a special soup that's your own recipe which will prove to be a great success in your own area.

Breads—
The Amazing Extra Money Maker
You Shouldn't Pass Up

There's nothing like homemade breads to go with homemade soups. People will flock to your "Soup Kitchen" not only for your soups, but for your breads as well. If you can't bake your own breads, don't be concerned. You can easily buy many varieties of commercial frozen bread. Of course, it's always more profitable for you if you can bake your own delicious breads to go with your homemade soups. There are many cookbooks available that offer recipes for homemade breads, and there are even some cookbooks devoted to breads alone.

Favorite Breads People Love to
Sink Their Teeth Into

Some of the breads people most enjoy with soups include black bread, pumpernickel, rye, French, and Italian bread. Perhaps you already bake some of these; if so, please continue to do so. If not, your library or local bookstore should be able to provide you with a few books on the subject. Right now, however, we'd like to offer two recipes for breads that are out of the ordinary and very satisfying. Both taste great with most soups.

Fast Peanut Bread

This bread is probably one of the quickest kinds to make. It should take no more than an hour and five minutes to bake, from start to finish. Take our word for it, it's delicious!

> 2 **tablespoons active dry yeast**
> 2 **teaspoons sea salt**
> 1¼ **cups warm water**
> ¼ **cup honey**
> ½ **cup shelled peanuts (unsalted),**
>   **very finely chopped**
> 1½ **cups whole wheat flour**
> 1½ **cups white flour**

Put yeast, sea salt, warm water and honey into a large bowl. Stir well.

Stir in shelled peanuts.

Mix in one cup of whole wheat flour and one cup of white flour. Beat hard for two minutes by hand or one minute by mixer. Stir in last half cup of whole wheat flour. Work in by hand last half cup of white flour, then work for 2 minutes more.

Grease 2 1-pound coffee cans. Divide batter in half and place into the 2 cans, pushing down into the corners and smoothing the tops.

Make an intial or design on top of each loaf.

Let bread rise for 20 minutes in a warm place. Put into an *un*heated oven and bake at 375 degrees for 30–35 minutes. Bread is done when it is golden brown and shrinks slightly from sides of pans. Turn out and cool on a wire rack.

Note: When you grease the coffee cans, grease well with butter or margarine. Cover the cans with a clean towel. When you are ready to bake the loaves, there will be little show of rising; don't panic, that's to be expected. When the bread is done, the sides and bottom have a dark golden brown look. The bread has an even, fine texture and slices beautifully.

There's nothing tastier than fresh creamy butter spread on a thick slice of this bread, accompanied by a hearty bowl of soup!

Banana Bread

This is a classic bread with which to spice up an ordinary soup, and an ideal way to use up some soft bananas. This recipe makes one loaf.

> ½ cup butter or margarine
> 2 medium eggs beaten
> 3 bananas on the soft side
> 1 teaspoon lemon juice
> 2 cups unbleached flour
> 3 teaspoons baking powder
> ½ teaspoon salt
> 3 dried figs
> 6 dried dates

Preheat your oven to 350 degrees. Grease and flour a 9-inch loaf pan.

Cream the butter, then add the beaten eggs.

Mash the soft bananas and blend in lemon juice.

Sift the flour, baking powder, and salt together. Stir these dry ingredients into the moist mixture ½ cupful at a time. Stir in the bananas. Cut the figs and dates into very small pieces. Stir them into the batter, distributing them throughout evenly.

Bake for 50 minutes to one hour, or until a toothpick inserted into the center of the loaf comes out clean. Cool on a rack.

Important

In addition to baking your own breads from scratch, you might want to buy commercial frozen doughs. They are inexpensive and simple to prepare. In any case, you'll want to vent the luscious aroma of baking bread into the seating area and out to the street. Smell is perhaps the most powerful allure of foods. You know that from your own experience! Use that technique to draw in crowds of customers.

It should be understood at this point that you *personally* won't have to bake the breads or prepare the soups. You'll certainly have a "say" in these matters, but you'll be hiring a chef who'll be responsible for the day-to-day operation of the restaurant.

How to Expand Your Menu So You Can Expand Your Profits

The Microwave oven you'll be installing will allow you to make even more profit. That way, you can include on your menu some items which require warming up—such as quiche, meat pies, and some dessert items. These items can be purchased wholesale and stored in your refrigerator.

Another profitable suggestion is to feature several heartier dishes on your evening menu. Items such as chicken, meat stews, and lasagna can all be bought frozen and stored in your restaurant freezer. Since they are already prepared, all you need to do is to heat them in the microwave oven when ordered.

As we've said before, salads are an extremely profitable item to feature on your menu. A crowd-pleasing salad includes three kinds of lettuce (iceberg, romaine, and Bibb), radishes, cherry tomatoes, endives, scallions, red cabbage, and watercress. You can offer toppings such as croutons, bacon bits, Parmesan cheese (grated), and chick peas. Be sure to have plenty of salad dressings on hand. People mostly go for creamy Italian, Thousand Island, and French, and Russian.

Remember that wine is a real profit generator and should be served by the glass, half and full liter. Keep red and white on hand. You'll be buying good but inexpensive domestic wines and serving them as "house" wines in your own carafes. In addition to the wines, you'll be serving foreign and domestic beers, soft drinks and milk.

What to Charge

Remember, the basic appeal of your Soup Kitchen is that it's a blessing in a tight economy. All signs indicate that the country is in for economic hard times *throughout* the 1980s. Thus the main attraction of your Soup Kitchen is good, filling meals at reasonable prices. The bulk of your clientele will be office workers looking to economize on lunch, so don't scare them off by charging high prices!

For an 8-ounce mug of soup, we suggest you charge $1.79, and $2.19 for a 16-ounce bowl. Get 99¢ for a bowl of salad, and $2.69 for a "lunch special" of a mug of soup and a salad. Wine generates large profits; you should charge 79¢ for a glass, $1.89 for a small carafe, and $3.49 for a large carafe. Be sure to give a slice of homemade bread and a pat of butter with every serving of soup.

You should also consider other items for your menu. Each of the following is very popular, comes frozen in single portions, and simply requires heating in the microwave oven. We suggest the following combinations and prices:

Veal Parmesan (& Salad) $3.89
Quiche (& Salad) $3.59
Beef or Chicken Pie (& Salad) $3.19
Lasagna (& Salad) $2.99

Important

Any prices we suggest are subject to change, depending on two factors (1) the competitive situation in your area; and (2) *inflation*—as the years go on, we expect prices to steadily increase, so you must pass them on to your customers!

Standard items such as beer (domestic and imported), soda,

milk, coffee, and tea will be competitive to other restaurants in your area.

Whom to Hire

Once you open a Soup Kitchen, the most important person in your life will be your manager. Unless you have previous experience in operating a restaurant, *don't* try to be a manager yourself. You'll have to rely on him or her for the day-to-day operation of the restaurant. Your manager should be hired one month before the doors open, and he (she) will assist you in hiring the personnel needed to staff the restaurant. A good manager has knowledge of local suppliers, understands inventory, and of course has previous restaurant experience.

You'll also need to hire a chef. His main job is to be responsible for a variety of truly delicious soups. In addition, he'll order all supplies needed and plan the work schedules of the kitchen personnel. To put it simply: the manager runs everything in the "front," and the chef is master in the "back." The chef will also help in baking breads, rolls, and some dessert items which can be baked on the premises (such as carrot cake).

For both the lunch and dinner shifts, you'll need two part-time workers to handle the serving of food. These are usually young people who can be paid the minimum wage. Two full-time workers on both shifts complete your staff needs.

A Day in the Life of a Soup Kitchen

As we've discussed, great-tasting soups are the heart of your restaurant. Previously in this chapter, we've given you some recipes, and we've told you where to write for others. In addition, you might have several of your own and several ideas for soups suggested by customers.

You'll want to feature four to six soups daily, including one that caters to vegetarians. We've found that there are two permanent soups you should list each day: Clam Chowder and Mushroom & Barley. Don't bother to print menus. Instead, have your items listed on a board behind the serving line. The menu for the day can either be written in chalk or printed on slats that can be changed daily.

At around 7:30 in the morning, the chef and his two assistants come to the restaurant to prepare the soups and salads for the lunch crowd. You personally should come at 10 A.M., to make sure that things are running smoothly and on schedule. You'll want to open your doors at 11 A.M., as your lunch crowd will start arriving from 11:30 on.

Your serving line should be organized so that your customers move through as smoothly as possible. As soon as they enter the line they should find trays, napkins, and eating utensils. As patrons continue along the line, two employees working this shift dish out soups, entrées, and whatever else is requested from your menu. You should be at the cash register at the end of the line, taking money and giving change. One important point: credit cards *should not* be accepted. This is a low-cost restaurant, and everyone should pay cash. (Better for you; you won't have to pay a percentage of your receipts to credit card companies.)

Your two full-time workers, who up until now have been assisting the chef in the preparation of lunch items, should now move to the seating area. Their job will be to clean off a table as soon as a customer departs. Only one worker is needed for this; the other can be washing the dishes. After lunch, both workers now clean the kitchen, work area, and bathrooms. Meanwhile, the workers who have been serving the food clean the counter and the seating area. You should remove all bills of large denominations from the cash register, and store them securely in the back—in a locked drawer or a small safe.

Between 3 and 5 P.M. is the time when activity will be at a minimum. During this period, the chef and his two evening assistants repeat the morning's routine in preparation for the dinner crowd.

In the evening, review the menu and prepare two soups to be featured the following day. They are refrigerated overnight, and heated the next morning on the serving line. At the same time, the chef is busy preparing two additional soups listed on that day's menu. Thus, you'll have four soups ready for the lunch crowd. These soups are on the serving line, freeing the kettles for preparation of the evening soups.

What time you close in the evening will depend on the size of your dinner crowd. You'll need to devote a full hour after closing to make certain that the entire premises is spotlessly clean for the next day's business.

A word about hiring: *be particular.* In a tight economy, you'll get plenty of job applicants, so look for men and women who are both attractive and well-qualified. Your manager should have good credentials in restaurant operations and he (she) should know how to relate to people—both to employees and customers. You'll want your chef to be attractive and pleasing also: in this type of "cozy" restaurant atmosphere, the chef should be visible to his customers.

Just as you want attractive-looking employees, so do your customers. That's why some sort of uniform is desirable. There are so many types to choose from that we recommend you look in the yellow pages of your phone book under "Uniforms." Shop around for uniforms that are inexpensive but visually appealing.

What It Takes to Become Successful

Not all soup kitchens hit it big—a lot depends on atmosphere and image. The majority of people in this country don't know what real homemade soup tastes like. Most people get their soup from cans; even worse is the growth of "instant soups." These are packages of dry ingredients to which you add boiling water. It makes no difference which kind you buy; both canned and "instant" soups are watered down imitations of the real thing. In other words, most people are "soup skeptics"; they tend to believe that all soups taste the same. With proper atmosphere, your Soup Kitchen can make them change their minds.

The "Early Americana" image can accomplish this. It will recall a time in this country when things tasted fresh and appetizing, a time when everything was honestly made.

We've given you the right image, but you've got to have the right follow-through. Your chef and manager are all-important to you! Experience makes all the difference in the world, and they've got it. Until you learn the business, let their know-how guide you on such crucial matters as what to buy and in what quantities, the maintenance of equipment, the daily operation of the restaurant, and the many details that come up in the restaurant business.

It's critically important that you have a fine relationship with your employees. Treat them well and they'll take their responsibilities seriously. You need them to work with maximum efficiency, because in this business *time is definitely money!* Your customers are the type who do not have the time to wait for their food, so your employees must produce and serve it on time. Your tables must be cleaned the moment customers leave, so that there's no delay in accommodating new arrivals. Treat your employees fairly; make them feel like they're part of a family, not just "hired hands."

The Secret to Hiring Dedicated Employees

Your restaurant operation is *different* than one of the typical nationwide fast-food franchises. They are gigantic and impersonal. On the other hand, your Soup Kitchen, with its wholesome menu, *can* attract a more dedicated employee. Of course, you'll have to pay your workers fairly—otherwise they'll leave. But often, money is just one factor. If your employees *believe* in what you're selling, they're apt to work hard for you. The greatest benefit from this is that a dependable staff means less turnover in personnel—and *that* means a consistently high level of quality in the operation of your Soup Kitchen. We can't overstress the importance of high quality—if it goes down, it'll bring you down with it. If it stays high, so will your profits!

The Two Professionals You Must Seek Out for Advice

If after reading this chapter you have a strong desire to open a Soup Kitchen restaurant, the first investment you must make is to hire an accountant and a lawyer. Your accountant knows bookkeeping and your lawyer knows regulations. One important point: when looking for an accountant and a lawyer, make sure the ones you hire have restaurant clients. That way, they'll already be familiar with the business you're entering. Their fees will vary, so shop around for the most reasonable rates.

The lawyer will advise on matters relating to insurance, permits, and licenses. A good lawyer knows a good insurance broker who will get you the maximum coverage to protect your operation against accidental food poisoning or any other business-related mishap. The lawyer will be responsible for thoroughly checking your lease and getting your health department certificate. He'll also secure a beer and wine license if it's required in your state.

The accountant has the extremely important job of balancing your books. (In a later chapter, we discuss how you can do your *own* bookkeeping. A restaurant operation, however, is so complex that you'll need an accountant when you first start out.)

Your Overall Expenses

As we discussed earlier in the chapter, all of the basic equipment you'll need will cost between $10,000 and $12,000. (Remember, that's *used* equipment; if you were to buy all that new, it would be *double* that price.) Then we included the optional equipment cost of about $7,500 if you decided to do your own baking. Then add another $2,000 for the miscellaneous supplies. This comes to a total of about *$21,000*. The other large expense is your cost of building preparation—establishing that "Early Americana" look. That will come to about *$8,000*. Therefore, your total expenses *before* you open the doors to do business on the first day will come to about *$29,000*. Again, please keep in mind that this will *vary* in different parts of the country, depending on labor costs, construction costs, and equipment availability.

The All-Important First 30 Days

When you open your doors the first day, you should have your operating expenses covered for *30 days*. That way you won't have to be in a "sweat" about needing the money from sales to meet your operating expenses. The two biggest expenses in your operating costs will be the *rent* for the premises and the *salaries* for your employees. With regard to the rent, we are talking about approximately 2,500 square feet for a Soup Kitchen that will accommodate 100 customers. We advise you to be prepared to pay $2,500. The landlord or owner of the space will want, in advance, the first month's rent plus a month's security. That's $5,000.

A Review of Your Total Investment

Your other large operating expense will be the salaries for your employees. Your chef, your manager and a staff of 6 to 8 employees will cost you about $7,500 a month. Also be prepared to have enough money on hand to be able to back up the cost of all your food over the first month period. You can estimate about $6,500 a month for your product cost. The other expenses in this first month period cover your utility costs, advertising and promotion, accounting and legal fees, insurance, permits and licenses, maintenance, laundry, disposable paper supplies, free employee meals, plus miscellaneous expenses. For this group of expenses, allow $3,500 for the month.

Summary

All Equipment (bought used)	$21,000
Decorating (Early Americana)	8,000
Rent (1 month + 1 month security)	5,000
Salaries (first month)	7,500
Food Costs (first month)	6,500
All Other Costs (first month)	3,500
	$51,500

So we're talking about a total investment—in round numbers—of about $50,000 to start up your Soup Kitchen.

By this time, you're probably in shock and saying, "I don't have that kind of money—where am I going to get it?" Our answer is, *there are ways!* (And we'll point them out to you in later chapters.) But first, let's look at the *good* side and mention some figures that point out how profitable this type of restaurant can be.

$50,000—Your Take-Home Pay

We conservatively estimate that an attractive, well-run Soup Kitchen can bring in approximately *$350,000* a year in gross sales. (This really *is* a conservative figure. Some Soup Kitchens are doing over $500,000 a year!) But on the basis of $350,000, that breaks down to a gross of about $30,000 a month. Your cost of doing this business each month—including your total product cost and the expenses of running your operation (rent, salaries, etc.) will come to about 70% of your gross, or about $21,000 a month. This leaves you a profit of about *$9,000 a month*, or a 30% net profit of your gross sales. On a yearly basis, that's *$108,000* before taxes. You personally could easily be drawing *$25,000 a year* as salary and then take another *$25,000* as a legitimate payout from profits. There's enough money left to pay taxes, and money left over from that to further expand the business or invest it in any other manner you so choose. Imagine if you had a *super* Soup Kitchen grossing *$500,000* a year. You'd easily earn *$75,000* a year.

Chapter 11

Everything You've Always Wanted to Know About Cooking ... But Were Afraid to Ask

Where to Get Cookbooks for Free

They say a good cook never has enough cookbooks! Well, that might be true, but we sure don't advocate spending a lot of money *buying* a bunch of cookbooks! Our first policy is to go to the library. It's free. See what they have there. And if their cookbook selection is thin, then urge them to stock more. You'd be surprised to know that librarians often take suggestions from the public about what new books might be ordered. It's understood that most libraries in the nation are under a financial squeeze, and they don't have money to throw around. But all you can do is ask! When they know that cooking is your *business,* they might well purchase a few cookbooks for their library that they normally wouldn't.

Learning About Other Cookbooks for Just $1

We'd like to give you the names and addresses of some folks who sell, via mail order, cookbooks and other information relating to "creative cooking." We're not suggesting that you spend a lot of money with them either; just look over what they have and judge for yourself.

JUST COOKBOOKS
P.O. Box 192
Palatine, Illinois 60087

If you send them $1.00 (no more) they'll send you their entire catalogue of all the cookbooks they have. They say that even their catalogue is a cookbook and that if you order a book through them, they'll deduct the $1 you sent them in the first place! (That sounds fair enough to us.)

It might be worth it to send $1.00 (no more) to:

KITCHEN BAZAAR
4455 Connecticut Avenue N.W.
Washington, D.C. 20008

For the $1 you get five publications a year relating to your business. They'll also send their latest Christmas catalogue. This $1 gamble also seems like a good investment.

Where to Get the Finest Gourmet Recipes for the Price of a Self-Addressed Envelope

We want to suggest an entirely different source of information; places where we think that for the cost of two stamps (one on your letter to them and one for your stamped, self-addressed envelope) you might pick up very valuable information. We're talking about the *gourmet* food stores in New York City. It's been understood that on the small island of Manhattan, they have more fine restaurants and more fancy gourmet food stores than anywhere else in the U.S. New York City is simply the gourmet capital of the world! That's not to say that there aren't fine restaurants in other cities in the country; it's just that the very best of them are in New York City. So are the most elegant of gourmet food shops.

New York is truly cosmopolitan in its tastes. It would be a good idea to find out what some of the city's fine gourmet food stores are carrying. Write each one and say, *"Would you be kind enough to send me any list you might have (prices included) of the foods and other delicacies you sell. I enclose a stamped, self-addressed envelope for your convenience."*

All of these stores are in *New York City, New York:*

Accents & Images
1020 Second Avenue
New York, N.Y. 10022

B. Altman & Company (Gourmet Food Dept.)
351 Fifth Avenue
New York, N.Y. 10016

Bloomingdale's (Gourmet Food Dept.)
59th Street & Lexington Avenue
New York, N.Y. 10022

Country Host
1435 Lexington Avenue
New York, N.Y. 10028

Just Desserts Ltd.
443 East 75th St.
New York, N.Y. 10021

Dean & DeLuca
121 Prince Street
New York, N.Y. 10013

E.A.T.
1064 Madison Avenue
New York, N.Y. 10028

Epicurean Gallery
17 East 70th Street
New York, N.Y. 10021

Fay & Allen's Foodworks
1241 Third Avenue
New York, N.Y. 10021

Donald Bruce White Caterers
159 East 64th St.
New York, N.Y. 10021

The Rosedale Market
1229 Lexington Avenue
New York, N.Y. 10021

Macy's (Gourmet Food Dept.)
Herald Square at 34th Street
New York, N.Y. 10001

Les Trois Petits Cochons
17 East 13th Street
New York, N.Y. 10003

Rosemary Miller's
197 East 76th Street
New York, N.Y. 10021

The Silver Palate
274 Columbus Avenue
New York, N.Y. 10023

William Poll
1051 Lexington Avenue
New York, N.Y. 10021

St. Remy, L'Herbier de Provence
156 East 64th Street
New York, N.Y. 10021

Schaller & Weber
1654 Second Avenue
New York, N.Y. 10028

Vermonti Enterprises, Inc.
35A Jane Street
New York, N.Y. 10014

Word of Mouth
1012 Lexington Avenue
New York, N.Y. 10021

Zabar's
2245 Broadway
New York, N.Y. 10024

The above list suggests twenty-one fancy gourmet food shops! They offer very fine products to people who are willing to pay extra for the superior quality that can't be found in the supermarket. None of these stores *replaces* the supermarket; they sell luxuries, *not* necessities. Yet they all do a very good business, because there are a lot of people who appreciate the finer things in life! Yes, even when it comes to food. As a matter of fact, *especially* when it comes to food!

Some of the stores might not send you their list, but we think the majority of them will. You might or might not be inclined to make what they make, but that isn't our point. We just want you to be *aware* of some very fancy specialties that are for sale in the "gourmet capital of the world." It's entirely possible that your particular specialty—the home-grown or home-baked food that you make—is the equal of anything they sell. Being fancy doesn't always mean being good. But, for the most part, these gourmet food shops buy from the best "Kitchen Ladies" (or "Kitchen Men") in the business. So we just want you to see what other talented cooks are doing.

An Important Note

Some of your letters might be returned due to the fact that some of the stores on the list might no longer be in business. But as this book is being written, they are very much in business. All it will cost you is a few stamps to find out. We think it's worth it as you can get some excellent ideas which you can cash in on in your own community!

An added tip: when you receive the lists from them, see if any *particular* food or delicacy interests you as something *you'd* like to add to your specialty. Then, *write* that store and ask for the recipe. The store owner *might* send you the details, since you probably live in another part of the country and pose no direct competition to his (her) New York City store. At any rate, it doesn't hurt to ask!

To Improve Your Cooking and/or Baking Skills, Here's a List of Schools Located Across the Country

None of the money-making ideas we have given you in our book—from chocolate chip cookies to the Soup Kitchen—require you to be a gourmet cook or fancy baker in order to profit by them. With the *simplest* of cooking and/or baking skills, you could cash in on any of these ideas right now!

But perhaps you've always had an ambition to become a really *excellent* cook and/or baker, the kind of person who goes on to achieve local, regional, and even national recognition. If that's been your heart's desire, then why not try to do it! In the next chapter, you're going to learn of a woman who made gourmet dishes her specialty, and today she owns a "take-out" gourmet food store that's earning her $10,000 a week—*yes,* $10,000 a *week!*

This can happen to you! But first, you'll need to substantially increase, or at the very least, polish your cooking and/or baking skills. For that reason, we'll now give you a state-by-state list (alphabetically arranged) of cooking schools located throughout the nation.

An Important Note!

We are not in the position to recommend *any* particular school on this list. We give you their names & addresses and when possible, their phone numbers. Otherwise, check your local directory. *Always* call before you visit, and on the phone, *ask* the following questions: (1) *What kinds of classes are taught?* (2) *How many students in each class?* (3) *How much do you charge?* (4) *What is the professional background of the owner or director?* (5) *Would you send me a brochure?*

The list we are providing you is a very *large* list. It is possible that some schools are no longer in existence. Some, being part of an educational system, could have been discontinued because of a cutback in funding. Other schools might not give actual cooking classes, but offer courses *related* to cooking and baking. But *most* of the schools will be able to give you what you're looking for. Make a few calls (asking the questions above) to find out which school *best suits your needs and your pocketbook!*

ALABAMA

Auburn   Auburn University
Auburn, Alabama 36830
(205) 826-4000

Birmingham   The Cooking School
2916 Linden Avenue
Birmingham, Alabama 35209
(205) 871-8785

Birmingham   The Kitchen Shoppe
2841 Cahaba Road
Birmingham, Alabama 35223
(205) 879-5277

Huntsville   Cooking School at Lawrens
809 Madison
Huntsville, Alabama 35801
(205) 539-3812

Mobile   Carver State Vocational & Technical Institute
Mobile, Alabama 36007

Tuskegee   Tuskegee Institute
Tuskegee, Alabama 36083
(205) 727-8011

ALASKA

Anchorage   Anchorage Community College
Anchorage, Alaska 99504

Fairbanks   University of Alaska
Fairbanks, Alaska 99701

Fairbanks   Tanana Valley College
Fairbanks, Alaska 99701

Seward   Human Resources Development
Center
Seward, Alaska 99664

Wassilla   Wassilla Youth Center
Wassilla, Alaska 99830

ARIZONA

Scottsdale   C. Steele
7303 East Indian School Road
Scottsdale, Arizona 85251
(602) 947-4596

Scottsdale   The House of Rice
3221 North Hayden Road
Scottsdale, Arizona 85251
(602) 947-6698

Tucson   Parisian Kitchen
6760 East Camino Principale
Tucson, Arizona 85715
(602) 886-5223

ARKANSAS

Little Rock   Marilyn Myers' Kitchen
115 South Victory
Little Rock, Arkansas 72201
(501) 372-2319

Little Rock   L'Ecole de Cuisine
10807 Crestdale Lane
Little Rock, Arkansas 72217
(501) 224-0542

Pine Bluff Pines Vocational Technical High
School
Pine Bluff, Arkansas 71601

CALIFORNIA

Belvedere Virginia Hjelte
P.O. Box 676
Belvedere, California 94920
(415) 937-0555

Berkeley Marinette Georgi Cuisine Minceur
2315½ Rose Street
Berkeley, California 94708
(415) 848-8736

Berkeley Joyce Esersky Goldstein
2515 Etna Street
Berkeley, California 94704
(415) 843-1074

Berkeley Cooking In The Country
Judith Lichez
2417 Cedar Street
Berkeley, California 94708

Berkeley Annie-May de Bresson
1438 Hawthorne Terrace
Berkeley, California 94708

Beverly Hills The Lillian Haines School of
Culinary Arts
P.O. Box 5248
Beverly Hills, California 90210
(213) 271-9173

Encino Microwave Cooking Center
17728 Marcello Place
Encino, California 91316
(213) 987-1701

Encino Walbert & Co.
17200 Ventura Boulevard
Encino, California 91316
(213) 789-7508   (213) 990-5761

Escondido	The Cupboard Felicita Village 330 West Felicita Avenue Escondido, California 92025 (714) 743-0421
Escondido	Frazier Farms Cooking School Creative Cuisinières 13th and Center City Parkway Escondido, California 92025 (714) 745-2141
Fremont	Mission Gourmet Cookware 165 Anza Street Fremont, California 94538 (415) 657-8062
Kentfield	Lenore Bleadon 170 Rancheria Road Kentfield, California 94904 (415) 461-0988
La Jolla	Low Cholesterol Cooking Jeanne Jones La Jolla, California (714) 459-1037
Long Beach	Long Beach City College 1305 East Pacific Coast Highway Long Beach, California (213) 420-4111
Los Altos	The Kitchen Emporium Cooking School 240 Main Street Los Altos, California 94022 (415) 941-1670
Los Angeles	The Von Welanetz Cooking Workshop The Cooking Store 8634 Sunset Boulevard Los Angeles, California 90069 (213) 657-1555

Los Angeles   Gourmet School of Cooking and
Entertaining
3915 Carnavon Way
Los Angeles, California 90027

Los Angeles   West Indian Dinner or Buffet
Thelma Williams
Los Angeles, California
(213) 674-4133 (213) 678-1958

Los Angeles   Lawry's California Center
568 San Fernando Road
Los Angeles, California 90065
(213) 225-2491 (Ext. 299)

Los Angeles   Microwave Oven Workshop
10988 West Pico Boulevard
Los Angeles, California 90064
(213) 474-3113

Los Angeles   Hayward School of Cookery and
Catering
3710 Fletcher Drive
Los Angeles, California 90065
(213) 257-3438

Los Angeles   Los Angeles Trade-Tech. College
400 W. Washington Boulevard
Los Angeles, California
(213) 746-0800

Los Gatos   Gourmet Kitchen
317 Montclair Road
Los Gatos, California 95030
(408) 354-4677

Menlo Park   Lesands Cooks
1139 Chestnut Street
Menlo Park, California 94025
(415) 325-1712

Napa Valley   Belle Rhodes
Napa Valley, California
(415) 547-0212

Oakland   Laney College
1001 3rd Avenue
Oakland, California
(415) 834-5740

Orinda   The Cookery at the Cove
c/o The Village Cookery
17 Orinda Way
Orinda, California 94563

Palo Alto   Helen Cassidy Page School of
Cooking
144 Melville Road
Palo Alto, California 94301

Pasadena   Inner Gourmet
691 La Loma Road
Pasadena, California 91105
(213) 441-2075

Redwood City   Charlotte Combe Cooking School
959 Woodside Road
Redwood City, California 94061
(415) 365-0548

Sacramento   William Glen
2651 El Paseo Lane
Sacramento, California 95821
(916) 483-2935

San Anselmo   The Cooking Craze
609 San Anselmo
San Anselmo, California 94960
(415) 459-1488

San Diego   Great Menus From Nouvelle Cuisine
Ann Otterson
San Diego, California
(614) 459-9344   (714) 454-1710

San Diego   Antonia Allegra Griffin
6845 Condon Drive
San Diego, California 92122
(714) 452-9427

San Diego Kitchen Liberation
Mission Valley Center West
824 Camino Del Rio North
San Diego, California
(714) 299-4040

San Diego Gibson Girl, The American School
of International Cuisine
University Towne Center
4405 La Jolla Village Drive
San Diego, California 92122
(714) 455-6255

San Diego The Perfect Pan
4040 Goldfinch Street
San Diego, California 92103
(714) 299-8442

San Francisco City College of San Francisco
Ocean and Phelan Aves.
San Francisco, California
(415) 239-3390

San Francisco Malvi Doshi's Cooking Classes
180 Blake Street
San Francisco, California 94118
(415) 387-3782

San Francisco John A. O'Connel Voc. & Tech.
Institute
San Francisco, California
(415) 648-1326

San Francisco Judith Ets-Hokin Culinary Institute
1802 Bush Street
San Francisco, California 94109
(415) 922-4603

San Francisco Classics & Basics
Mary Risley
San Francisco, California
(415) 771-8667

San Francisco   Maybelle Iribe
1913 Grant Avenue
San Francisco, California 94133
(415) 421-4164

San Francisco   Chinese—Northern, Central,
Southern Cuisine
Barbara Tropp
San Francisco, California
(415) 922-4789

San Francisco   Emalee Chapman
405 Davis Court
San Francisco, California 94111
(415) 397-8088

San Francisco   Simplified French Classics
Paul Mayer
San Francisco, California
(415) 474-7221

San Francisco   Hyde and Green Company
1898 Hyde Street
San Francisco, California 94109
(415) 441-2130

San Francisco   The Great Chefs of France
at the Robert Mondavi Winery
1496 Dolores Street
San Francisco, California 94110
(415) 648-0909

San Francisco   California Culinary Academy
215 Fremont Street
San Francisco, California 94105
(415) 543-2764

San Francisco   Rosemary Hinton
34B Hill Street
San Francisco, California 94110
(415) 285-6482

San Francisco   La Grande Bouffe
2235 Greenwich Street
San Francisco, California 94123
(415) 931-4152

San Francisco　The Wine Country Cooking School
393 Cumberland Avenue
San Francisco, California 94114

San Francisco　Jenny Chen Cooking School
175 Villa Terrace
San Francisco, California 94114
(415) 863-5765

San Francisco　Charcuterie Cooking School
25 Buena Vista Terrace
San Francisco, California 94117
(415) 431-0211

San Francisco　Tante Marie's Cooking School
271 Francisco Street
San Francisco, California 94133
(415) 771-8667

San Francisco　Loni Kuhn's Cook's Tour
91 Commonwealth Avenue
San Francisco, California 94118
(415) 752-5265

San Francisco　The Jack Liro Cooking School
757 Monterey Boulevard
San Francisco, California 94127
(415) 587-8908

San Francisco　The Mandarin Salon de Cuisine
Ghirardelli Square
900 North Point
San Francisco, California 94109
(415) 673-8812

San Pablo　Contra Costa College
2801 Castro Road
San Pablo, California
(415) 235-7800

Santa Monica　Jean Brady Cooking School
680 Brooktree Road
Santa Monica, California 90402
(213) 454-4220

Seal Beach   La Bonne Cuisine
(School of French & European
Cooking)
1435 Main Street
Seal Beach, California 90740
(213) 430-2157

Sherman Oaks   Candy Factory/Chocolate Specialties
Alan Badger & Gerilyn Wilson
Sherman Oaks, California
(213) 784-9141

Sherman Oaks   Le Kookery Cooking School
13624 Ventura Blvd.
Sherman Oaks, California 91423
(213) 995-0568

Tarzana   Marlene Sorosky's Cooking Center
18440 Burbank Blvd.
Tarzana, California 91356
(213) 345-4003

Visalia   Helen's Happy Thought
3338-B South Mooney Blvd.
Visalia, California 93277
(209) 733-4747

Walnut Creek   Janice Lowry
14 San Antonio Court
Walnut Creek, California 94958
(415) 937-0587

COLORADO

Boulder   Peppercorn Gourmet Goods & Cooking School
2040 Broadway #100
Boulder, Colorado 80302
(303) 449-5847

Denver   Emily Griffith Opportunity School
12th & Welton Streets
Denver, Colorado
(303) 572-8218

Ft. Collins   Colorado State University
Ft. Collins, Colorado 80521

Golden   Lynne Kasper's Lid and Ladle
Cooking School
2575 Youngfield Street
Golden, Colorado 80401
(303) 232-7288

CONNECTICUT

Farmington   Ann Howard Cookery
Brickwalk Lane
Farmington, Connecticut
(203) 678-9486

Greenwich   Cook's Corner
115 Mason Street
Greenwich, Connecticut 06830
(203) 869-2653

Greenwich   Ron Buebendorf Chinese Cooking
Classes
44 W. Putnam Ave.
Greenwich, Connecticut
(203) 869-7139

Greenwich   Polly Fritch's Cooking Classes
969 North Street
Greenwich, Connecticut 06830
(203) 661-7742

Greenwich   Greenwich Public Schools Adult
Education
Greenwich High School
11 Hillside Rd.
Greenwich, Connecticut
(203) 869-9400 ext. 32

Greenwich   Greenwich Y.W.C.A.
259 East Putnam Avenue
Greenwich, Connecticut
(203) 869-6501

Greenwich   Pottery, Etc.
935 Poquonock Rd.
Greenwich, Connecticut
(203) 445-5151

Guilford   Cuisinier
943A Boston Post Road
Guilford, Connecticut 06437
(203) 453-6127

Guilford   Michel LeBorgne
61 Woodside Road
Guilford, Connecticut 06437
(203) 453-9724

New Haven   The Culinary Institute of America
387 Prospect Street
New Haven, Connecticut 06509

New Milford   The Silo
Hunt Hill Farm
Upland Road
New Milford, Connecticut 06776
(203) 355-0300

Old Greenwich   The Constance Quan Cooking
School
39 Lockwood Drive
Old Greenwich, Connecticut 06870
(203) 637-9302

W. Hartford   The China Closet
West Hartford, Connecticut
(203) 236-2772

Westport   Joanne Hush Chinese Cooking
School
The Greens Farms Bookstore
1254 Post Road
Westport, Connecticut 06880
(203) 227-4151

Westport   Rose Chann Gray
24 Meeker Road
Westport, Connecticut
(203) 227-9056

Westport   Cook's Corner
11 Sherwood Square
Westport, Connecticut 06880
(203) 227-9554

Wilton   Culinary Arts Cooking School
Gateway Shopping Center
Wilton, Connecticut 06897
(203) 762-7575

Wilton   Potsanjammer School of Natural
Cooking
Wilton's Natural Living Center
33 Danbury Road
Wilton, Connecticut 06897
(203) 762-0247

DELAWARE

Hockessin   Carmen's Cuisine
516 Faraday Road
Hockessin, Delaware 19707
(302) 239-2996

Newark   Creative Cooking
536 Christiana Mall
Newark, Delaware 19702
(302) 366-7484

DISTRICT OF
COLUMBIA

Washington   Carol Mason's Food Originals
2723 P Street N.W.
Washington, D.C. 20007
(202) 333-2448

Washington   The Renaissance Chefs Cooking
School
2450 Virginia Ave. N.W.
Washington, D.C. 20037
(202) 659-5735

Washington   Anna Burdick Voc. High School
1300 Allison St., N.W.
Washington, D.C.
(202) 576-6241

Washington   John A. Chamberlain
14th and Potomac Ave., S.E.
Washington, D.C.
(202) 724-4648

Washington   Margaret Murray Washington Voc.
High School
Washington, D.C.
(202) 673-7224

FLORIDA

Hallandale   Ralph Varketta's Cooking School
428 South West 11th St.
Hallandale, Florida 33009
(305) 458-4946

Lakeland   Kettles Culinary Supplies
1074 S. Florida Avenue
Lakeland, Florida 33803
(813) 688-0130

S. Miami   Bobbi and Carole's Cooking School
7251 Southwest 57th Court
South Miami, Florida 33143
(305) 667-5957
(*or*)
8507 S.W. 136th Street
Miami, Florida 33156
(305) 232-0343

Miami   Lindsey Hopkins
Educational Center
1410 Northeast 2nd Ave.
Miami, Florida
(305) 350-3010

Sarasota   Sally Fine's Cuisine Classics
5029 Oxford Drive
Sarasota, Florida
(813) 349-7626

St. Petersburg   The Stock Pot
7020 Central Avenue
St. Petersburg, Florida 33707
(813) 381-2179

Tallahassee   Betty Griffith Cooking School
2317 Clare Drive
Tallahassee, Florida 32308
(904) 893-4889

Tallahassee   Florida State University
Tallahassee, Florida
(904) 644-2525

GEORGIA

Atlanta   Diane Wilkinson's Cooking School
4365 Harris Trail
Atlanta, Georgia 30327
(404) 233-0366

Atlanta   Ursula's Cooking School & Catering
1764 Cheshire Bridge Road N.E.
Atlanta, Georgia 30324
(404) 876-7463

Atlanta   The Cooking School
Rich's Department Store (Downtown)
45 Broad St.
Atlanta, Georgia 30303
(404) 586-4727

Atlanta   Kathy Hendricks' The Compleat Cook
230 The Prado
Atlanta, Georgia 30309
(404) 892-2417

Atlanta   Truffles Gourmet Cooking School
Andrews Square
56 East Andrews Drive N.W.
Atlanta, Georgia 30305
(404) 237-7005

Savannah   Bailee's Best
107 E. Jones Street
Savannah, Georgia 31401
(912) 234-4178

White	Fran Crisco Cooks at Home and Away Route 1, Box 84 White, Georgia (404) 382-5659

HAWAII

Honolulu	Honolulu Community College Honolulu, Hawaii 96817
Honolulu	Kapiolani Community College Honolulu, Hawaii 96814
Honolulu	University of Hawaii Honolulu, Hawaii 96822
Kahului	Maui Community College Kahului, Hawaii 96732
Lihue	Kauai Community College Lihue, Hawaii 96766
Pearl City	Leward Community College Pearl City, Hawaii 96782

IDAHO

Boise	Boise State University Boise, Idaho 83707
Boise	School of Voc. & Tech. Education Boise, Idaho 83707
Coeur D'Alene	Peppermill Coeur D'Alene Mall Annex Coeur D'Alene, Idaho 83814 (208) 664-2926
Pocatello	Idaho State University Pocatello, Idaho 83209
Twin Falls	College of Southern Idaho Twin Falls, Idaho 83301

ILLINOIS

Barrington   Helen Baetz Cooking School
225 Bellingham Drive
Barrington, Illinois 60010
(312) 381-5931

Chicago   University of Chicago
Chicago, Illinois
(312) 753-1234

Chicago   Cook's Mart Ltd.
609 North LaSalle Street
Chicago, Illinois 60610
(312) 642-3526

Chicago   American Institute of Baking
400 East Ontario Street
Chicago, Illinois 60611

Chicago   Jane Salzfass Freiman Cooking Class
837 West Oakdale Ave.
Chicago, Illinois 60657
(312) 549-7526

Chicago   Cooking and Catering School
127 North Dearborn St.
Chicago, Illinois 60602

Chicago   Monique's
684 West Irving Park Road
Chicago, Illinois 60613
(312) 935-9019

Chicago   Oriental Food Market and Cooking
School
7411 North Clark Street
Chicago, Illinois 60626
(312) 274-2826

Chicago   Culinarion
113 East Oak Street
Chicago, Illinois 60611
(312) 266-7840

Chicago	Washburn Trade School 3100 S. Kedzie Chicago, Illinois (312) 641-4800
Chicago	Alma Lach 710 North Rush Street Chicago, Illinois 60611 (312) 664-7800
Chicago	City Colleges of Chicago Chicago, Illinois 60601
Chicago	Westinghouse Area Voc. High School Chicago, Illinois 60624
Elk Grove Village	William Rainey Harper College Elk Grove Village, Illinois 60007
Fairview Heights	Tin Pan Galley 271 St. Clair Square Fairview Heights, Illinois 62208 (618) 632-1210
Geneva	Persimmon Tree 127 South Third Street Geneva, Illinois 60134 (312) 232-6446
Glencoe	Abby Cooks & Cooks & Cooks P.O. Box 118 Glencoe, Illinois 60022 (312) 835-1134
Glen Ellyn	City College of DuPage Glen Ellyn, Illinois 60137
Glen Ellyn	Microcookery Center, Inc. 413 Main Street Glen Ellyn, Illinois 60137 (312) 858-2853
Glenview	Dumas Père L'Ecole de la Cuisine Française 1129 North Depot Street Glenview, Illinois 60025 (312) 729-4823

Glenview   The Complete Cook
222 Waukegan Road
Glenview, Illinois 60025
(312) 729-7687

Hazel Crest   Ruth's Kitchen
3206 Maple Lane
Hazel Crest, Illinois 60429
(312) 335-4758

Hinsdale   Shirley Waterloo Culinary
Instruction
307 North Quincy
Hinsdale, Illinois 60521
(312) 323-3903

Hinsdale   What's Cooking
P.O. Box 323
Hinsdale, Illinois 60521
(312) 986-1595

Lake Bluff   Tin Pan Galley
P.O. Box 445
Lake Bluff, Illinois 60044
(312) 234-0346

Lincoln   Lincoln Area Voc. Center
Lincoln, Illinois 62656

Maple Park   Kaneland Area Voc. Center
Maple Park, Illinois 60151

Marion   Marion Area Vocational Center
Marion, Illinois 62959

Moline   Moline Area Voc. Center
Moline, Illinois 61265

Mt. Prospect   Continental Cookery
1144 South Elmhurst
Mt. Prospect, Illinois 60056
(312) 593-3020

Naperville   Napercurean House, Inc.
28 West Chicago Ave.
Naperville, Illinois 60540
(312) 357-4100

Pekin   Pekin Area Vocation Center
Pekin, Illinois 61554

Peoria   Proper Pan Cooking School
4620 North University
Metro Center
Peoria, Illinois 61614
(309) 692-6382

Peoria   Holt's Culinary School, Inc.
521 Fulton Street
Peoria, Illinois 61602

Peoria   Le Petit Bedon
1319 West Devereux
Peoria, Illinois 61614
(309) 692-4524

Pontiac   Pontiac Area Voc. Center
Pontiac, Illinois 61764

River Grove   Triton College
River Grove, Illinois 60171

Urbana   University of Illinois
Urbana, Illinois
(217) 333-1000

Wilmette   Charie's Kitchen
2111 Beechwood
Wilmette, Illinois 60091
(312) 256-3979

INDIANA

Bloomington   Indiana University
Bloomington, Indiana
(812) 332-0211

Evansville   Indiana Vocational Technical
College
Evansville, Indiana
(812) 426-2865

Fort Wayne   Chef's Connection
9324 Thunder Hill Place
Fort Wayne, Indiana 46804
(219) 432-4221   (219) 745-0458

Indianapolis	Indiana Vocational Technical College Indianapolis, Indiana (317) 635-6100
Indianapolis	The Pan Handler 8702 Keystone Crossing Indianapolis, Indiana 46240 (317) 844-8160
Lafayette	The Eight Mice Market Square Lafayette, Indiana 47904 (317) 447-5255
Lafayette	Purdue University Lafayette, Indiana (317) 749-8111
Michigan City	Michigan City Area Voc. School Michigan City, Indiana 46360
Muncie	Microwave Kitchen Shop 3506 West Jackson Muncie, Indiana 47304 (317) 282-7555
Terre Haute	Indiana State University Terre Haute, Indiana 47809
Valparaiso	The Creative Cook 56 West Indiana Valparaiso, Indiana 46383 (219) 464-3398
Versailles	Southeastern Indiana Voc. School Versailles, Indiana 47042
Vincennes	Vincennes University Vincennes, Indiana (812) 882-3350
West Baden	Northwood College Cooking School West Baden, Indiana 47469

IOWA

Ames Iowa State University
Ames, Iowa 50010

Burlington Southeastern Community College
Burlington, Iowa 52601

Cedar Falls Iowa State College
Cedar Falls, Iowa 60513

Creston Southwestern Community College
Creston, Iowa 50801

Des Moines Des Moines Technical High School
Des Moines, Iowa
(515) 284-7846

Dubuque Clarke College
Dubuque, Iowa 52001

Iowa City Chez Mimi
621 Holt Avenue
Iowa City, Iowa 52240
(319) 351-4071

Mason North Iowa Area Community
College
Mason, Iowa 50401

Mt. Pleasant Iowa Wesleyan University
Mt. Pleasant, Iowa 52641

KANSAS

Atchinson Northeast Kansas Area Voc. Tech.
School
Atchinson, Kansas 66002

Manhattan Kansas State University
Manhattan, Kansas 66502

Overland Park The Back Burner
6964 West 105th Street
Overland Park, Kansas 66204

Shawnee Mission   Culinary Art
9321 Alhambra
Shawnee Mission, Kansas 66204
(913) 381-2122

Wichita   Tin Pan Galley
3700 East Douglas
Wichita, Kansas 67208
(316) 684-9651

KENTUCKY

Berea   Berea College
Berea, Kentucky
(606) 986-9341

Bowling Green   Bowling Green Area Vocational
School
Bowling Green, Kentucky 42101

Harlan   Harlan Area Voc. School
Harlan, Kentucky 40831

Hazard   Hazard Area Voc. School
Hazard, Kentucky 41701

Lexington   Central Kentucky Area Voc. School
Lexington, Kentucky

Louisville   The Baker's Rack
Plainview Village
9952 Linn Station Road
Louisville, Kentucky 40223
(502) 425-2900

Louisville   Central High School
12th and Chestnut
Louisville, Kentucky
(502) 584-6193

Louisville   Adult & Vocational Education
Louisville, Kentucky 40208

LOUISIANA

Baton Route Louisiana Cooking School
8742 West Fairway Drive
Baton Rouge, Louisiana 70809
(504) 927-2369

Baton Rouge Capitol Area Vocational School
1500 S. 13th Street
Baton Rouge, Louisiana
(504) 342-6828

New Orleans Delgrado Trade & Tech. Institute
615 City Park Ave.
New Orleans, Louisiana
(504) 483-4114

New Orleans Orleans Area Voc.-Tech. School
P.O. Box 8202
New Orleans, Louisiana
(504) 945-8080

New Orleans Lee Barnes Cooking School
7808 Maple Street
New Orleans, Louisiana 70118
(504) 866-0246

MAINE

Bangor Eastern Maine Voc.-Tech. Institute
Bangor, Maine 04401

Bridgton Bridgton Tech.-Voc. Center
Bridgton, Maine 04009

Calais Washington County Voc.-Tech.
Institute
Calais, Maine 04619

East Blue Hill Suzanne Taylor's Cooking Classes
Meadow Rue
East Blue Hill, Maine 04629
(207) 374-9948

Orono University of Maine
Orono, Maine
(207) 581-1110

South Portland Southern Maine Voc.-Tech. Institute
South Portland, Maine
(207) 799-7303

Waterville Waterville Tech.-Voc. Center
Waterville, Maine 04901

Westbrook Westbrook Tech.-Voc. Center
Westbrook, Maine 04092

MARYLAND

Annapolis Le Fourneau
101 Annapolis Street
Annapolis, Maryland 21401
(301) 268-5999

Baltimore Chinese Cooking School of the
International Gourmet Center
323 Park Ave.
Baltimore, Maryland 21201
(301) 752-5501

Baltimore Carver Voc.-Tech. High School
Baltimore, Maryland
(301) 396-0553

Baltimore Les Deux Gourmettes
2015 Skyline Road
Baltimore, Maryland 21210
(301) 828-6586

Baltimore Mergenthaler Voc.-Tech
High School
Baltimore, Maryland
(301) 396-6496

Baltimore Culinary Arts
5701 Newbury Street
Baltimore, Maryland 21209
(301) 542-6100

Baltimore The Junior Chef's Kitchen
3607 Barberry Court
Baltimore, Maryland 21208
(301) 486-2814

Bethesda   L'Academie De Cuisine
5021 Wilson Lane
Bethesda, Maryland 20014
(301) 986-9490

College Park   University of Maryland
College Park, Maryland
(301) 454-3311

Cresaptown   Allegany County Voc.-Tech. School
P.O. Box 5387
(Mrs. Lucille Mudrich)
Cresaptown, Maryland 21502

Elkton   Cecil Voc.-Tech. Center
Elkton, Maryland 21921

Hagerstown   Hagerstown Junior College
Hagerstown, Maryland 21740

Newark   Worcester County Voc. Center
Newark, Maryland 21841

Rockville   What's Cooking
Phyliss Frucht
1776 East Jefferson
Rockville, Maryland 20852
(301) 881-2430

Westminster   Carroll County Voc.-Tech. Center
Westminster, Maryland 21157

MASSACHUSETTS

Amherst   University of Massachusetts
Amherst, Massachusetts 01002
(413) 545-0111

Beverly   Endicott Junior College
Beverly, Massachusetts
(617) 927-0585

Boston   La Cuisine Cooking Classes
92 Charles St.
Boston, Massachusetts 02114
(617) 227-7340

Boston   Boston University
              685 Commonwealth Ave.
              Boston, Massachusetts
              (617) 353-2000

Boston   Boston Trade High School Annex
              (Dorchester) 690 Washington St.
              Boston, Massachusetts

Boston   Simmons College
              300 The Fenway
              Boston, Massachusetts
              (617) 738-2000

Boston   Miss Farmer's Cooking School
              Boston, Massachusetts 02115

Cambridge   Creative Cuisine
              2020 Massachusetts Ave.
              Cambridge, Massachusetts 02140
              (617) 354-3836

Fitchburg   Montachusett Regional Voc-Tech.
              School
              1050 Westminster St.
              Fitchburg, Massachusetts 01420

Framingham   Framingham State Teachers College
              Framingham, Massachusetts 01701

Hyannis   Cape Cod Community College
              Hyannis, Massachusetts 02601

Natick   The Every Day Gourmet
              Mill and Speen Streets
              Natick, Massachusetts 01760
              (617) 653-8010

Natick   Denise Schorr
              50 Hartford St.
              Natick, Massachusetts 01760
              (617) 653-5188

Newton Centre Modern Gourmet
              81 Union St.
              Newton Centre, Massachusetts
              02159
              (617) 969-1320

Winchester   Jeanne Tahnk's Gourmet Kitchen,
Inc.
910 Main Street
Winchester, Massachusetts 01890
(617) 729-8027

MICHIGAN

Albion   Albion College
Albion, Michigan
(517) 639-5551

Ann Arbor   Complete Cuisine, Ltd.
322 South Main Street
Ann Arbor, Michigan 48104
(313) 662-0046

Battle Creek   Calhoun County Vocational Center
475 East Roosevelt Ave.
Battle Creek, Michigan 49017

Detroit   Chadsey High School
5535 Martin Street
Detroit, Michigan
(313) 361-1400

Detroit   Wayne State University
Detroit, Michigan
(313) 577-3611

Detroit   Wilbur Wright Cooperative H.S.
Detroit, Michigan
(313) 895-2550

Grand Haven   Kitchen Mechanics
945 Robbins Road
Grand Haven, Michigan 49417
(616) 846-3630

Grand Rapids   Grand Rapids Junior College
Grand Rapids, Michigan 49502

Grosse Point   Le Petit Cordon Bleu School
of International Cuisine
591 Fisher Road
Grosse Point, Michigan 48230
(313) 885-2124

Harrison Mid-Michigan Community College
Harrison, Michigan 48625

Lansing Lansing Community College
Lansing, Michigan 48914

Mt. Pleasant Central Michigan University
Mt. Pleasant, Michigan 48859

Royal Oak Southeast Oakland
Educational Center
Royal Oak, Michigan 48073

Scottville West Shore Community College
Scottville, Michigan 49454

MINNESOTA

Bloomington Normandale Community College
Bloomington, Minnesota 55431

Canby Canby Vocational-Technical
Institute
Canby, Minnesota 56220

Duluth Beatrice Ojakangas
1150 Emerson Road
Duluth, Minnesota 55803
(218) 721-3026

Duluth Duluth Area Voc.-Tech. School
East London Rd.
Duluth, Minnesota
(218) 728-5107

Edina La Bonne Cuisine
6716 Samuel Road
Edina, Minnesota 55435
(612) 944-2485

Golden Valley La Cuvette, Inc.
250 Paisley Lane
Golden Valley, Minnesota 55422
(612) 545-9554

Minneapolis Minneapolis Vocational High School
Minneapolis, Minnesota
(612) 370-9400

Minneapolis	Marvel Chong's Cantonese Cooking School 75 West Island Avenue Minneapolis, Minnesota 55401 (612) 679-2335
Minneapolis	Judith Bell's Cooking Kitchen 3940 West 50th St. Minneapolis, Minnesota 55424 (612) 926-7262
Minnetonka	Rosa Isleib 18316 Woolman Drive Minnetonka, Minnesota 55343 (612) 474-3716
New Brighton	Elizabeth B. Germaine Cookery Demonstrations 2945 Torchwood Drive New Brighton, Minnesota 55112 (612) 636-5750
St. Paul	TH'RICE 1086½ Grand Avenue St. Paul, Minnesota 55105 (612) 225-0513
St. Paul	St. Paul Voc.-Tech. Institute St. Paul, Minnesota (612) 221-1300

MISSISSIPPI

Gautier	Mississippi Gulf Coast Junior College Gautier, Mississippi 39501
Gulfport	Mississippi Gulf Coast Junior College District Gulfport, Mississippi 39573
Handsboro	Jefferson Davis Junior College Handsboro, Mississippi 39554
Hattiesburg	University of Southern Mississippi Hattiesburg, Mississippi 39401

Jackson	Hinds Junior College Jackson, Mississippi 39205
Perkinston	Mississippi Gulf Coast Junior College Perkinston, Mississippi 39573

MISSOURI

Cape Girardeau	Southeast Missouri State College Cape Girardeau, Missouri 63701
Hillsboro	Jefferson Junior College Hillsboro, Missouri 63050
Joplin	Missouri Southern College Joplin, Missouri 64801
Kansas City	Penn Valley Community College Kansas City, Missouri 64111
Kirkwood	Kitchen Klutter 113 West Argonne Kirkwood, Missouri 63122 (314) 822-0666
Neosho	Crowder College (Mrs. Farrell Siddens) Neosho, Missouri 64850
St. Louis	Marianist Culinary Institute St. Louis, Missouri 63112
St. Louis	The Pampered Pantry 8139 Maryland Ave. St. Louis, Missouri 63105
St. Louis	Forest Park Community College 5600 Oakland Ave. St. Louis, Missouri 63110
Warrensburg	Central Missouri State University (Contact: Department Head) Warrensburg, Missouri 64093

MONTANA

Billings	Billings Vocational-Technical Center Billings, Montana

Bozeman   Montana State College
Bozeman, Montana 59715

Missoula   University of Montana
Missoula, Montana 59801
(406) 243-0211

NEBRASKA

Hastings   Central Nebraska Voc.-Tech. School
P.O. Box 1024
Hastings, Nebraska 68901
(Robert P. Harrington)

Lincoln   University of Nebraska
Lincoln, Nebraska
(402) 472-7211

Lincoln   Union College of
Occupational Foods
Lincoln, Nebraska 68508

Omaha   Omaha Technical High School
3201 Cumming St.
Omaha, Nebraska
(402) 554-6700

NEVADA

Las Vegas   University of Nevada
4505 Maryland Parkway
Las Vegas, Nevada 89109

Las Vegas   Southern Nevada Voc.-Tech. Center
Las Vegas, Nevada

Las Vegas   Clark County Voc.-Tech. Center
Las Vegas, Nevada 89109

NEW HAMPSHIRE

Berlin   New Hampshire Voc.-Tech. College
Berlin, New Hampshire 03570

Durham   University of New Hampshire
Durham, New Hampshire 03824
(603) 862-1234

NEW JERSEY

Cresskill Chingwan Tcheng's Chinese Cooking
40 6th Street
Cresskill, New Jersey 07626
(201) 567-5310

Cresskill Irene Feigelis
2 Palisades Court
Cresskill, New Jersey 07626
(201) 568-6480

Eatontown Contempra Cooking Center
Monmouth Hall
Eatontown, New Jersey 07724
(201) 542-3031

Edison Edison Adult School
J.P. Stevens High School
(Chinese Cooking Class)
Edison, New Jersey
(201) 287-4433

Emerson Carole's Capers
5 Lexington Ave.
Emerson, New Jersey 07630
(201) 967-9545

Englewood Cliffs Silvia Lehrer's School of Cookery
34 Stephen Drive
Englewood Cliffs, New Jersey
(201) 567-4549

Hackensack Bergan County Voc. & Tech. High
Hackensack, New Jersey
(201) 343-6000

Hillsdale Sue Lyon's Essencial Cooking
School
43 Saddle Ranch Lane
Hillsdale, New Jersey 07642
(201) 664-8775

Lebanon Kitchen Caboodle
Mountainville
Route #2
Lebanon, New Jersey 08833
(201) 832-7218
(201) 832-7445

Madison Mai Leung Thayer
Madison, New Jersey
(201) 822-2293

Madison Teal & Marien's Cooking School
Madison, New Jersey
(201) 822-3474

Merchantville Camden County Vocational School
Browning Road
Merchantville, New Jersey
(609) 767-7000

Midland Park Epicure School of Fine Cooking
200 Franklin Ave.
Midland Park, New Jersey 07432
(201) 445-2776

Montclair Eileen Yin-Fei-Lo Cooking School
Montclair, New Jersey
(201) 783-9416

Montclair (Upper) Sheila Donahue Carter
201 Fernwood Avenue
Upper Montclair, New Jersey
(201) 783-9047

Mt. Holly Burlingtown County Vocational &
Technical School
Mt. Holly, New Jersey 08060
(Contact: Program Director)

New Brunswick Cook College, Rutgers University
New Brunswick, New Jersey 08903

Newark Essex County Voc. & Tech. High
School
Newark, New Jersey 07170

Paramus   Emilie Taylor's Meat School
             189 Kaywin Road
             Paramus, New Jersey 07652
             (201) 265-4145

Park Ridge   East/West Cooking School
             137 Sibbald Drive
             Park Ridge, New Jersey 07656
             (201) 391-7068

Pennsauken   Camden County Voc. & Tech. High
             School
             Pennsauken, New Jersey 08109

Teaneck   Look & Cook
             433 Cedar Land
             Teaneck, New Jersey 07666
             (201) 836-0833

Tenafly   Cooktique
             9 Railroad Ave.
             Tenafly, New Jersey 07670
             (201) 568-7990

Windsor (East) Le Petit Village
             Rt. 130 Warren Plaza West
             E. Windsor, New Jersey
             (609) 448-6670

Woodbridge   Middlesex County Voc. & Tech.
             High
             Woodbridge, New Jersey
             (201) 634-5858

Wyckoff   La Cuisine
             396 Franklin Avenue
             Wyckoff, New Jersey 07481
             (201) 891-4161

Wyckoff   Italian Kitchen
             309 Newton Road
             Wyckoff, New Jersey 07481
             (201) 447-0696

NEW MEXICO

Albuquerque   L'Epicure
First Plaza Galeria
Albuquerque, New Mexico 87102
(505) 242-0430

Espanola   Northern New Mexico Voc.-Tech.
School
Espanola, New Mexico

Las Vegas   Highlands University
Las Vegas, New Mexico 87701

Portales   Eastern New Mexico University
Portales, New Mexico
(505) 562-1011

Santa Fe   College of Santa Fe
Santa Fe, New Mexico 87501

Santa Fe   International Banquet
Rosa Rajovic
Santa Fe, New Mexico
(505) 242-0430
(505) 344-9242

NEW YORK

Ardsley   Cooking With Mady
(Mady Brown)
20 Bramble Brook Road
Ardsley, New York 10502
(914) 693-2698

Buffalo   Par Avion Pantry
361 Delaware Avenue
Buffalo, New York 14202
(716) 853-2900

Buffalo   Emerson Vocational High School
1405 Sycamore Street
Buffalo, New York
(716) 892-7451

Croton-on-the Hudson Mattimore Cooking School
Oak Place
Croton-on-the-Hudson, New York
10520
(914) 271-3142

East Hampton The 1770 House Cooking School
143 Main Street
East Hampton, New York 11937
(516) 324-1770

Great Neck Les Chefettes Cooking School, Inc.
123 Middle Neck Road
Great Neck, New York 11021

Hyde Park Culinary Institute of America
Route 9
Hyde Park, New York 12538
(914) 452-9600

Mount Vernon Continental Cooking
34 Parkway West
Mount Vernon, New York 10552
(914) 664-8482

New Hyde Park Libby Hillman's Cooking School
17 Lawrence Street
New Hyde Park, New York 11040
(516) 437-6155

New Rochelle Alice M. Perlmutter Cooking School
67 Interlaken Ave.
New Rochelle, New York 10807
(914) 235-4528

North Salem Rowan Tree Farm
Route 116
North Salem, New York 10560
(914) 669-8362

Rochester Rochester Institute of Technology
65 Plymouth Ave. South
Rochester, New York
(716) 475-2411

Scarsdale   In Julie's Kitchen
1527 Weaver Street
Scarsdale, New York 10583
(914) 723-8870

Syracuse   Syracuse University
Syracuse, New York
(315) 423-1870

Valhalla   Westchester Community College
75 Grasslands Avenue
Valhalla, New York
(914) 347-6800

NEW YORK CITY
(& Its Boroughs)

Donna Adams Cooking Classes
445 East 86th St.
New York, N.Y. 10028
(212) 831-8864

A la Bonne Cocotte
23 Eighth Avenue
New York City, N.Y. 10014
(212) 675-7736

Alliance Française La Cuisine
22 East 60th Street
New York, N.Y. 10021
(212) 355-6100

Andrée's Mediterranean Cooking
School
354 East 74th Street
New York, N.Y. 10021
(212) 249-6619

Annemarie's Cooking School
164 Lexington Avenue
New York, N.Y. 10016
(212) 685-5685

James A. Beard Cooking School
167 West 12th Street
New York, N.Y. 10011
(212) 675-4984

Brantès-Autet Cuisine, Inc.
160 East 64th Street
New York, N.Y. 10021
(212) 759-3505

Helene Borey School of Creative
Cooking
255 East 71st Street
New York, N.Y. 10021
(212) 249-3883

The French Way
Apartment 7B
60 West 76th Street
New York, N.Y. 10023
(212) 362-2305

Giuliano Bugialli Cooking Classes
18 East 81st Street
New York, N.Y. 10028
(212) 472-0760

Anna-Teresa Callen's Italian
Kitchen
59 West 12th Street
New York, N.Y. 10011
(212) 929-5640

Madame Chu's Chinese Cooking
Classes
370 Riverside Drive
New York, N.Y. 10025
(212) 663-2182

Miriam Brickman
175 West 13th Street
New York, N.Y. 10011
(212) 929-5812

Cake Decorating
45 East 89th Street
New York, N.Y. 10028
(212) 876-7403

China Institute In America
125 East 65th Street
New York, N.Y. 10021
(212) 744-8181

Cooking With Class
226 East 54th Street
New York, N.Y. 10022
(212) 355-5021

Epicurean Gallery Ltd.
17 East 70th Street
New York, N.Y. 10021
(212) 861-0453

John Clancy's Kitchen Workshop
324 West 19th Street
New York, N.Y. 10011
(212) 243-0958

Mary Beth Clark Cooking School
1841 Broadway Suite 1000
New York, N.Y. 10023
(212) 755-8938

The Helen Worth Cooking School
106 East 31st Street
New York, N.Y. 10016
(212) 532-2185

Scuola Italiana di Cucina of the
America-Italy Society
667 Madison Avenue
New York, N.Y. 10021
(212) 744-0500

International School of Cooking
143 West 94th Street
New York, N.Y. 10025
(212) 749-5000

Jerome Walman
400 East 59th Street
New York, N.Y. 10022
(212) 832-6659

Margaret Spader's Chinese Cooking
School
235 East 50th Street
New York, N.Y. 10022
(212) 755-2661

Murray Hill School of Cooking
125 East 36th Street
New York, N.Y. 10016
(212) 684-4299

Anna Muffoletto's Cordon Bleu of
New York, Ltd.
332 East 84th Street
New York, N.Y. 10028
(212) 628-0264

Marique School of French Cooking
170 East 83rd Street
New York, N.Y. 10028
(212) 879-4229

Virginia Lee Chinese Cooking
Classes
201 East 28th Street (Apt. 21D)
New York, N.Y. 10016
(212) 689-8723

Madhur Jaffrey's Cooking Classes
Apt. 14N
101 West 12th Street
New York, N.Y. 10011
(212) 924-6287

Peter Kump Cooking School
333 East 69th Street
New York, N.Y. 10021
(212) 628-1778

Mexican Cooking Classes
333 East 69th Street
New York, N.Y. 10021
(212) 628-1778

Lilah Kan's Chinese Cooking Classes
884 West End Avenue
New York, N.Y. 10025
(212) 749-0550

Do It The French Way
60 West 76th Street
New York, N.Y. 10024
(212) 362-2305

La Cuisine Sans Peur
216 West 89th Street
New York, N.Y. 10024
(212) 362-0638

Le Cordon Bleu—New York
155 West 68th Street
New York, N.Y. 10023
(212) 873-2434

Michele Urvater
200 West 86th Street
New York, N.Y. 10024
(212) 595-0768

The Mandarin Inn
Peter Wong
14 Mott Street
New York, N.Y. 10002

Anne Sekely School for Cooking
229 East 79th Street
New York, N.Y. 10021
(212) 744-0500

Elisa Celli's Light & Natural
Italian Cooking School
108 East 35th Street
New York, N.Y. 10016
(212) 532-7221

Moore-Betty School of Fine Cooking
162 East 92nd Street
New York, N.Y. 10028
(212) 860-4922

School of Contemporary Cooking
75 East End Avenue
New York, N.Y. 10028
(212) 794-2041

Karen Lee Cooking Classes
142 West End Avenue
New York, N.Y. 10023
(212) 787-2227

The Perla Meyers International
Cooking School
19 East 88th Street
New York, N.Y. 10028
(212) 289-0556

The Marcella Hazan School of
Classic Italian Cooking
155 East 76th Street
New York, N.Y. 10021
(212) 861-2825

The Natural Gourmet Cookery
School
365 West End Ave.
Apartment 1103
New York, N.Y. 10024
(212) 580-7121

Edith Themal's Gourmet Cooking
513 East 82nd Street
New York, N.Y. 10028
(212) 268-7955

Waldorf-Astoria Cooking School
c/o Learning With Professionals
325 East 57th Street
New York, N.Y. 10022
(212) 935-4874

Anna Wong, Society of Ethical
Culture
2 West 64th Street
New York, N.Y. 10023
(212) 874-5280

Robert Schneiderman's Cooking
Classes
203 East 72nd Street
New York, N.Y. 10021
(212) 988-0810

Stuyvestant Adult Center
225 East 23rd Street
New York, N.Y. 10010
(212) 254-2890

Cordon Rose
110 Bleeker Street (Apt. 7D)
New York, N.Y. 10003
(212) 475-8856

Culinary Concepts
1945 Adam C. Powell Jr. Blvd.
Apt. 1-South
New York, N.Y.
(212) 864-1750

Culinary Center of New York
100 Greenwich Avenue
New York, N.Y. 10011
(212) 255-1414

French Pastry Chef
56 West 88th Street
New York, N.Y. 10024
(212) 874-5727

Macy's Department Store
(8th Floor)
151 West 34th Street
New York, N.Y. 10001
(212) 560-4661

Feats Unlimited
46 West 83rd Street
New York, N.Y. 10024
(212) 799-1085

New York Institute of Dietetics
154 West 14th Street
New York, N.Y. 10011
(212) 675-6655

Mabel D. Bacon Vocational High
School
22nd & Lexington Avenue
New York, N.Y. 10010
(212) 475-6875

Hunter College
695 Park Avenue
New York, N.Y. 10021
(212) 570-5118

New York City Community College
300 Jay Street
Brooklyn, New York 11201
(212) 643-8595

Clara Barton Vocational High
School
901 Classon Avenue
Brooklyn, New York
(212) 636-4900

Sarah J. Hale Vocational High
School
345 Dean Street
Brooklyn, New York
(212) 855-2412

Ann Amendolara Nurse's Cooking
Classes
414 East 2nd Street
Brooklyn, New York
(212) 436-1054

Brooklyn Skills Exchange
2242 East 28th Street
Brooklyn, New York
(212) 646-6800

The Hot Wok
151 Sixth Avenue, Park Slope
Brooklyn, New York
(212) 857-1323

Indian Cooking School
101 Clark Street
Brooklyn Heights, New York
(212) 625-3958

Kingsborough Community College of
the City University of New York
Oriental Blvd., Manhattan Beach
Brooklyn, New York
(212) 934-5051

La Cuisine School of Cooking
155 Clinton Street
Brooklyn Heights, New York
(212) 522-3074

Woks On Wheels
76 Pierrepont Street
Brooklyn Heights, New York
(212) 522-0495

Kennedy Adult Center
99 Terrace View Avenue
Bronx, New York
(212) 786-0800

Jane Addams
Vocational High School
900 Tinton Avenue
Bronx, New York
(212) 292-4513

North Bronx
Adult Educational System
Harry S. Truman H.S.
750 Baychester Avenue
Bronx, New York
(212) 653-0747

Forest Hills Adult Education Center
67-01 110th Street
Forest Hills, Queens
New York
(212) 263-8066

Lee Gold Cooking School
43-19 168th Street
Auburndale, Queens
New York
(212) 539-7836

Ann Mariotti Cooking School
70-37 Ingram Street
Forest Hills, Queens
New York 11375
(212) 263-5540

Bryant Adult Center
48-10 31st Avenue
Long Island City, Queens
New York
(212) 728-5275

Vegetarian Cooking Classes
For Beginners
65-68 Elwell Crescent
Rego Park, Queens
New York
(212) 261-3219

McKee Vocational & Technical H.S.
290 St. Mark's Place
St. George, Staten Island
New York
(212) 273-4000

College of Staten Island
100 Stuyvesant Place
St. George, Staten Island
New York
(212) 390-7707

Carol's Cuisine
18 Scranton Street
Grasmere, Staten Island
New York
(212) 987-1219

NORTH CAROLINA

Asheville   Asheville-Buncombe
Technical Institute
Asheville, North Carolina 28801

Boone   Appalachian State University
Boone, North Carolina 28607

Charlotte   West Charlotte High School
Charlotte, North Carolina
(704) 392-0157

Fayetteville   Ecole de Cuisine Lafayette
P.O. Box 53445
Fayetteville, North Carolina 28305
(919) 484-0652

Goldsboro   Wayne Community College
Goldsboro, North Carolina 27530

Greensboro   Anne Byrd's Cookery
225 Florence Street
Greensboro, North Carolina 27401
(919) 275-7024

Pinehurst   The Pinehurst Cooking School
P.O. Box 4000
Pinehurst, North Carolina 28374
(Toll Free) 800-334-9560

Wilkesboro   Wilkes Community College
Wilkesboro, North Carolina 28697

NORTH DAKOTA

Bismarck   Bismarck Junior College
Bismarck, North Dakota 58501

Devil's Lake   Lake Region Junior College
Devil's Lake, North Dakota 58301

Fargo   North Dakota State University
Fargo, North Dakota 58102

Grand Forks   University of North Dakota
Grand Forks, North Dakota 58201

Williston   University of North Dakota
              Williston Center
              Williston, North Dakota 58801

OHIO

Ashland   Ashland College
              Ashland, Ohio 44805

Athens   Ohio University
              Athens, Ohio
              (614) 594-5511

Centerville   Mr. Pots & Pans, Inc.
              986 West Centerville
              Centerville, Ohio 45459
              (513) 434-6635

Cincinnati   University of Cincinnati
              Cincinnati, Ohio
              (513) 475-8000

Cincinnati   Everything Microwave
              340 Northland Boulevard
              Cincinnati, Ohio 45246
              (513) 771-4935

Cincinnati   HURRAH!
              Kitchen Shop and Cooking School
              8008 Hosbrook Road
              Cincinnati, Ohio 45236

Cleveland   Cuyahoga Community College
              Metropolitan Campus
              2900 Community College Ave.
              Cleveland, Ohio 44115

Cleveland   Jane Addams Vocational
              High School
              4940 Carnegie Avenue
              Cleveland, Ohio 44103
              (216) 621-2131

Cleveland   Case/Western Reserves University
              2023 Adelbert Road
              Cleveland, Ohio
              (216) 368-2000

Cleveland   Iris Bailin Cooking School
18405 Van Aken Boulevard
Shaker Heights
Cleveland, Ohio 44122
(216) 921-5267

Cleveland   La Cuisinique School of Cookery
20696 South Woodland Road
Shaker Heights
Cleveland, Ohio 44122
(216) 751-7026

Columbus   Ohio State University
Columbus, Ohio 43210
(614) 422-6446

Columbus   Good Things
2390 East Main Street
Columbus, Ohio 43209
(614) 237-8668

Columbus   Columbus Technical Institute
550 East Spring Street
Columbus, Ohio 43215

Columbus   La Belle Pomme
1412 Presidential Drive
Columbus, Ohio 43212
(614) 488-3898

Columbus   A Matter Of Taste
92 West Fifth Avenue
Columbus, Ohio 43201
(619) 299-1714
(619) 294-0452

Dayton   Drannon's Gourmet Cooking School
Aledo Drive
Dayton, Ohio 45430
(513) 426-6316

Dayton   Sinclair Community College
Dayton, Ohio 45402

Hudson	Zona Spray Cooking School 140 North Main Street Hudson, Ohio 44236 (216) 653-9727
Jefferson	Ashtabula Joint Vocational School Jefferson, Ohio 44047
Mt. Vernon	Knox County Joint Vocational School Mount Vernon, Ohio 43050
Oberlin	Lorain County Joint Vocational School Oberlin, Ohio 44074
Rocky River	Pandemonium 19300 Detroit Road Rocky River, Ohio 44116 (216) 331-0964
Springfield	Springfield-Clark County Joint Vocational School Springfield, Ohio 45505
Toledo	The University of Toledo (Community & Technical College) Toledo, Ohio 43606
Toledo	Whitney Vocational High School Washington St. at 17th Toledo, Ohio (419) 243-2212
Xenia	Greene County Joint Vocational School Xenia, Ohio 45385
Youngstown	Choffin Vocational Center Youngstown, Ohio
Zanesville	Muchingum Area Joint Vocational School Zanesville, Ohio 43701

OKLAHOMA

Ardmore Southern Oklahoma Area Vocational
& Technical School
Ardmore, Oklahoma 73401

Burns Flat Western Oklahoma Area Vocational
& Technical School
Burns Flat, Oklahoma 73623

Norman University of Oklahoma
Norman, Oklahoma 73069

Oklahoma City Creative Cookery
6509 North May Avenue
Oklahoma City, Oklahoma 73116

Stillwater Oklahoma State University
Stillwater, Oklahoma 74074

Tulsa Tin Pan Galley
144 Woodland Hills Mall
Tulsa, Oklahoma 74133
(918) 252-1212

Tulsa Winifred Cowan
344 East 29th Place
Tulsa, Oklahoma 74114
(918) 747-6000

Tulsa Sue Schempf
1215 East 20th Street
Tulsa, Oklahoma 74120
(918) 585-5023

Tulsa The Fair Culinary Shop
5201 A South Sheridan
Tulsa, Oklahoma 74145

Tulsa Colonial Cooking School
3948 East 31st Street
Tulsa, Oklahoma 74105
(918) 742-8730

Tulsa Mary Gubser's Cooking School
2499 East 49th Street
Tulsa, Oklahoma 74105
(918) 742-2200

OREGON

Albany   Linn-Benton Community College
Albany, Oregon 97331

Corvallis Oregon State University
Corvallis, Oregon 97331

Eugene   Lane Community College
P.O. Box 1E
4000 East 30th Avenue
Eugene, Oregon 97405

Lynnwood   Edmonds Community College
Lynnwood, Oregon 98036

Milwaukie Creative Cooking Center
14631 S.E. McLoughlin
Milwaukie, Oregon 97222
(503) 653-5544

Portland   The Food Experience
525 S.W. 12th Street
Portland, Oregon 97205

Portland   Richard Nelson
1151 S.W. King Avenue
Portland, Oregon 97025
(503) 227-0254

Portland   Greb's
5027 N.E. 42nd Street
Portland, Oregon 97218
(503) 284-7023
(503) 284-0083

Portland   Portland Community College
12000 S.W. 49th Avenue
Portland, Oregon 97219

Salem   Chemeketa Community College
Salem, Oregon 97308

PENNSYLVANIA

Bethlehem Bethlehem Area Vocational & Technical School
Bethlehem, PA 18018

Blue Bell   Montgomery County Community
College
340 Dekalb Pike
Blue Bell, PA 19422
(Contact: Program Director)

Coatesville   Central Chester County Area
Vocational & Technical School
1635 East Lincoln Highway
Coatesville, PA 19320
(Contact: Program Director)

Fairless Hills   Bucks County Area Tech. School
Wistar Road
Fairless Hills, PA 19030
(215) 949-1700

Harrisburg   Harrisburg Area Community College
Harrisburg, PA 17110

Haverford   La Bonne Cuisine
Golf House Road
Haverford, PA 19041

Lehigh   Lehigh Valley Area Community College
Lehigh, PA

Merion   The Potpourri School of Cooking
515 N. Latches Lane
Merion, PA 19066
(215) 667-3898
(215) 544-8394

Nanticoke   Luzerne County Community College
Prospect Street & Middle Road
Nanticoke, PA 18634

Philadelphia   Julie Dannenbaum's Creative Cooking, Inc.
2044 Rittenhouse Square
Philadelphia, PA 19103
(215) 546-0442

Philadelphia   International Cuisine, Inc.
Chestnut Hill Hotel
8229 Germantown Avenue
Philadelphia, PA 19118
(215) 247-2100

Philadelphia   Dobbins Tech. High School
Lehigh Ave. at 22nd
Philadelphia, PA

Philadelphia   Drexel Institute of Technology
32nd & Chestnut Sts.
Philadelphia, PA
(215) 895-2000

Philadelphia   Bok Voc.-Tech. School
8th and Mifflin Sts.
Philadelphia, PA
(215) 463-6060

Philadelphia   Temple University
Div. of Vocational Teacher
Education
Philadelphia, PA
(215) 787-8376

Philadelphia   The Restaurant School
2129 Walnut Street
Philadelphia, PA 19103
(215) 561-3446

Pittsburgh   Arsenal Middle Voc. High School
40th & Butler
Pittsburgh, PA
(412) 622-5960

Pittsburgh   Carnegie College, Women's Div.
Schenley Park
Pittsburgh, PA
(412) 578-2000

Pittsburgh   University of Pittsburgh
Div. of Voc. Teacher Education
Pittsburgh, PA
(412) 624-4141

Pittsburgh   The Classic Cook Ltd.
                    Station Square
                    Pittsburgh, PA 15219
                    (412) 261-9196

Schnecksville   Lehigh County Community College
                    Schnecksville, PA 18104

Sewickley   Marlene Parrish
                    428 Woodland Road
                    Sewickley, PA 15143
                    (412) 741-3207
                    (412) 741-3112

University Park Pennsylvania State University
                     University Park, PA 16802
                     (814) 865-4700

RHODE ISLAND

Kingston   University of Rhode Island
                    Kingston, Rhode Island 02881
                    (401) 792-1000

Providence   Bryant College
                    Providence, Rhode Island 02906

SOUTH CAROLINA

Clemson   Clemson University
                    Clemson, South Carolina 29631

Columbia   Le Pot De Chocolat
                    #17 Forest Lake Shopping Center
                    Columbia, South Carolina 29206
                    (803) 738-9585

Orangeburg   South Carolina State College
                    Orangeburg, South Carolina 29115
                    (803) 536-7000

SOUTH DAKOTA

Aberdeen   Presentation College
                    Aberdeen, South Dakota 57401

Brookings   South Dakota State University
                    Brookings, South Dakota 56006

Flandreau	Flandreau Indian School Flandreau, South Dakota 57028
Freeman	Freeman Junior College Freeman, South Dakota
Mitchell	Mitchell Area Voc.-Tech. School Mitchell, South Dakota 57301
Rapid City	National College of Business Rapid City, South Dakota 56006
Springfield	University of South Dakota Springfield, South Dakota 56062

TENNESSEE

Chattanooga	Happy Baker 608 Georgia Avenue Chattanooga, Tennessee 37403 (615) 756-4222
Chattanooga	Howard School 2500 Market St. Chattanooga, Tennessee (615) 267-9589
Chattanooga	Kirkman Tech. High School 215 Chestnut Street Chattanooga, Tennessee (615) 226-8163
Chattanooga	Chattanooga State Community College Chattanooga, Tennessee 37406
Franklin	Cooking Under Glass 1111 Columbia Avenue Franklin, Tennessee 37064 (615) 794-0927
Knoxville	Austin East Knoxville, Tennessee (615) 522-3125
Knoxville	The University of Tennessee 220 Harris Building Knoxville, Tennessee 27916

Knoxville   Fulton High School
2509 N. Broadway, N.E.
Knoxville, Tennessee
(615) 524-3001

Memphis   John Simmons Cooking School
416 Grove Park Road
Memphis, Tennessee 38117
(901) 767-0428

Memphis   Forty Carrots School of Creative
Cookery
2087 Madison
Memphis, Tennessee 38104
(901) 726-1667

Morristown   Walters State Community College
Morristown, Tennessee 37814

Nashville   The Cook's Nook Inc.
4004 Hillsboro Road
Nashville, Tennessee 37215
(615) 383-5492

TEXAS

Austin   Irene Wong's Great Asia Cooking
School
803-B Robert E. Lee Road
Austin, Texas 78704
(512) 441-5983

Austin   University of Texas
Austin, Texas
(512) 471-3434

Beaumont   Lamar State College
Beaumont, Texas
(713) 838-7011

Corpus Christi   Del Mar College
Corpus Christi, Texas 78404

Dallas   Creative Cookery
2945 Walnut Hill Lane
Dallas, Texas 75229

Dallas   Edible Arts
7230 Mason Dells Drive
Dallas, Texas 75230

Denton   North Texas State College
Denton, Texas 76201

Fort Worth   Florence Simon
3669 Manderly Place
Fort Worth, Texas 76109
(817) 926-5566

Greenville   Nancy Parker
1615 Walworth Street
Greenville, Texas 75401
(214) 455-6723

Houston   La Cuisine Culinary Arts Center
1114 Barkdull
Houston, Texas 77006
(713) 521-9900

Houston   Batterie De Cuisine Inc.
4360 Westheimer on Mid Lane
Houston, Texas 77027
(713) 961-1373

Houston   University of Houston
Houston, Texas 77004

Houston   Edmond Foulard at Foulards'
10001 Westheimer Road
Houston, Texas 77027
(713) 789-1661

Houston   The Cooking School
2520½ Westcreek
Houston, Texas 77027
(713) 626-8360

Houston   Sharon Oswald
1136 Berthea
Houston, Texas 77026
(713) 528-3661

Houston   Gertrude Yang
(Chinese Cooking)
Houston, Texas
(713) 729-0996

Round Rock Inn at Brushy Creek
Round Rock, Texas 78664

San Antonio Southwest Craft Center
300 Augusta Street
San Antonio, Texas 78205

Tyler Tyler Junior College
Tyler, Texas
(214) 597-4281

UTAH

Logan Utah State University
Logan, Utah 84320
(801) 750-1000

Ogden Weber State College
Ogden, Utah 84408

Price College of Eastern Utah
Price, Utah 84501

Provo Brigham Young University
Provo, Utah 84602

Salt Lake City University of Utah
Salt Lake City, Utah 84112
(801) 581-7200

St. George Dixie College
St. George, Utah 84770

VERMONT

Burlington Burlington High School
Burlington, VT
(802) 863-4521

Rutland Rutland Community Center
Rutland, VT 05701

Springfield Springfield High School
Springfield, VT
(802) 885-5141

West Dover The Ironstone Restaurant
(Libby Hillman)
Route 100
West Dover, Vermont
(802) 464-3796

VIRGINIA

Annandale Northern Virginia
Community College
Annandale, Virginia 22003

Bridgewater Bridgewater College
Bridgewater, Virginia 22812

Falls Church Madame Colonna's
School of Cooking
102 North Oak Street
Falls Church, Virginia 22046
(703) 534-7787

Harrisonburg Madison College
Harrisonburg, Virginia 22801

Norfolk Virginia State College
Norfolk, Virginia
(804) 625-9334

Norfolk Old Dominion College
Norfolk, Virginia 23508

Radford Radford University
Radford, Virginia 24141
(804) 731-5000

Virginia Beach The Kitchen Barn
1600 Hilltop West Executive Center
Virginia Beach, Virginia 23451
(803) 422-4777

WASHINGTON

Bellevue Sunshine Kitchen Co.
14603 N.E. 20th Street
Bellevue, Washington 98007
(206) 641-4520

Bellevue Yankee Kitchen School of Cookery
10108 Main Street
Bellevue, Washington 98004
(206) 455-0614

Bellingham Bellingham Technical School
3028 Lindberg Ave.
Bellingham, Washington
(206) 676-6490

Everett Everett Community College
Everett, Washington 98201

Mercer Island Sharon's Kitchen
2852 80th S.E.
Mercer Island, Washington 98040

Seattle Mary Pang's
Chinese Cooking School
811 7th Street
Seattle, Washington 98104
(206) 622-3524

Seattle The Good Wife
17171 Bothell Way N.E.
Seattle, Washington 98155
(206) 524-3575

Seattle Esther Chen's
Chinese Cooking School
5230 University Way N.E.
Seattle, Washington 98105

Seattle House of Rice
4112 University Way N.E.
Seattle, Washington 98105
(206) 633-5181
(206) 633-0738

Seattle La Cuisine School of Cooking
7812 Lake City Way N.E.
Seattle, Washington 98115
(206) 522-6718

Seattle   Lorraine Arnold's
International Kitchen
2201 N.E. 65th Street
Seattle, Washington 98115
(206) 524-4004

Seattle   Karen Gregorakis Creative Cookery
& Catering
5604 17th Avenue N.E.
Seattle, Washington 98105
(206) 523-9823

Seattle   Shoreline Community College
Seattle, Washington 98133

Spokane   Spokane Community College
Spokane, Washington 99202

Tacoma   Tacoma Voc.-Tech. School
1101 S. Yakima Ave.
Tacoma, Washington
(206) 597-7220

Vancouver   Clark College
1925 Fort Vancouver Way
Vancouver, Washington
(206) 694-6521

WEST VIRGINIA

Mercer County   Mercer County Voc.-Tech. Center
Mercer County, West Virginia

Putnam County   Putnam County Voc.-Tech. Center
Putnam County, West Virginia

Raleigh   Raleigh County Voc.-Tech. Center
Raleigh, West Virginia 25911

White Sulphur Springs   The Greenbrier Cooking School
White Sulphur Springs,
West Virginia
(800) 624-6070
(304) 536-1110

WISCONSIN

Fond du Lac   The Postillion School of
Culinary Arts
615 Old Pioneer Road
Fond du Lac, Wisconsin 54935
(414) 922-4170

Madison   University of Wisconsin
Madison, Wisconsin 53706
(608) 262-1234

Milwaukee   Jill Heavenrich Cooking School
2443 North Wahl Avenue
Milwaukee, Wisconsin 53211
(414) 961-0213

Milwaukee   The Postillion School of
Culinary Arts
775 North Jefferson
Milwaukee, Wisconsin 53202
(414) 276-4141

Milwaukee   Wholistic Nutrition Center
3902 North Mayfair Road
Milwaukee, Wisconsin 53222
(414) 463-1707

Pewaukee   Waukesha County
Technical Institute
Main Street
Pewaukee, Wisconsin 53072
(Contact: Richard P. Hollender)

Rhinelander   Nicolet College &
Technical Institute
Box 518
Rhinelander, Wisconsin 54501

WYOMING

Casper   Casper College
Casper, Wyoming 82601

Chapter 12

Want to Earn $10,000 a Week? Meet a Woman Who Really Did

The Most Amazing Kitchen Lady Success Story We've Ever Heard

Nadine Kalachnikoff* started from scratch, just like all of us. She went all the way: opening a fancy store and putting in a 14-hour day selling her specialties to prominent people in Washington, D.C.

She makes fabulous, delicious-tasting specialties, charging $10 to $15 a pound for some of them. If you also happen to be a gourmet cook, you might want to open up this type of store in your *own* city. Her story is an inspiration to all of us. It simply says that there's no telling how far you can go.

Overnight success was the one thing Miss Kalachnikoff had not counted on. "I don't understand any of it," she said. She

*Actual name.

223

sank into a chair in the office over the store, Pasta Inc., and brushed back her hair.

Imagine—$75,000 Earned in Her First Six Weeks of Business

She had been there since eight that morning and it was now 11 A.M. The doors had just opened to a stream of customers who had lined up outside. They were buying fresh pasta, a variety of sauces, pastries, salads, and an array of other specialties. In the first six weeks the store grossed more than $75,000, and one recent Saturday it took in $4,500.

Not bad for a woman who is so new to business that when her banker asked how she planned to pay back a loan she was seeking, she thought he wanted to know if she planned to make payment by check or cash. But the store has been the road to survival for the 34-year-old Nadine Kalachnikoff, who was born in Paris to a Spanish mother and a Russian father.

A Husband Walking Out on You Doesn't Mean the End of the World

When she and her former husband, Howard Joynt, separated several years ago, leaving her with two small boys, she was in shock and wondered what she could do. Since she had cooked all her life and had a passion for food, her first thought was to open a restaurant, she said. But Miss Kalachnikoff felt the hours would be too inflexible and demanding, leaving her little time for her children.

How Nadine Got the Idea to Go Into Business

One evening when she had a sudden yearning for some risotto, she thought: what if there were a place where people could drop in and buy an entire meal—from first course through dessert and wine? All they would need would be a pot of boiling water. So Pasta Inc., an elegant carry-out, was born.

She mortgaged her 1753 Georgetown house for $100,000 and sold "the car, the paintings and everything I own" to put together some working capital, then headed for Milan, Italy, to check out pasta machines and to New York to visit such places as Pasta & Cheese, Dean & DeLuca, and The Silver Palate.

Familiar with the Silver Palate label, she called on Julie Rosso, one of the owners. "I discovered she had started out in more or less the same way that I did," Miss Kalachnikoff said, "and she encouraged me tremendously."

How to Create the Perfect Atmosphere

Pasta Inc. is located at 2805 M Street in Georgetown, which is a very desirable section in our nation's capital. The store has pristine white walls, a starkly white ceramic tile floor, white ceiling fans, shiny metal racks, baskets of tulips and daisies everywhere, copper pots and dried herbs suspended from the skylight over a counter where tempting salads and fresh ricotta and mozzarella cheese are displayed.

In the window are a pasta machine, a drying rack, and a tortellini machine spinning forth curlicues of pasta. The pasta (spinach, tomato, egg, and whole wheat) sells for $2.69 a pound and can be purchased in five different widths ranging from tagliatelle (five-eighths of an inch) to capelli d'angelo (one-eighth of an inch).

Some of Nadine's Specialties

The nine freshly prepared sauces range in price from $2.85 to $6.50 for containers that are normally 14 ounces, and include pesto, summer and winter tomato, Trastevere, Lombarda, and nutmeg. And there is ravioli at $5.95.

The pastries include chocolate truffles, orange tarts, canoli, fresh peach mousse, delicate meringue doves, chocolate cups piled high with chocolate mousse, and a house specialty, St. George's cake.

Except for the bread, everything is made on the premises, and Miss Kalachnikoff has been putting in 14-hour days with a kitchen staff of five.

Sometimes You Have to Make a Personal Sacrifice

The success of the operation has meant that she is able to spend less time with her children than she wants to, but, she said, "I realize that the most important thing in my life right now is the store because it is going to pay for their schooling." The boys often come to the store on weekends and they take late naps so they can stay up for dinner with their mother.

"At 7:30 I stop and go home and have an hour with the children," she said, "then I come back to do the mozzarella or whatever."

Since she suffers from dyslexia and has never measured an ingredient in her life, her manager, David Dennison, who first came to work as an electrician, follows her about as she cooks— notebook in hand—to try to get a handle on food costs.

"I am embarrassed and shocked at the prices I have to charge," she said. "It is all that Swiss chocolate and butter."

People Will Pay $13.75 a Pound for Gourmet Food

The store also has different specials each day, such as lentils and sausage, blanquette de veau, and pâté de foie de volailles at $13.75 a pound. Her Corfu salad at $10.25 a pound includes fish, squid, scallops, shrimps, clams, celery, scallions, parsley, and garlic.

A recent addition to the operation is an "in-home pasta man" who will go to a house and cook to order, preparing sauces in chafing dishes and serving freshly tossed pasta and salad to any number of guests. The "pasta man," along with a cook, costs $150 an evening in addition to the food.

Nadine Was in Such Demand That They Sent for Her by Private Plane

Miss Kalachnikoff has also started a catering service and has done some dinner parties for Evangeline Bruce ("I nearly died, I was so nervous I forgot to string the snow peas for the vegetable aspic"), the John Sherman Coopers, and the Charles Percys. On a recent Saturday, Mr. and Mrs. Kiki Costa-Lobo of Atlanta sent a private plane to fly her and a catered meal to Atlanta for the day.

"Sometimes I think it would have been simpler to go to Europe and find a rich man," she says with a weary smile.

The copy in the above story about Nadine Kalachnikoff was written by Barbara Gamarekian and appeared in the *New York Times.*

We are thrilled with Nadine Kalachnikoff's great success. What a wonderful feeling it is to start from scratch and grow to achieve such financial security. However, we would like to comment in passing on Nadine's last statement. *No,* it wouldn't have been simpler to go to Europe and find a rich man! Kitchen Ladies don't agree on everything, but most agree that a good man is hard to find. Many of us are divorced—like Miss Kalachnikoff—or widowed. We urge her to stay on the job. Let her get rich; she seems to be well on her way. *Then* a good man is not hard to find!

The Two Factors for Success in a Gourmet Take-Out Store

Nadine has two important things going for her: (1) she is an excellent gourmet cook; and (2) she lives in an area where customers can afford to pay gourmet prices for truly fine food. If this set of conditions applies to you, then you can repeat her success. All you need is the desire.

Redo
Dan + Sar
Spelling
2 lessons per week

Chapter 13

How Good Will You Be in Business? Test Yourself!

How Well Do You Know Yourself?

We've given you many ideas up to this point, and we've spelled out the details of how to make them pay off. In later chapters, we'll even tell you how and where to get the money to get started in business. We'll also teach you how to run a business and make the most profit from it.

But now, we'd like to take time out to focus on the most important subject of all—YOU! Let's begin with a little personal examination and stock-taking. How well do you really know yourself? How long has it been since you've taken a penetrating unbiased look at yourself, your capabilities, your goals, and your ambitions?

229

More importantly, when did you last equate your talents and capabilities with the progress you are making toward the realization of those goals and ambitions? In other words, who are you? Why do you want to go into business? What makes you think you can succeed?

Take the following questions seriously. Take time to think about them. Answer them carefully and honestly. Knowing *yourself* is the first step toward making good business decisions. In the final analysis, your response to these questions may help you determine the pattern for the rest of your life.

Getting to Know Me

Who Am I?

1. My physical health is ____ excellent ____ good ____ fair ____ poor

2. As a problem-solver, I am ____ good ____ average ____ poor

3. I get along with people ____ very well ____ well ____ rarely

4. I take direction ____ very well ____ well ____ reluctantly

5. I take the initiative ____ usually ____ sometimes ____ seldom ____ never

6. My self-confidence is ____ very high ____ high ____ moderate ____ shaky

7. I work better ____ under supervision ____ with a group ____ alone

8. In an emergency ____ I need support ____ I am usually the stronger one

9. As a risk-taker ____ I like a sure thing ____ I'm careful ____ I'm a high-flyer

10. I make decisions ____ quickly ____ slowly ____ seldom ____ alone ____ in consultation

Why Do I Want To Go Into Business?

1. My personal responsibilities have ＿＿ increased ＿＿ decreased ＿＿ no one needs me any more

2. I need more money for ＿＿ necessities ＿＿ extras ＿＿ financial independence

3. To be my own boss ＿＿

4. To market my own skill or product ＿＿

5. I can't find a job I like ＿＿

6. I've helped someone run a business for years, and now I want to do it on my own ＿＿

7. My family has always been in business ＿＿

8. It would be the culmination of all my hopes and plans ＿＿

9. I have to prove that I can ＿＿ for myself ＿＿ for my family

10. It would make me feel like a human being again ＿＿

What Makes Me Think I Can Succeed?

1. My financial assets are ＿＿ limited ＿＿ fair ＿＿ sufficient for a year

2. My business experience has been ＿＿ limited to selling ＿＿ managerial ＿＿ primarily bookkeeping and secretarial ＿＿ varied and long ＿＿ extremely limited

3. Experience in my chosen field has been ＿＿ nil ＿＿ short term ＿＿ long enough to convince me that I can do it

4. Responsibility is ＿＿ new to me ＿＿ not new to me ＿＿ important to me

5. I expect to work ＿＿ long hours ＿＿ less than I do now ＿＿ to fit my own life pattern

6. Immediate profits are ____ important to me ____ not important to me

7. My expectations are ____ high ____ realistic ____ unsure

8. I have volunteer experience as a ____ major fund-raiser ____ administrative officer ____ other _____
                                        (specify)

When Did I Decide To Go Into Business?

1. On the spur of the moment, after ____ fight with boss ____ quitting dead-end job ____ suggestions of friends ____ other

2. Decision thrust on me ____ by divorce ____ widowhood ____ husband lost job ____ husband simply not bringing home enough

3. Thoughtful, planned decision is ____ logical next step in career pattern ____ in family tradition ____ characteristics of business leadership evident since childhood

4. Decision is ____ definite ____ still being weighed ____ tentative

Report Card Time

There is no automatic grading process for the questions you have just answered. No one can assure you that checking the "correct" answers in any test will guarantee business success. What these questions are primarily for is to *make you think*. No matter what your answers seem to indicate, if you are *truly* interested in a business of your own, don't be discouraged. Women who, on the surface, at least, seemed the least likely candidates for careers in small business ownership have achieved spectacular success. Others who seemed to have all the necessary attributes for success never quite made it.

Test #2

This second test is one that we'd also like you to take. Again, answer each question with complete honesty. At the conclusion, we do have a scoring system. But before we tell you what it is, first answer all of the following questions.

Are you a self-starter?

_____ I do things on my own. Nobody has to tell me to get going.

_____ Once someone gets me started, I keep going all right.

_____ Easy does it. I don't put myself out until I have to.

How do you feel about other people?

_____ I like people. I can get along with just about anybody.

_____ I have plenty of friends—I don't need anyone else.

_____ Most people irritate me.

Can you lead others?

_____ I can get most people to go along with something I start.

_____ I can give the orders if someone tells me what we should do.

_____ I let someone else get things moving. Then I go along if I feel I like it.

Can you take responsibility?

_____ I like to take charge of things and see them through.

_____ I'll take over if I have to, but I'd rather let someone else be responsible.

_____ There's always some eager beaver around wanting to show how smart he is. I say let him.

How good an organizer are you?

_____ I like to have a plan before I start. I'm usually the one to get things lined up when the group wants to do something.

_____ I do all right unless things get too confused. Then I quit.

_____ I get all set and then something comes along and presents too many problems. So I just take things as they come.

How good a worker are you?

_____ I can keep going as long as I need to. I don't mind working hard for something I want.

_____ I'll work hard for a while, but when I've had enough, that's it.

_____ I can't see that hard work gets you anywhere.

Can you make decisions?

_____ I can make up my mind in a hurry if I have to. It usually turns out O.K., too.

_____ I can if I have plenty of time. If I have to make up my mind fast, I think later that I should have decided the other way.

_____ I don't like to be the one who has to decide things.

Can people trust what you say?

_____ You bet they can. I don't say things I don't mean.

_____ I try to be on the level most of the time, but sometimes I just say what's easiest.

_____ Why bother if the other fellow doesn't know the difference?

Can you stick with it?

_____ If I make up my mind to do something, I don't let *anything* stop me.

_____ I usually finish what I start—if it goes well.

_____ If it doesn't go well right away, I quit. Why beat your brains out?

How good is your health?

_____ I *never* run down.

_____ I have enough energy for most things I want to do.

_____ I run out of energy sooner than most of my friends seem to.

Score Your Answers Honestly

Now count the checks you made. There were ten questions.

How many checks are there beside the *first* answer
to each question?   _____

How many checks are there beside the *second* answer to each question?   _____

How many checks are there beside the *third* answer to each question?   _____

Don't Be Discouraged— Just Make Improvements

If most of your checks are beside the first answers, you probably have what it takes to run a business. If not, you're likely to have some difficulty. In this event it is sometimes a good idea to find a partner who is strong on the points you're not. If many checks are beside the third answer, then not even a good partner will be able to shore you up. But remember this: if at this moment you honestly see too many weaknesses and you don't want to take a partner into business with you, then *work on your weak points!* If you have check marks in #2, work on it so you can honestly make it a #1. If you have several #3 check marks, improve yourself so they become #2's. Nobody's perfect, but we can keep working on it! *Don't be discouraged!*

Chapter 14

The U.S. Government Will Help You Financially —Here's How to Get Your Share

Women and the U.S. Small Business Administration

Helping women become successful independent entrepreneurs is a major goal of the U.S. Small Business Administration. While women make up more than half the population of the country, they own fewer than five percent of its businesses. To the extent that women are interested in operating their own small businesses, SBA is committed to an all-out effort to assist them. The Agency can be an important source of aid and of information. But no entrepreneur should overlook other public and private sources of management and financial assistance, to which SBA can be of help in referring you.

SBA services are provided through offices in 96 different

cities located in all 50 states, Puerto Rico, and Guam. You will find a list of offices midway through this chapter. In addition, SBA has a central office in Washington, D.C., and 10 regional headquarters in major cities where broad administrative advice can be obtained.

SBA services fall into four general categories: financial assistance, management assistance, procurement assistance, and advocacy.

Contact your nearest SBA district office for program details or publications describing services or offering useful information.

Publications

Each SBA office has a library of over 300 titles which cover specific problems and give advice on specific businesses. All publications and services are either free or available at a nominal cost.

SBA publications are listed on two forms. Form 115A lists free publications; Form 115B, publications for sale. Both the lists and the publications are available from SBA district offices, or by calling a toll-free number: (800) 433-7212. For residents of Texas the number is (800) 792-8901.

Single copies of free publications should be ordered through the toll-free numbers listed above. For-sale publications are ordered from the Government Printing Office, Washington, D.C. 20402.

A special publication, "Women's Handbook—How SBA Can Help You Go Into Business" is available through all district offices. The handbook describes the various programs useful to women business owners and potential women business owners and a step-by-step outline of how to apply for a loan.

Business Loan Programs

SBA has several loan programs to meet a variety of a business person's needs. The regular business loan program, known as

7(a) is by far the largest. The majority of 7(a) business loans are made cooperatively with local private banks under an arrangement in which the bank disburses the money to the borrower, and the SBA guarantees to repay the bank up to 90 percent of the loan value, if the loan goes into default.

Loan proceeds can be used for working capital, purchase of inventory, equipment and supplies, or for building construction or expansion.

To be eligible for an SBA business loan, a small firm must be turned down by a bank (by two banks in cities of 200,000 and over population) and must be able to show an ability to repay the loan. An applicant is required to present historical financial statements, if the business has been in operation, and also to furnish appropriate financial projections.

To help small business people who cannot get credit even under the bank guarantee plan, SBA has a limited amount of money it can lend directly to the applicant.

Economic Opportunity loans are available to help persons who are socially or economically disadvantaged.

SBA also makes loans to help small businesses comply with Federal air and water pollution regulations and occupational safety and health requirements; to offset problems caused by Federal actions, e.g., highway or building construction or the closing of military bases; and to relieve economic injuries suffered by a small business as a result of energy or material shortages, or temporary economic dislocations.

"Key Features," publication OPI-7 gives details on these programs.

Venture Capital

Money for "venture" or "risk" investments is difficult for small businesses to obtain. SBA licenses, regulates, and provides financial assistance to privately owned and operated Small Business Investment Companies (SBICs). Their major function is to make "venture" or "risk" investments by supplying equity capital and extending unsecured loans, and loans not fully collateralized to small enterprises that meet their investment criteria. SBICs are privately capitalized in participation with the government and are intended to be profit-making corporations. Due to their own economics, most SBICs do not make very small investments.

SBICs finance small firms in two general ways—by straight loans and by equity-type investments which give the SBIC actual or potential ownership of a portion of a small business' equity securities. Some SBICs provide management assistance to the companies they finance.

SBA also licenses a specialized 301(d) SBIC known as a Minority Enterprise Small Business Investment Company (MESBIC) solely to assist small businesses owned and managed by socially or economically disadvantaged persons.

Write the SBIC or MESBIC Program, U.S. Small Business Administration, Washington, D.C. 20416 for information on how to contact an SBIC or a MESBIC or how to form one.

Disaster Loans

When the President or the Administrator of SBA declares a specific geographic area a disaster area as a result of a natural disaster such as a hurricane, tornado, flood, or earthquake, owners of small and large businesses and homeowners and renters within the area can apply to SBA for disaster recovery loans to repair or replace their damaged or destroyed real or personal property.

Owners of small businesses who have suffered economic losses as a result of the disaster can apply to SBA for economic injury disaster loans for working capital and funds to pay financial obligations that they would have met if the disaster had not occurred. Your local SBA office can provide details.

Management Assistance

Basic information or advice on every aspect of forming and managing a business is available through training courses, workshops, seminars, films, counseling, and publications. Much of the formal training is co-sponsored with educational institutions, professional associations, and local civic or business organizations, for little or no charge.

In-depth counseling is provided on an individual basis by SBA management assistance staff augmented by over 12,000 experienced business people from SCORE (Service Corps of Retired Executives) and ACE (Active Corps of Executives), who volunteer their services. Appointments with these counselors can be made at any SBA district office.

Small business people can also get help from SBA's Small Business Institute program, in which over 20,000 business administration students from 450 colleges and universities are participating.

Teams of students working with faculty advisors take on the solving of specific problems of small business clients for a semester, as part of their academic curriculum.

Two special training programs are available for women. An in-depth 45-hour training course in small business management subjects is being presented through local community and junior colleges, co-sponsored by SBA. Many offices are also providing special seminars on franchising and its uses as a business entry procedure for women. A general training program, geared especially for the visual arts, will also be available in early 1981 through district offices and local and state arts councils.

All counseling is given without charge. See SBA publications MA-1 about SCORE and ACE and MA-6, "Management Assistance."

Pre-Business Workshops

For the prospective small business owner, attendance at a pre-business workshop offered by all SBA district offices is a "must." These are held once or twice each month. In general, they are one-day sessions to help participants determine their readiness to go into business. Over the years, the numbers of women attendees has been growing. At the present time, 50 percent of workshop audiences are women. Once potential owners decide to go ahead, SBA will help them develop a workable business plan and arrange follow-up management assistance.

Minority Small Business and Capital Ownership Development Program

This program has undertaken a special outreach effort to provide eligible minority women with financial, contracting, technical, and management assistance.

Through the 8(a) business development program, SBA assists small firms owned and controlled by socially and economically disadvantaged persons to develop the capability to compete in the open market.

If eligible, women may become 8(a) contractors and also may receive management and technical assistance under SBA's call contracting program.

Details are available at all SBA offices.

Advocacy

SBA's Advocacy office has a number of responsibilities to defend and champion the cause of small business throughout the Federal Government and with state and local governments; to work with trade and professional organizations to advance the cause of small business; to determine and help to lessen the impact of Federal regulations on small business; and to encourage the involvement of women in small business.

National Women's Business Ownership Campaign

This ongoing Campaign was started by SBA in August 1977. Under the leadership of the Deputy Administrator of SBA, the

Agency's second-highest-ranking official, the Campaign is directed by the Office of Women-in-Business and a top level coordinating committee in the Washington office. The purpose is to raise significantly the number of women actively involved in the small business sector of the economy by increasing women's ownership of small, profitable companies.

How to Apply for a Loan

To summarize, the step-by-step procedures to be followed in applying for a business loan are as follows:

A. *For a New Business*

1. Write a detailed description of the business to be established.

2. Describe your experience and management capabilities.

3. Prepare an estimate of how much money you and/or others have to invest in the business, and how much you will need to borrow.

4. Prepare a current financial statement listing all your personal assets and liabilities.

5. Prepare a detailed projection of earnings anticipated for your first year in business.

6. List collateral you can offer as security for the loan, including an estimate of the present market value of each item.

7. Take all the above with you to your banker. Ask for a direct loan. If the direct loan is declined, ask the bank to (a) give you a loan under SBA's Loan Guaranty Plan, or (b) participate with SBA in a loan. If the bank is interested, ask the banker to discuss your application with the SBA. In most cases, SBA deals directly with the bank on these two loans.

8. If neither the guaranty or participation loan is available to you, visit or write the nearest SBA office. (See SBA Field Offices listing on the following page.) Take your financial information with you on your first office visit or include it in your first letter.

B. *For an Established Business*

1. Prepare a current financial statement listing all assets and listing all liabilities of the business; do not include personal items.

2. Prepare an earnings (profit and loss) statement for the previous full year, and for the current period to the date of the balance sheet.

3. Prepare a current personal financial statement of the owner, or each partner or stockholder owning 20 percent or more of the stock in the business.

4. List collateral to be offered as loan security, with your estimate of the present market value of each item.

5. State amount of loan requested, and explain exact purposes for which it will be used.

6. Take the above financial information with you to your banker. Ask for the direct loan. If the direct loan is declined, ask the banker to (a) give you a loan under SBA's Loan Guaranty Plan, or (b) participate with SBA in a loan. If the bank is interested, ask the banker to discuss your application with the SBA. In most cases, SBA deals directly with the bank on these two loans.

7. If neither the guaranty nor the participation loan is available to you, visit or write your nearest SBA office. Take your financial information with you on your first office visit, or include it in your first letter.

Wherever You Live, There's a
Small Business Administration Office
There to Help You

SBA Field Office Addresses

Alabama 35205	Birmingham, 908 South 20th Street
Alaska 99501	Anchorage, 1016 West Sixth Ave., Suite 200
Alaska 99701	Fairbanks, 101 12th Ave.
Arizona 85012	Phoenix, 3030 North Central Ave.
Arkansas 72201	Little Rock, 611 Gaines Street
California 93712	Fresno, 1229 N Street
California 90071	Los Angeles, 350 South Figueroa Street
California 95825	Sacramento, 2800 Cottage Way
California 92188	San Diego, 880 Front Street
California 94105	San Francisco, 211 Main Street
Colorado 80202	Denver, 721 19th Street
Connecticut 06103	Hartford, One Financial Plaza
Delaware 19801	Wilmington, 844 King Street
D.C. 20417	Washington, 1030 15th St., NW, Suite 250
Florida 33134	Coral Gables, 2222 Ponce de Leon Blvd.
Florida 32202	Jacksonville, 400 West Bay Street
Florida 33602	Tampa, 700 Twiggs Street
Florida 33402	West Palm Beach, 701 Clematis Street
Georgia 30309	Atlanta, 1720 Peachtree Road, NW
Guam 96910	Agana, Pacific Daily News Building
Hawaii 96850	Honolulu, 300 Ala Moana
Idaho 83701	Boise, 1005 Main Street

Illinois 60604	Chicago, 219 South Dearborn Street
Illinois 62701	Springfield, 1 North Old State Capitol Plaza
Indiana 46204	Indianapolis, 575 North Pennsylvania Street
Iowa 50309	Des Moines, 210 Walnut Street
Kansas 67202	Wichita, 110 East Waterman Street
Kentucky 40202	Louisville, 600 Federal Place, Room 188
Louisiana 70113	New Orleans, 1001 Howard Ave.
Louisiana 71101	Shreveport, 500 Fannin Street
Maine 04330	Augusta, 40 Western Ave., Room 512
Maryland 21204	Baltimore, Towson, 8600 La Salle Road
Massachusetts 02114	Boston, 150 Causeway Street
Massachusetts 01050	Holyoke, 302 High Street
Michigan 48226	Detroit, 477 Michigan Ave.
Michigan 49885	Marquette, 540 West Kaye Ave.
Minnesota 55402	Minneapolis, 12 South Sixth Street
Mississippi 39530	Biloxi, 111 Fred Haise Boulevard
Mississippi 39201	Jackson, 200 East Pascagoula Street
Missouri 64106	Kansas City, 1150 Grand Ave.
Missouri 63101	St. Louis, Mercantile Tower, Suite 2500
Montana 59601	Helena, 301 South Park
Nebraska 68102	Omaha, Nineteenth and Farnam Streets
Nevada 89101	Las Vegas, 301 East Stewart
Nevada 89505	Reno, 50 South Virginia Street
New Hampshire 03301	Concord, 55 Pleasant Street
New Jersey 08104	Camden, 1800 East Davis Street
New Jersey 07102	Newark, 970 Broad Street, Room 1635
New Mexico 87110	Albuquerque, 5000 Marble Ave., NE

New York 12210	Albany, 3100 Twin Towers Building
New York 14202	Buffalo, 111 West Huron Street
New York 14901	Elmira, 180 State Street, Room 412
New York 11746	Melville, 425 Broad Hollow Road
New York 10007	New York, 26 Federal Plaza, Room 3100
New York 14014	Rochester, 100 State Street
New York 13260	Syracuse, 100 South Clinton St., Room 1071
North Carolina 28202	Charlotte, 230 South Tryon St., Suite 700
North Carolina 27834	Greenville, 215 South Evans Street
North Dakota 58102	Fargo, 657 2nd Ave., North, Room 218
Ohio 45202	Cincinnati, 550 Main Street, Room 5028
Ohio 44199	Cleveland, 1240 East 9th St., Room 317
Ohio 43215	Columbus, 85 Marconi Boulevard
Oklahoma 73102	Oklahoma City, 200 N.W. 5th Street
Oregon 97204	Portland, 1220 South West Third Ave.
Pennsylvania 17101	Harrisburg, 100 Chestnut Street
Pennsylvania 19004	Philadelphia, Bala Cynwyd, 1 Bala Cynwyd Plaza
Pennsylvania 15222	Pittsburgh, 1000 Liberty Avenue
Pennsylvania 18702	Wilkes-Barre, 20 North Pennsylvania Ave.
Puerto Rico 00919	Hato Rey, Chardon and Bolivia Streets
Rhode Island 02903	Providence, 57 Eddy Street
South Carolina 29201	Columbia, 1801 Assembly Street
South Dakota 57701	Rapid City, 515 9th Street
South Dakota 57102	Sioux Falls, 8th and Main Avenue
Tennessee 37902	Knoxville, 502 South Gay Street, Room 307
Tennessee 38103	Memphis, 167 North Main Street

Tennessee 37219	Nashville, 404 James Robertson Pkway, Suite 1012
Texas 88408	Corpus Christi, 3105 Leopard Street
Texas 75242	Dallas, 1100 Commerce Street
Texas 79902	El Paso, 4100 Rio Bravo, Suite 300
Texas 78550	Lower Rio Grande Valley, Harlington, 222 East Van Buren
Texas 77002	Houston, 1 Allen Center, 500 Dallas St.
Texas 79401	Lubbock, 1205 Texas Avenue
Texas 75670	Marshall, 100 South Washington St., Room G12
Texas 78206	San Antonio, 727 East Durango, Room A–513
Utah 84138	Salt Lake City, 125 So. State St., Rm. 2237
Vermont 05602	Montpelier, 87 State St., P.O. Box 605
Virginia 23240	Richmond, 400 N. 8th Street, Room 3015
Virgin Islands 00801	St. Thomas, Federal Office Bldg., Veteran's Dr.
Washington 98174	Seattle, 915 Second Avenue
Washington 99120	Spokane, Courthouse Bldg., Room 651
West Virginia 25301	Charleston, Charleston Nat'l Plaza, Suite 628
West Virginia 26301	Clarksburg, 109 N. 3rd Street
Wisconsin 54701	Eau Claire, 500 So. Barstow St., Rm. B9AA
Wisconsin 53703	Madison, 122 West Washington Ave.
Wisconsin 53202	Milwaukee, 517 East Wisconsin Ave.
Wyoming 82601	Casper, 100 East B Street, Room 4001

Small Marketers' Aids

These leaflets provide suggestions and management guidelines for small retail, wholesale, and service firms. To receive copies of them, write down the numbers and titles of your selections, plus your name and address, and mail to:

Small Business Administration
P.O. Box 15434
Fort Worth, Texas 76119

Or call toll free 800-433-7212
(Texas only, call 800-792-8901)

_____ 71. Checklist For Going Into Business

_____ 118. Legal Services For Small Retail and Service Firms

_____ 121. Measuring The Results Of Advertising

_____ 126. Accounting Services For Small Service Firms

_____ 129. Reducing Shoplifting Losses

_____ 130. Analyze Your Records to Reduce Costs

_____ 133. Can You Afford Delivery Service?

_____ 134. Preventing Burglary and Robbery Loss

_____ 135. Arbitration: Peace-Maker in Small Business

_____ 137. Outwitting Bad Check Passers

_____ 138. Sweeping Profit Out the Back Door

_____ 139. Understanding Truth-in-Lending

_____ 140. Profit By Your Wholesalers' Services

_____ 141. Danger Signals in a Small Store

_____ 142. Steps in Meeting Your Tax Obligations

Small Business Bibliographies
(no mailing list for this series)

These leaflets furnish reference sources for individual types of business.

_____ 1. Handicrafts

_____ 2. Home Business

_____ 3. Selling by Mail Order

_____ 9. Marketing Research Procedures

_____ 10. Retailing

_____ 12. Statistics and Maps for National Market Analysis

_____ 13. National Directories for Use in Marketing

_____ 15. Recordkeeping Systems—Small Store and Service Trade

_____ 18. Basic Library Reference Sources

_____ 20. Advertising—Retail Store

_____ 29. National Mailing-List Houses

_____ 31. Retail Credit and Collections

_____ 37. Buying for Retail Stores

_____ 53. Hobby Shops

_____ 55. Wholesaling

_____ 64. Photographic Dealers and Studios

_____ 66. Motels

_____ 67. Manufacturers' Sales Representative

_____ 72. Personnel Management

_____ 75. Inventory Management

_____ 77. Tourism and Outdoor Recreation

_____ 78. Recreation Vehicles

_____ 79. Small Store Planning and Design

_____ 80. Data Processing for Small Businesses

_____ 85. Purchasing for Owners of Small Plants

_____ 86. Training for Small Business

_____ 87. Financial Management

_____ 88. Manufacturing Management

_____ 89. Marketing for Small Business

_____ 90. New Product Development

Free Management Assistance Publications

Management Aids

These leaflets deal with functional problems in small manufacturing plants and concentrate on subjects of interest to administrative executives.

_____ 170. The ABC's of Borrowing

_____ 171. How to Write A Job Description

_____ 178. Effective Industrial Advertising for Small Plants

_____ 179. Breaking the Barriers to Small Business Planning

_____ 186. Checklist for Developing a Training Program

_____ 187. Using Census Data in Small Plant Marketing

_____ 188. Developing a List of Prospects

_____ 189. Should You Make or Buy Components?

Chapter 15

Need Money from Banks? Here's How to Talk a Banker's Language

Why You Should Never Walk In Off the Street to Open a Bank Account

Before opening a business bank account, interview the managers of the banks in your area by phone. Tell them what kind of business you're in and what your needs will be. Explain to them that you want to put your "Kitchen Lady" operation on a business-like basis.

With this approach, you'll earn the respect of the bank manager with whom you'll do business. During your telephone conversation with him, set a specific time and date to meet him at the bank. This is a far more professional way of establishing a business bank account than if you were to walk in off the street and speak to a new-accounts clerk.

If You Can't Deal with the Manager, Don't Deal with the Bank at All

Make sure that when you call, you speak only to the manager. If his secretary tells you that he's busy and tries to switch you to a new-accounts clerk, your reply should be, "No thanks, I'll call back." We give you this advice because it's been our experience that clerks shift jobs far more frequently than managers do. And you want to establish a personal and lasting relationship with a bank. Besides, why not practice the time-honored rule of "going to the top."

Before you have that first meeting with the manager of the bank, study the following terms you'll need to know in order to speak the bank's language.

Banking Terms You Should Know

☐ A BALANCE SHEET is a current financial statement. It is a dollars-and-cents description of your business, existing or projected, which lists all your assets and liabilities.

☐ A PROFIT AND LOSS STATEMENT is a detailed earnings statement for the previous full year (if you are in business) or a projected full year (if you are going into business). Existing businesses are usually also required to show a Profit and Loss Statement for the current period to the date of the Balance Sheet.

☐ ASSETS (if you are already in business) are your accounts receivable (money customers owe you), inventory (stock or merchandise), equipment (furniture, fixtures, machinery, delivery trucks); anything that can generate cash.

☐ LIABILITIES (if you are already in business) include accounts payable (money you owe to suppliers), plus all current costs of doing business (mortgage payments, insurance, taxes, salaries, utilities).

☐ A CASH FLOW PROJECTION is a forecast of the cash (checks or money orders) a business anticipates receiving and disbursing during the course of a given span of time—frequently a month. It is useful in anticipating the cash position of your business at specific times during the period being projected. Well-managed, the Cash Flow should be sufficient to meet the cash requirements for the following month. If there is too little cash, you may need an additional loan, or you are paying out too much cash. If the end of the month finds you with a surplus of cash, on the other hand, either you have borrowed too much money and are paying unnecessary interest, or you have idle money that should be put to work.

☐ Your PERSONAL FINANCIAL HISTORY is a picture of your personal financial condition to date. It is a very important part of any loan application and/or interview, especially when a loan for a projected new business is under consideration. A complete Personal Financial History is a record of all borrowing and repayments, an itemized listing of your personal assets and liabilities. It will list your sources of income such as salary, personal investments (stocks, bonds, real estate, savings accounts)—all of which are called Assets. Your Liabilities in the form of personal debts (installment credit payments, life insurance premiums, mortgage status, etc.) must also be listed in detail.

☐ COLLATERAL is a favorite word in the banking community. It means property, stocks, bonds, savings accounts, life insurance and current business assets—any or all of which may be held or assumed to insure repayment of your loan.

There are, of course, many other banking terms and phrases. However, an understanding of the above and—what is more important—a responsible integration of them into your loan application with all the necessary data, will probably serve your needs adequately.

Why You Shouldn't Open an Account with a Big Bank

Of the various bank managers you will be talking to, we advise you—if you have a choice—to establish yourself with a *small* bank. The reason is simple: you'll have a small account to start with, and you'll simply be overlooked in a large bank. In a small bank, the personnel see to it that even the smallest accounts get proper attention.

How to Get Banks to Trust You

Try to make the first bank you pick be the one you stay with. In any business, you need to establish references. If you're always shifting your account, you're never in any one bank long enough to establish your credibility.

Most of us, whether we have a business account, or a personal account, never take the time to have a heart-to-heart talk with a bank manager. Whatever kind of money problem you're having, don't be afraid to discuss it with your banker. For a lot of people, their entire relationship with a bank consists of opening and closing accounts. Make the bank manager aware of all the financial aspects of a "Kitchen Lady" operation and get his professional insight into how to make it succeed. The reason you want to take him into your confidence when you first open your account is that when you need him later—particularly for a *loan*—you're not coming to him as a total stranger. Very often, that makes all the difference between an approved loan and a rejected one.

Study These Banking Questions and You'll Get the Loan You Need

When you're at the stage when you need a loan, be prepared to answer the following questions:

Is Your Firm Credit-Worthy?

The ability to obtain money when you need it is as necessary to the operation of your business as is a good location, or the right equipment, reliable sources of supplies and materials, or an adequate labor force. Before a bank or any other lending agency will lend you money, the loan officer must feel satisfied with the answers to the five following questions:

1. What sort of person are you, the prospective borrower? By all odds, the character of the borrower comes first. Next is his ability to manage his business.

2. What are you going to do with the money? The answer to this question will determine the type of loan—short- or long-term. Money to be used for the purchase of seasonal inventory will require quicker repayment than money used to buy fixed assets.

3. When and how do you plan to pay it back? Your banker's judgment as to your business ability and the type of loan will be a deciding factor in the answer to this question.

4. Is the cushion in the loan large enough? In other words, does the amount requested make suitable allowance for unexpected developments? The banker decides this question on the basis of your financial statement, which sets forth the condition of your business and/or on the collateral pledge.

5. What is the outlook for business in general and for your business particularly?

Adequate Financial Information Is a "Must"

The banker wants to make loans to businesses that are solvent, profitable, and growing. The two basic financial statements he uses to determine those conditions are the balance sheet and profit-and-loss statement. The former is the major yardstick for solvency and the latter for profits. A continuous series of these two statements over a period of time is the principal device for measuring financial stability and growth potential.

In interviewing loan applicants and in studying their records, the banker is especially interested in the following facts and figures.

GENERAL INFORMATION: Are the books and records up-to-date and in good condition? What is the condition of accounts payable? Of notes payable? What are the salaries of the owner-manager and other company officers? Are all taxes being paid currently? What is the order backlog? What is the number of employees? What is the insurance coverage?

ACCOUNTS RECEIVABLE: Are there indications that some of the accounts receivable have already been pledged to another creditor? What is the accounts receivable turnover? Is the accounts receivable total weakened because many customers are far behind in their payments? Has a large enough reserve been set up to cover doubtful accounts? How much do the largest accounts owe and what percentage of your total accounts does this amount represent?

INVENTORIES: Is merchandise in good shape or will it have to be marked down? How much raw material is on hand? How much work is in process? How much of the inventory is finished goods?

Is there any obsolete inventory? Has an excessive amount of inventory been consigned to customers? Is inventory turnover in line with the turnover for other businesses in the same industry? Or is money being tied up too long in inventory?

FIXED ASSETS: What is the type, age, and condition of the equipment? What are the depreciation policies? What are the details of mortgages or conditional sales contracts? What are the future acquisition plans?

What Kind of Money?

When you set out to borrow money for your firm, it is important to know the kind of money you need from a bank or other lending institution. There are three kinds of money: short-term money, term money, and equity capital.

Keep in mind that the purpose for which the funds are to be used is an important factor in deciding the kind of money needed. But even so, deciding what kind of money to use is not always easy. It is sometimes complicated by the fact that you may be using some of various kinds of money at the same time and for identical purposes.

Keep in mind that a very important distinction between the types of money is the source of repayment. Generally, short-term loans are repaid from the liquidation of current assets which they have financed. Long-term loans are usually repaid from earnings.

Short-Term Bank Loans

You can use short-term bank loans for purposes such as financing accounts receivable for, say 30 to 60 days. Or you can use them for purposes that take longer to pay off—such as for building a seasonal inventory over a period of 5 to 6 months. Usually, lenders expect short-term loans to be repaid after their purposes have been served: for example, accounts receivable loans, when the outstanding accounts have been paid by the borrower's customers, and inventory loans, when the inventory has been converted into saleable merchandise.

Banks grant such money either on your general credit reputation with an unsecured loan or on a secured loan—against collateral.

The *unsecured loan* is the most frequently used form of bank credit for short-term purposes. You do not have to put up collateral because the bank relies on your credit reputation.

The *secured loan* involves a pledge of some or all of your assets. The bank requires security as a protection for its depositors against the risks that are involved even in business situations where the chances of success are good.

Term Borrowing

Term borrowing provides money you plan to pay back over a fairly long time. Some people break it down into two forms: (1) intermediate—loans longer than 1 year but less than 5 years, and (2) long-term loans for more than 5 years.

However, for your purpose of matching the kind of money to

the needs of your company, think of term borrowing as a kind of money which you probably will pay back in periodic installments from earnings.

Equity Capital

Some people confuse term borrowing and equity (or investment) capital. Yet there is a big difference. You don't have to repay equity money. It is money you get by selling a part interest in your business.

You take people into your company who are willing to risk their money in it. They are interested in potential income rather than in an immediate return on their investment.

How Much Money?

The amount of money you need to borrow depends on the purpose for which you need funds. Figuring the amount of money required for business construction, conversion, or expansion—term loans or equity capital—is relatively easy. Equipment manufacturers, architects, and builders will readily supply you with cost estimates. On the other hand, the amount of working capital you need depends upon the type of business you're in. While rule-of-thumb ratios may be helpful as a starting point, a detailed projection of sources and uses of funds over some future period of time—usually for 12 months—is a better approach. In this way, the characteristics of the particular situation can be taken into account. Such a projection is developed through the combination of a predicted budget and a cash forecast.

The budget is based on recent operating experience plus your best judgment of performance during the coming period. The cash forecast is your estimates of cash receipts and disbursements during the budget period. Thus the budget and the cash forecast together represent your plan for meeting your working capital requirements.

To plan your working capital requirements, it is important to know the "cash flow" which your business will generate. This involves simply a consideration of all elements of cash receipts and disbursements at the time they occur.

What Kind of Collateral?

Sometimes, your signature is the only security the bank needs when making a loan. At other times, the bank requires additional assurance that the money will be repaid. The kind and amount of security depends on the bank and on the borrower's situation.

If the loan required cannot be justified by the borrower's financial statements alone, a pledge of security may bridge the gap. The types of security are: endorsers, co-makers, and guarantors; assignment of leases; trust receipts and floor planning; chattel mortgages; real estate; accounts receivables, savings accounts; life insurance policies; and stocks and bonds. In a substantial number of States where the Uniform Commercial Code has been enacted, paperwork for recording loan transactions will be greatly simplified.

Endorsers, Co-makers, and Guarantors

Borrowers often get other people to sign a note in order to bolster their own credit. These *endorsers* are contingently liable for the note they sign. If the borrower fails to pay up, the bank expects the endorser to make the note good. Sometimes, the endorser may be asked to pledge assets or securities that he owns.

A *co-maker* is one who creates an obligation jointly with the borrower. In such cases, the bank can collect directly from either the maker or the co-maker.

A *guarantor* is one who guarantees the payment of a note by signing a guaranty commitment. Both private and government lenders often require guarantees from officers of corporations in order to assure continuity of effective management. Sometimes, a manufacturer will act as guarantor for one of his customers.

Assignment of Leases

The assigned lease as security is similar to the guarantee. It is used, for example, in some franchise situations.

The bank lends the money on a building and takes a mortgage. Then the lease, which the dealer and the parent franchise company work out, is assigned so that the bank automatically receives the rent payments. In this manner, the bank is guaranteed repayment of the loan.

Chattel Mortgages

If you buy equipment such as a cash register or a delivery truck, you may want to get a chattel mortgage loan. You give the bank a lien on the equipment you are buying.

The bank also evaluates the present and future market value of the equipment being used to secure the loan. How rapidly will it depreciate? Does the borrower have the necessary fire, theft, property damage, and public liability insurance on the equipment? The banker has to be sure that the borrower protects the equipment.

Real Estate

Real estate is another form of collateral for long-term loans. When taking a real estate mortgage, the bank finds out: (1) the location of the real estate, (2) its physical condition, (3) its foreclosure value, and (4) the amount of insurance carried on the property.

Accounts Receivable

Many banks lend money on accounts receivable. In effect, you are counting on your customers to pay your note.

The bank may take accounts receivable on a notification or a nonnotification plan. Under the *notification* plan, the purchaser of the goods is informed by the bank that his account has been assigned to it and he is asked to pay the bank. Under the *nonnotification* plan, the borrower's customers continue to pay him the sums due on their accounts and he pays the bank.

Savings Account

Sometimes, you might get a loan by assigning to the bank a savings account. In such cases, the bank gets an assignment from you and keeps your passbook. If you assign an account in another bank as collateral, the lending bank asks the other bank to mark its records to show that the account is held as collateral.

Life Insurance

Another kind of collateral is life insurance. Banks will lend up to the cash value of a life insurance policy. You have to assign the policy to the bank.

If the policy is on the life of an executive of a small corporation, corporate resolutions must be made authorizing the assignment. Most insurance companies allow you to sign the policy back to the original beneficiary when the assignment to the bank ends.

Some people like to use life insurance as collateral rather than borrow directly from insurance companies. One reason is that a bank loan is often more convenient to obtain and usually may be obtained at a lower interest rate.

Stocks and Bonds

If you use stocks and bonds as collateral, they must be marketable. As a protection against market declines and possible expenses of liquidation, banks usually lend no more than 75 percent of the market value of high grade stock. On Federal Government or municipal bonds, they may be willing to lend 90 percent or more of their market value.

The bank may ask the borrower for additional security or

payment whenever the market value of the stocks or bonds drops below the bank's required margin.

What Are the Lender's Rules?

Lending institutions are not just interested in loan repayments. They are also interested in borrowers with healthy profit-making businesses. Therefore, whether or not collateral is required for a loan, they set loan limitations and restrictions to protect themselves against unnecessary risk and at the same time against poor management practices by their borrowers. Often some owner-managers consider loan limitations a burden.

Yet others feel that such limitations also offer an opportunity for improving their management techniques.

Especially in making long-term loans, the borrower as well as the lender should be thinking of: (1) the net earning power of the borrowing company, (2) the capability of its management, (3) the long-range prospects of the company, and (4) the long-range prospects of the industry of which the company is a part. Such factors often mean that limitations increase as the duration of the loan increases.

What Kinds of Limitations?

The kinds of limitations which an owner-manager finds set upon the company depends, to a great extent, on the company. If the company is a good risk, only minimum limitations need be set. A poor risk, of course, is different. Its limitations should be greater than those of a stronger company.

Look now for a few moments at the kinds of limitations and restrictions which the lender may set. Knowing what they are can help you see how they affect your operations.

The limitations which you will usually run into when you borrow money are:

(1) Repayment terms.

(2) Pledging or the use of security.

(3) Periodic reporting.

A loan agreement, as you may already know, is a tailor-made document covering, or referring to, all the terms and conditions of the loan. With it, the lender does two things: (1) protects his position as a creditor (he wants to keep that position in as well a protected state as it was on the date the loan was made) and (2) assures himself of repayment according to the terms.

The lender reasons that the borrower's business should *generate enough funds* to repay the loan while taking care of other needs. He considers that cash inflow should be great enough to do this without hurting the working capital of the borrower.

Covenants—Negative and Positive

The actual restrictions in a loan agreement come under a section known as covenants. Negative covenants are things which the borrower may not do without prior approval from the lender. Some examples are: further additions to the borrower's total debt, nonpledge to others of the borrower's assets, and issuance of dividends in excess of the terms of the loan agreement.

On the other hand, positive covenants spell out things which the borrower must do. Some examples are: (1) maintenance of a minimum net working capital, (2) carrying of adequate insurance, (3) repaying the loan according to the terms of the agreement, and (4) supplying the lender with financial statements and reports.

Overall, however, loan agreements may be amended from time to time and exceptions made. Certain provisions may be waived from one year to the next, with the consent of the lender.

You Can Negotiate

Next time you go to borrow money, thrash out the lending terms before you sign. It is good practice no matter how badly you may need the money. Ask to see the papers in advance of the loan closing. Legitimate lenders are glad to cooperate.

Chances are that the lender may "give" some on the terms. Keep in mind also that, while you're mulling over the terms, you may want to get the advice of your associates and outside advisors. In short, try to get terms which you know your company can live with. Remember, however, that once the terms have been agreed upon and the loan is made, you are bound by them.

Never Be Intimidated

Always remember: banks are in business to *make* loans, not deny them. To get any loan you'll need to expand your business, follow the advice of the Boy Scout motto: *be prepared.* Have all your facts and figures in front of you when you meet your banker. Always believe that your banker *wants* to lend you money. And he really does; that's how banks stay in business!

Chapter 16

Now That You're in Business, Learn How to Be Your Own Bookkeeper

Everybody who goes into this business goes into it for one basic reason: *to make money!* There is also a lot of pride involved, the pride of having more and more people compliment you on the delicious homemade specialty you're turning out. Compliments are well and good, but you're working awfully hard at what you're doing. You want, and deserve, the financial rewards that go with it! That's why you have to pay attention to *how much money is coming in and how much is going out!*

You're Already Better Trained to Be a Bookkeeper Than You Realize!

It's not all that hard to "take care of the books"; after all, even before you got into this business, you've been working within a budget all your life. Just plain day-to-day living meant managing a household budget; you had so much each week to manage on. This same principle is now applied to your new business.

The difference is the *unpredictability* of the situation. In business, you cannot predict events as simply as you could when you had a set amount of money to run a house. You had fairly predictable expenses week after week, so you allotted a certain amount of money for rent, food, clothing, etc. In starting a business, you're starting from *scratch*. Both aspects of a business—how much you'll be *spending* and how much you'll be *earning*—can change week-to-week, even day-to-day. It's no problem to handle it if you are fully prepared for it. What we want to do is to show you all the steps to take so you can maintain your business on a profitable basis!

The Very First Thing You'll Need to Go Into Business

The first thing you'll need is a *business checking account.* A few hundred dollars put into it starts you off. This business account should stay completely separate from your personal account. The business account starts up a bookkeeping system for you. It tells you what business expenses you are incurring and what income from sales you are depositing. This business checking account is your *one and only guideline* as to the profitability or lack-of-profitability of your business. If you make the mistake of paying your business expenses in cash and neglect to get receipts, you'll never really know what your costs are. *If* there's a time when you don't have your checkbook with you and you need to run in for something, you *must* get a receipt for it.

Keeping accurate records of your expenditures is all-important; it's the only way of knowing for certain whether your business is making a profit or not. Try to pay by check as often as possible, and *only* out of your business account. Each and every time a "buyer" pays you for your specialty, record it on your business deposit slip. As often as possible pay everything by check, even that bag of sugar that you had to run into the supermarket for at the last moment. You'll find that you get awfully proud of yourself when you keep completely detailed records of the money you're paying out and the money you're taking in. Your checkbook becomes your *instant picture* of how you're doing in the business. As your business gets bigger and there becomes need for an *accountant,* your business checkbook is what he needs to figure your *deductions* when you have to pay taxes.

The accountant, with the following basic records, sets up a system according to your particular need.

Cash Receipts

Used to record the cash which the business receives.

Cash Disbursements

Used to record the firm's expenditures.

Sales

Used to record and summarize monthly income.

Purchases

Used to record the purchases of merchandise bought for processing or resale.

Payroll

Used to record the wages of employees and their deductions, such as those for income and Social Security taxes.

Equipment

Used to record the firm's capital assets, such as equipment, office furniture, and motor vehicles.

Inventory

Used to record the firm's investment in stock which is needed for arriving at a true profit on financial statements and for income tax purposes.

Accounts Receivable

Used to record the balances that customers owe to the firm.

Accounts Payable

Used to record what the firm owes its creditors and suppliers.

Who Keeps the Books?

Once a system of records has been set up, the question is: Who will keep the books?

Four possibilities are open. The public accountant who has set up the books may keep them himself and provide the greatest accuracy. But you must weigh the cost because he has to charge for his time, operating expenses, and profit. However, his professional advice can frequently increase your profits to more than cover his expenses.

If you have the time and inclination, you can keep the books yourself.

Another possibility is to hire someone to work part-time. Then there is the free-lance bookkeeper who works full-time but allots his talent among several firms.

Drawing the Picture

A set of books is like a roll of exposed film. The latter must be developed before you can see the picture.

Similarly, your books contain facts and figures that make up a picture of your business. They have to be arranged into an order before you see the picture.

The accountant draws such a picture by preparing financial statements, such as a profit-and-loss statement. The P-and-L statement shows what profit or loss your business had in a certain time period.

Your system of keeping records need not be elaborate, but it should be complete and well organized. Unless you have training or experience in accounting, it will pay you to have a professional accountant set up a system for you and explain its use. Some Kitchen Ladies, instead of keeping the records themselves, employ a public accountant continuously on a part-time basis. Even if you do this, you should understand the system he uses—how it works and how you can get information you want from it.

Your record-keeping system should include the following elements, at least:

A chronological record (journal) and a classified record (ledger of accounts) of the following types of transactions: cash receipts; cash payments; customer charges and credits; cash and credit sales; other income; expenses (direct labor, supplies, delivery expense, depreciation allowance, and so on); other payments.

A system for safeguarding your cash, including accounting for petty cash, daily proof of cash, and daily bank deposits.

A record of each credit customer's account.

A record of each employee's earnings and deductions.

A record of purchases and accounts payable.

A record of equipment and depreciation.

A record of your physical inventory. Essential to making buying and selling decisions, this record is also necessary to provide required information when you file your income tax return.

Small Business
Financial Status Review

DAILY   1. Cash on hand.

           2. Bank balance (keep business and personal funds separate).

           3. Daily Summary of sales and cash receipts.

4. That all errors in recording collections on accounts are corrected.

5. That a record of all monies paid out, by cash or check, is maintained.

WEEKLY 1. Accounts Receivable (take action on slow payers).

2. Accounts Payable (take advantage of discounts).

3. Payroll (records should include name and address of employee, social security number, number of exemptions, date ending the pay period, hours worked, rate of pay, total wages, deductions, net pay, check number).

4. Taxes and reports to State and Federal Government (sales, withholding, Social Security, etc.).

MONTHLY 1. All journal entries are classified according to like elements (these should be generally accepted and standardized for both income and expense) and posted to general ledger.

2. A Profit-and-Loss Statement for the month is available within a reasonable time, usually 10 to 15 days following the close of the month. This shows the income of the business for the month, the expense incurred in obtaining the income, and the profit or loss resulting. From this, take action to eliminate loss (adjust mark-up? reduce overhead expense? pilferage? incorrect tax reporting? incorrect buying procedures? failure to take advantage of cash discounts?).

3. That a Balance Sheet accompanies the Prof-

it-and-Loss Statement. This shows assets (what the business has), liabilities (what the business owes), and the investment of the owner.

4. The Bank Statement is reconciled. (That is, the owner's books are in agreement with the bank's record of the cash balance.)

5. The Petty Cash Account is in balance. (The actual cash in the Petty Cash Box plus the total of the paid-out slips that have not been charged to expense total the amount set aside as petty cash.)

6. All Federal Tax Deposits, Withheld Income and FICA Taxes (Form 501), and State Taxes are made.

7. Accounts Receivable are aged, i.e., 30, 60, 90 days, etc., past due. (Work all bad and slow accounts.)

8. Inventory Control is worked to remove dead stock and order new stock. (What moves slowly? Reduce. What moves fast? Increase.)

Chapter 17

Preparing Yourself for That Day— April 15: Income Tax Time

April 15—Income Tax Day

This is a mirror that reflects all the business days of the year for sole proprietors and partners. It is a confused reflection for some owner-managers of small firms because of poor record-keeping. It is a clear reflection for other owner-managers because of good recordkeeping.

Day by day, week by week, and month by month, good records accumulate the facts an owner-manager needs for income tax reporting. These facts help him to report his income properly, to take the proper tax deductions, and to back up that report should he be asked to do so.

No Set Records Required

The Internal Revenue Service (IRS) prescribes no specific accounting records, documents, or systems. However, the IRS requires that the owner-manager maintain permanent books of accounts or records which can be used to identify his firm's income, expenses, and deductions. Where inventories are factors in determining income correctly, or when travel and entertainment deductions are taken, special supporting details are required.

Although IRS requires no particular form of records, your records must be accurate and reflect taxable income and allowable deductions. Records must also be kept so that they are available for inspection by IRS officers.

In most tax matters, the burden of proof lies with the taxpayer. Therefore, your records must reflect *all* your income and *all* your expenses, just in case they are inspected by an IRS agent. Otherwise, he may disallow any deductions which you have made and cannot substantiate. As a result, you may have to make an additional payment.

In addition, if you have adequate records, all the facts you need for filing a tax return are easily accessible. You are less likely to make a late filing for which there are severe charges and penalties. Moreover, you remove any suspicion of willful negligence and fraud for which a person can be fined or imprisoned.

A Simple System

If your small business is a sole proprietorship, you can use a simple set of records to capture facts for income tax reporting. Such a system consists of a checkbook, a cash receipts journal, a cash disbursements journal, and a petty cash fund.

Checkbook

All funds that pass in and out of your store or service shop should go through a checking account that you set up for your business. (The owner-manager should handle his personal expenses in a separate checking account.) When used with your other records, the checkbook helps you to prove how much money was handled, how much was taxable income, and what amounts were deductible for income tax reporting. You should reconcile your bank statement monthly, using the proof totals from your receipts and disbursements journals to check your work.

Cash Receipts Journal

All receipts should be entered in a receipts journal. In this manner, income that is not realized from sales—for example, advertising allowances—is separated from receipts that have to be reported as "gross receipts or gross sales." Sales taxes which you collect for the local or state government should also be kept separate because they are not business income.

Cash Disbursements Journal

All funds that are paid out should be recorded in a cash disbursements, purchases, and expense journal. The best practice is to enter daily in this journal each check you write. Each entry should show the nature or classification of the disbursement—merchandise, office supplies, rent, and employee wages, to mention a few examples. You can summarize the expense classifications by extending each entry into a column for a particular class of expenses and adding the columns monthly. This type of journal may be created by either posting each check stub regularly to a line in the journal or by using one of the "one-write" pegboards which are available from several commercial suppliers.

Petty Cash Fund

You should keep a petty cash fund with voucher slips to document each expenditure. In this manner, you can prove that cash expenditures—those of an amount too small to justify writing a check—are deductible for tax filing. A petty cash fund also eliminates your paying for miscellaneous small expenses out of your own pocket.

Other Records

Under even the simplest system, a fixed asset record is needed. In this manner, you record all equipment, buildings, vehicles, and other depreciable assets.

In addition, there is a variety of depreciation techniques such as accelerated methods and special "first year" additional depreciation which, in some cases, should be used to defer or reduce tax costs. (Investment credit applicability is also a factor. A good record of your assets is essential to plan for and get maximum tax advantages in these areas of fixed assets.) Under the Revenue Procedure 62–21, depreciation schedules and records must be kept for at least as long as the replacement cycle to substantiate the guideline lives which IRS allows.

Employers who withhold taxes from wages have to keep additional and extensive records. If you have one or more employees, you may be required to withhold Federal income tax from their wages. Your payroll records must include the amounts and dates of all employee wage payments subject to withholding taxes. You should keep such records for at least four years after the date the tax becomes due or is paid, whichever is later. (For additional details see "Steps in Meeting Your Tax Obligations," Small Marketers' Aids No. 142, free from SBA, P.O. Box 15434, Fort Worth, TX 76119).

Corporations and Partnerships

If your business is a small corporation or a partnership, your records must cover situations that do not exist in a sole proprietorship. In a corporation, the records must show the salaries paid to its officers and the dividends paid to stockholders. The owner-manager is an officer of the corporation responsible for filing an income tax return for the company. In addition, he files a personal return to pay income tax on his salary and the dividends he receives from the corporation. If the business is a partnership, it files an information return on Form 1065 indicating the income or loss assignable to each partner. Each partner then files a personal return and includes his share of partnership income with his other taxable income. The legal form of your organization can have a substantial effect on taxes, and both legal and accounting advice will be important in selecting the best form of business for your particular needs.

Retaining Records

You should keep the records which you use to prepare your firm's income tax return. However, there is no fixed answer to the question on how long to retain such records. You should keep them as long as their contents may become material in the administration of any Internal Revenue law. Ordinarily, the statute of limitations for such records expires three years after the return is due to be filed.

Generally, the Internal Revenue Service cannot bring assessment or collection proceedings for a given taxable year after three years has elapsed from the due date of the return or the date it was filed, whichever is later. The major exception to this time period are in cases where the taxpayer omitted over 25 percent of gross income or filed a false or fraudulent return.

However, you should keep in mind that this three-year period is a minimum. Many of your records should be kept for a longer period.

Among records often considered permanent are cash books, depreciation schedules, general ledger, journals, financial statements, and audit reports. Records to be retained six to seven years often include accounts payable and receivable, cancelled checks, inventory schedules, payroll records, and sales vouchers, and invoice details.

Copies of income tax returns should always be retained. Retaining records helps the taxpayer as well as the IRS because it is often to the taxpayer's advantage to use carry-back claims and amended returns. In such cases, you must be able to prove that your tax returns are correct.

Plan with Records

The owner-manager of a small business should use his records to plan his income tax. The Government wants you to pay only your legal obligation—no more and no less.

This fact has been best expressed by the late Judge Learned Hand. He said:

> Over and over again courts have said there is nothing sinister in arranging one's affairs to keep taxes as low as possible. Everybody does so, rich or poor; and all do right, for nobody owes any public duty to pay more than the law demands.

Your accounting system should provide a current indication of the profitability of your business. Thus, your records help you to make a sound estimate of taxable income for the year, and consequently, the projected tax bracket of your business. You should review these figures at least once each quarter during the year to see what, if any, steps you can take to minimize your tax.

When making tax payments, it is essential that your accounting system provide a basis for your estimate. Where underpayment has already occurred, the system should substantiate the timing of income to avoid or mitigate penalties.

An employee benefit plan may offer tax advantages. For the smallest entrepreneur, the self-employed retirement deduction can be very beneficial. However, as in the case of any pension or profit sharing plan, the decision of whether or not to adopt such a plan or on what basis, depends on what your accounting system projects for profits and available cash.

Outside Help

Unless the owner-manager's background includes bookkeeping or accounting, he should use outside help in setting up his records. An accountant can help you determine what records to keep. He can advise on techniques which will insure that you don't pay unnecessary tax.

For example, because of poor records one small businessman unnecessarily included $30,000 of installment sales in his income even though they would not be earned for two or three years. At a 22 percent tax rate, he paid more than $6,500 "extra" taxes.

Inventory costing is another example of the need for sound records. Your records should allow you to substantiate a correct but minimum income valuation.

An accountant can also advise you on the most economical way of maintaining records. For example, some small businesses need only a part-time bookkeeper or can use a bookkeeping service. Still other firms need a full-time employee to keep records up-to-date.

In addition, accountants and lawyers can advise of changes in tax laws that may require adjustments in the kinds of facts necessary for tax reporting.

You'll also need an outside accountant to assist you in the preparation of payroll records and payroll taxes.

If you have any employees at all, you have certain obligations to the Federal Government for payment of payroll taxes and withholding of income taxes in connection with the sala-

ries of your employees. You will probably have similar obligations for payroll and/or withholding taxes to the State and
perhaps to the local jurisdiction—it depends on where your
business is located. Contact city and state authorities for information about payroll and withholding taxes under their ju-
risdictions.

The outside accountant will also help you with the collection
and recording of sales taxes.

When and how you pay sales taxes will depend on the regulations of the taxing authority in your area. Be sure that you
understand what is required of you.

When you make the payment, it will be entered in the Cash
Disbursements Journal. The account is shown as "Sales Tax"
and the amount is entered in the Amount-of-Check column
and in the debit column under General Ledger Items. The
debit entry will later be posted to the Sales-Tax-Payable account in the General Ledger.

Chapter 18

Every Business Needs One: What a Good Lawyer Will Do for You

A Lawyer Can Help in Ways You Didn't Know About

Many small business owners consider legal services only when their firms are in trouble. They fail to realize that legal troubles can be reduced or avoided by a program of consultation which is carried out on a continuing basis. The advice and suggestions of a lawyer on day-to-day operations help prevent costly and time-consuming problems.

As you read this, you should keep in mind that a lawyer's job, properly done, is to see that his clients adhere to the law and thus prevent inadvertent violations and near-violations which may turn out to be costly.

The legal services which a lawyer provides the owner-manager of a small retail or service firm can be summed up in four words: checking, advising, guiding, and representing.

Your lawyer can *check* past actions to determine if you have unintentionally violated the law. For example a retailer may have failed to get a license for a new line of merchandise because he wasn't aware that one was required.

Such a check may sometimes turn up facts that can be used to improve the firm. For example, the lawyer's examination may show that another form of business organization from the one used in the past may be much better for the owner-manager and his family.

In *advising,* the lawyer can explain the legal principles involved in the various courses of action which are open to the owner-manager under the law. A decision will be easy when but one action is allowed. *Making* a judgment may be difficult, however, when the law allows several courses of action.

At this point, a lawyer's *guidance* can be valuable. While the ultimate decision must rest with the owner-manager in all cases, the lawyer because of his experience, can help evaluate the courses of action and materially assist in making this decision.

In *representing* the owner-manager, the lawyer speaks as one specialist to other specialists. He knows and can talk the language of licensing boards, regulatory bodies, town courts, and other governmental agencies. Equally as important, is the representation which your lawyer provides in negotiating and drawing up contracts. You can be sure your interest is protected, for example, when your lawyer sits down with his counterpart to negotiate a lease. He can protect you from unknowingly placing restrictions on future expansion plans or obligating yourself to pay the renovation costs if your rented store or shop is damaged by a fire.

Organization

The financial future of a retail or service business will be affected by the initial decision of the owner as to the form to be

used in its organization. There are certain incidents attached
to any form selected which make it imperative that an attorney discuss fully the consequences with the owner.

Three forms generally are available to the owner—sole ownership, partnership, or a corporation. Each form has distinct
rules applicable to it regarding taxation, management, liabilities of the owner, and division of profits. Only after being advised as to all of these may an intelligent decision be made as
to which form is most suitable.

Legal services are a necessity when the choice of organization requires contracts, partnership agreements, or the filing
of certificates. There are many municipal and State law requirements attached to the beginning of any new business.
Full compliance can be best assured with legal advice.

Even after the business is established, periodic checks
should be made as the business progresses, particularly from a
tax standpoint. For example, a sole proprietorship may have
been desirable in the early years when losses were incurred
and could be used to offset other income of the owner.

However, when a firm grows and profits are being shown,
the owner-manager may desire to incorporate in order to obtain a tax advantage and at the same time reduce personal
liability for any losses of the business. As management responsibilities increase, he may wish to form a partnership to help
carry the load. Or he may wish to realize on the increasing
value of the business by incorporating and selling shares in the
business to the public.

Acquiring Property

Acquiring property is another area in which legal services can
be helpful and profitable. This is true whether the property is
real estate or merchandise.

Real Property

In many cases, the owner-manager's concern with real estate is
through a landlord. He rents space in which to operate his

retail or service business. In such cases, a lawyer always should check the provisions of the lease.

The lawyer can explain in lay language the consequences an owner-manager may suffer because of provisions in a lease. Some of the more important considerations when signing a lease are: (1) title to and cost of any improvements to be made to the property; (2) ownership of these improvements when the lease ends; (3) renewal provisions; (4) any restriction on competitive operation by the lessee or others; (5) provisions as to compensation in case of fire or condemnation of the property; (6) provisions for assignment or subletting of the premises; and (7) the means of determining and measuring your sales— an important item when the amount of rent is to depend on a percentage of sales.

Your lawyer also will call to your attention any reciprocal restrictions as to the use of the premises, such as are commonly found in shopping center leases. Sometimes, the provisions in the leases of other stores may severely restrict your operations as well as future development of the shopping center.

If you buy a store building, the services of a lawyer are essential. In those states where title abstract companies do not operate, a lawyer will examine and certify title to the real estate to insure that you own what you are paying for. Also, he can explain the meaning and impact of any mortgage or other type of instrument necessary to finance such a purchase.

Title to Merchandise

If you buy a stock of merchandise from another retailer, or another business, your lawyer can tell you whether you are complying with the applicable provisions of the Uniform Commercial Code or the Bulk Sales Law of the state in which you and the seller are located.

Basically, these laws require that the creditors of the *seller* be protected in any outright sale of a stock of merchandise to another. Your title to the goods may be jeopardized if you fail to examine and comply with these laws. Your lawyer can also check for any security interests that may be outstanding against the goods, and insure that you have proper title before you close the transaction.

Inventory and Other Financing

No retail business can operate without an inventory. Rarely is this purchased for cash by the owner, and some form of financing is essential. If you borrow against inventory, for example, your lawyer should be consulted to make sure that the contracts and security documents are in order and help make clear what commitments you are making.

The basic idea behind inventory financing is that the seller does not turn the goods loose completely. Some form of security or other interest in the property is held by the seller until the merchandise is sold or paid for. Your lawyer can make sure that the security restrictions incurred by you are fully understood so that the method of financing does not unduly hamper the conduct of the business.

Aside from financing inventory, funds may be obtained by short- or long-term bank loans either secured or unsecured. In any such borrowing, your lawyer's help and advice can be especially helpful because such borrowing puts limitations on your firm. For example, in the term-loan agreement, the bank or lending institution may impose certain restrictions as to the operations of your business. You may obtain funds by assigning your accounts receivable to a lending institution. Here also a lawyer should be consulted.

Legal advice is a must, if and when, you seek funds through equity financing. Here you raise funds by selling a part of your business to another person—bringing him in as a part-owner. If you do this by offering stock to the general public, your lawyer will have to make sure that your firm meets the requirements set by the Securities and Exchange Commission and by any state regulatory body.

Taxes

There are innumerable instances in which the advice of an attorney with tax experience is essential in complying with tax laws. Among the factors in tax planning about which you may want to seek legal advice are: (1) the fiscal year you use; (2) the legal aspects of adopting a profit-sharing or pension plan; (3) the means and methods of capitalizing your business to minimize taxation; (4) the availability of stock-option plans to the owners, if you operate as a corporation; (5) the legal implications of insurance programs which your firm can adopt; and (6) the election as to the form of taxation available to you.

Advice and assistance on such matters can be helpful not only when the business is showing profits, but also when it has losses. For example, the effects of a loss when a newly established firm is trying to reach its break-even point sometimes may be softened measurably by using the loss in relation to other income.

Legal advice also should be sought by the owner-manager in making plans for the continuation of his business in event of his death. Such long-range plans for transferring ownership of the firm to the next generation should be made early in the firm's existence, as such planning may be difficult if not impossible at a later date.

Laws Affecting Employees

Advice and assistance on laws covering employees is another helpful legal service. For example, a lawyer can point out and help the owner-manager to observe the requirements that Federal and state laws set on wages, employees' hours, workmen's compensation, and unemployment compensation.

Legal assistance can be useful also when, and if, you employ workers represented by a labor union. It is essential in collective bargaining, and contract negotiations.

You will also want your lawyer to check to insure that your

employment practices comply with any applicable fair employment legislation.

Litigation

Of course, you'll use a lawyer to defend your firm if someone should sue it or if you should have to sue someone. The fire has to be put out.

However, it is easier when you have a regular lawyer. Because he is already familiar with your business, you will spend less time away from your work in such cases. This familiarity, which your lawyer gets from working with your firm on a regular basis, can also enable him to help you prevent situations which might lead to trouble. Such preventive law can keep your business out of the court room. Thus you avoid time-consuming and expensive attempts to rescue a situation after things have gotten out of hand.

Operating without litigation also helps your store's image. Some customers and prospective customers prefer not to deal with a business when its name is frequently in the court news.

Credit Problems

Sometimes a small retailer gets in trouble because he is unable to pay his debts. If things have not progressed too far, a lawyer may be able to work out an arrangement that will allow the store to pay its debts on an installment plan, over an extended period of time and out of current income. In other cases, the lawyer may help to reorganize the store's financial structure so its creditors can receive a reasonable amount while the business continues to operate.

On the other hand, if the creditors insist on closing, the lawyer can work to prevent them from taking unfair advantage of the retailer—prevent his sacrificing his business and insulate him from any undue personal liability for the debts of the business.

Something Extra Important
to Keep in Your Mind

As you start making money in this business, start thinking about making your specialties away from your own kitchen. In some cities they say you're operating a business and you shouldn't do that in a residential zone. In some other cities they might say that the kitchen you use to prepare food for your family, shouldn't be the same kitchen you use to prepare food for sale. Mind you, right this very moment, thousands of women all over the country are preparing their delicious specialties from their own kitchens and selling them. Both they and their customers are positively delighted. You could go on for years working this way and it's no problem. But, should it ever develop into a problem, fear not. You have many alternatives, and sometimes these alternatives turn out to be a blessing in disguise. You'll end up making even *more* money. Here are the options:

(1) If you're told you can't use your family kitchen for commercial purposes, then consider these other alternatives: (a) If you live in a house, set up a "mini-kitchen" (with refrigerator and oven) in another area, perhaps the basement or another room. (b) If that's not possible, then rent existing kitchen facilities elsewhere: a cooking school, a club, a camp, even a restaurant. There are many kitchen facilities that you can rent on a part-time basis.

(2) If you live in an apartment and you're told you can't use your kitchen (and of course there's no room for a second kitchen), then you can also rent another facility as detailed above.

(3) Yet another possibility is to *hire* someone to do your work. There are two women living in New York City who have a flourishing mail-order cookie business, and they hire a baker who does all the baking on his premises. These women have already outgrown their own apartments they used for packaging the cookies, so now they rent a basement in a nearby

church four mornings a week. When your business grows, just grow with it.

(4) If your specialty is catering meals to people's homes, there's no problem at all if you're told you can't use your own kitchen. Use the kitchens where you do your catering! Your customers are often delighted because they learn a great deal from watching you.

(5) When you start to outgrow your own kitchen, form a cooperative arrangement with a group of other Kitchen Ladies. All of you keep your eyes peeled for a small luncheonette or coffee shop that's going out of business. Hire a lawyer to go in and take a lease on the premises and buy out the existing kitchen equipment. Because the store is going out of business, your group will be able to buy everything for a fraction of the original purchase price. From these premises, each woman will prepare her own specialty and everyone will mutually share in the profits.

(6) Another alternative is to eventually form a partnership with another woman and open up a combined cooking school and gourmet food store. In the back, cooking classes are held, and in the front, you sell a complete line of gourmet foods. You can also sell kitchen equipment and utensils.

To summarize: Every Kitchen Lady we know gets started in this business from her own kitchen. Many stay that way and continue to enjoy an excellent income. If a legal hassle develops and you have to work elsewhere, it often ends up turning out for the best. There are times in life when we're forced to do something we think we're not ready for, but when we do it, we succeed beyond our wildest dreams. Many Kitchen Ladies were *pushed* into becoming more successful. This can easily happen to you. Throughout all of this, look to your lawyer for guidance, that's what you hired him for. But no matter what happens, never fear the future. Remember: "Cream always rises to the top!"

Chapter 19
A Talk with Sylvia Caudell, The "Happy Kooker"

The editors of Pantry Press felt it would be a good idea to sit down and have a heart-to-heart talk with one of the Kitchen Ladies. We felt this would give our readers a special insight into how one woman got started in this business and how she's getting along. Sometimes, an open and honest question-and-answer session is the best way to accomplish this. There's probably a lot of truth to the old expression, "You learn a lot by asking questions."

We're particularly pleased—and we hope you will be too—with the woman we'll be talking to. Her name is Sylvia Caudell,* a housewife who is divorced and living in New York City. She's a very sweet and sincere woman, nothing fancy about her; she doesn't put on any "airs." She's living in New York City now, but when she talks, she's all "down-home" country. She does a fine business selling her cakes to fancy gourmet food stores and her private customers. (At the end of this chapter, we'll be giving you Sylvia's recipes.)

Do you recall earlier in the book when we told you always to make up labels with your name on it? Well, we just have to pass along to you what Sylvia Caudell has on her labels. She has her phone number, of course. But, instead of her name, she goes by the name of THE HAPPY KOOKER! We wouldn't say that if it weren't true.

Now to the questions and answers. We (Pantry Press—PP) will be asking the questions; Sylvia (SC) will do the answering.

PP: Sylvia, where were you born and raised?

SC: I was born and raised in a small town called Wallace, in North Carolina. It's on the coast, near Wilmington.

PP: As a young girl, did you show any special interest in cooking or baking?

SC: I didn't have any choice! (Laughs.) You see, my mother was a home economics teacher and to earn extra money, she took jobs catering dinner parties; she quickly made me her assistant.

PP: About how old were you when you started helping your mother in catering?

SC: I was nine years old.

PP: To whom would she generally cater?

SC: To private clubs mostly, like the Lions Club.

PP: It sounds like a lot of work.

---

* Actual name.

SC: It was trying. I'd say about twenty to thirty people would come to the club, so my mother needed each of her three children to be assistants.

PP: What types of food specialties would your mother make? Tell us what made up a typical dinner she would cater.

SC: It would mainly be Southern food. It would either be a chicken or beef or pork dinner; along with a starch and two vegetables—and especially her homemade dinner rolls, and of course her desserts. They were excellent. My mother prided herself on being a very good cook and baker—and she was a very gracious hostess.

PP: If she would cater to a group of twenty or thirty people at a dinner party—at the Lions Club— how much time did she allow to prepare everything?

SC: I would say two days in advance.

PP: Where did your mother do her shopping?

SC: Well, back then, all of her vegetables were out of our garden so the expense was not much. And then she'd usually have a friend that either had the chickens or the pigs and she would buy from them. So everything was local. It was not something she would have to go to a wholesaler for. And everything was homemade, even to the relishes and the preserves she had to serve with the rolls. She did *everything*. And it was great fun. I remember it. I even remember what great fun I had watching her carve chickens. I mean, pick and pluck chickens as well as clean them. It goes back to age three and how fascinated I was in watching her. Then she would talk about what a chicken was like—its stomach, its gizzard, and all. It was a tremendous fascination to us—my sisters and me. And my mother was such a fast worker in the kitchen. She was just all over the place. I was never able to actually cook or bake anything until my mother would say, "I'm going downtown to get some groceries. Would you like to go, Sylvia?" I'd say, "Oh, no, I think I'll stay home." And while she was gone, I'd whip up a batch of fudge or a cake and my next door neighbor, Catherine, received so many cakes and batches of fudge that she had to come to my mother and say, *"Stop Sylvia!"* Mother had no idea I was practicing on the dear soul everytime she went out for the groceries.

PP: You were only nine years old and were already making batches of fudge and cakes?

SC: Oh sure, and it was all just observing my mother. She had no recipes on paper; it was all in her head, and so I had to pick it up from just watching. And it was great fun. You know, I remember getting out of college and all my friends would say, "Can you cook?" And I said, "No, but I had a feeling if I get into a kitchen, I'd be able to use all that I remember."

PP: Was there a time in your life when you got some professional instruction?

SC: Oh yes. I was teaching school in Germany in the early '60s and I decided to spend a summer in Paris and I attended the famous Cordon Bleu school for five weeks. And I didn't speak a word of French; the chef knew I didn't and laughed. But I observed *everything* that was going on. I went three days a week to his class, and every afternoon, for five weeks, I attended the demonstration classes. I learned a lot: there was puff pastry, mousse, fish, chicken dishes, everything. And then, still, I decided that one day I would do more. And then in the early '70s, the first woman chef was written up in *The New York Times.* It said that she was working at the Waldorf-Astoria Hotel on Park Avenue. And so if I wanted to get that far ahead, I decided that maybe I ought to go back

to Paris and study again. And I did. But it was too expensive to spend a full year there. So I returned to New
York to my manager's position at Bonwit Teller. One of
my employees there told me about New York City Community College in Brooklyn; that's where the first woman
chef went. So I made the decision to stop my work at
Bonwit's and go to the school full-time. And while I was
taking classes there, I decided to try a few specialties to
sell to local restaurants and gourmet shops. In that way, I
could pick up some money to help me through school.

PP: **What made you decide which specialties could do
best? And ones that you would feel would have
the best commercial value?**

SC: Well, how I came to make the carrot cake, which is a very
popular cake of mine, is kind of an interesting story. It
sort of shows how much I *didn't* know when I first started out. I was selling a few cakes to one of the health
stores in New York when the manager asked me to make
her a carrot cake. I smiled at this and said, "Yes, of
course I would." Well, I ran home frantic, because I never
heard of a carrot cake. But I would never say no, so I
went through all the recipe books—especially Southern
cookbooks, and I found a recipe there. I began des-
perately pulling a little information from here, from
there . . . and tried my first few cakes. The manager said,
"Not bad, not bad." Well, I knew that meant not good
enough. You see, she was a lady from California and she
knew what good carrot cake tasted like. It's been popular
out there with natural food stores for years. To me what I
had was really no more than a spice cake, and so I started
to add some raisins and nuts. Well, before I knew it, she
started buying and buying them. That's how I started to
get into business with my carrot cakes.

PP: **How did you arrive at what to *charge* for your
carrot cakes? That's always the hardest thing to**

decide when you first start out in this business. Did anyone give you any advice?

SC: Yes. I asked a professor at school and he said, "You charge one-third for your ingredients; one-third for your time; and one-third goes for profit and overhead. Let me work it out in dollars and cents. I allow $2.65 for the recipe for my 8 inch tube-size carrot cake. I add another $2.65 for my time, and that includes shopping, baking, and delivery. Then another $2.65 for my overhead, such as energy costs, and my profit is in there as well. And so it's one-third for the ingredients, the same one-third amount for time, and one-third for overhead and profit. And three times $2.65 is $7.95, and so I charge the restaurant $8 for my 8-inch, sometimes up to 10-inch carrot cake. Another way some people figure out what to charge is *triple* the cost of your ingredients. And so it comes out to the same three times the $2.65—$7.95 or $8. Now mind you, it's important that your readers understand that prices vary in different parts of the country. As they say, it's all according to what the "traffic will bear."

PP: Talking about "what the traffic will bear," what does the restaurant charge their patrons for each slice of your cake?

SC: They get about triple of what the cake costs them. I know they get $2.25 for each slice of my cake. And they get ten slices out of one of my cakes, depending how they cut it. And at $2.25 each, they get $22.50 for my cake. And so that's nearly three times the $8 they pay me for the cake. But of course they have a very big overhead, what with the high rent they pay and the salaries of the help. But I can tell you a funny little story about how one restaurant was losing money on my carrot cakes.

PP: How could that happen?

SC: Anita, who was the owner of this one restaurant, would

walk among the diners after she started buying my cakes, to see how the customers were enjoying it. Well, she noticed, after a time, that none of the customers were eating it. When she checked up, she found that some of the waiters and waitresses were helping themselves to my cake in the kitchen, and there was nothing left over for the customers. The waiters and waitresses kept telling them, "I'm sorry, it's all sold out."

PP: **What a terrific compliment to you!**

SC: I thought so. But Anita didn't think it was so funny. She went ahead and saw to it that my cakes were kept, not in the kitchen, but in the office, on top of the safe. From then on, every waiter and waitress had to come to Anita for the key to get my cake. And Anita would only give it to them if she then saw 'em bring slices out to the customers. And each time they had to return the key to her.

PP: **Well, when they start keeping your cakes under lock and key, then you know you *really* have something!**

SC: Well, it was a lot of fun to hear that.

PP: **Can you give some advice to our readers about taking that very first step in selling what you make. Say a woman has baked some cakes and she's ready to sell them to a restaurant or gourmet shop. Does she ask for money right away? Does she leave some samples and wait to hear from them? What does she do?**

SC: When I first started out, my way was *not* to ask for money. Sometimes you put your new customer on the defensive that way. They don't know you, so make it easy for them. You walk in, always dressed nicely and filled with confidence. After all, you've made something delicious and you're proud of it. You might offer them a slice of your cake right then and there. If they feel uncomfortable with that idea, then just leave it and say you'll call them tomorrow. Even if a store or restaurant owner says, "I'm sorry, we really have all we need," don't accept that for a final answer yet. You answer with, "Try it, you have nothing to lose, and your customers will love it." Chances are he won't refuse you. A man or woman running some type of food business has to keep an open mind; they're always looking for some new taste treat to sell their customers. So you just have to keep knocking on doors. When you have something good, sooner or later you'll be getting more orders than you can handle.

PP: It's been said that you actually make the most money from your cakes by selling them to your private customers. Is that true?

SC: Yes, it is; there's no middle man that way. Let me explain to you how it works. I also bake my carrot cakes into small loaves. Each carrot loaf is about six inches long, about three inches wide and runs about three inches deep. Now I use one complete recipe at a cost to me of $2.65—like I mentioned before—and from that I can get four small loaves. I can sell each of those loaves privately for $2.50; that's $10 for the 4 of them. That's my best mark-up of all. Sometimes though, I would sell the loaves right to a gourmet shop, but they only pay $1.50 for each of them, for a total of $6 for four of them. So I do less well that way. You always make more when you sell direct to your own private customers. Selling to the gourmet shops is always a steady business. You get a certain amount of orders every week and you know you can count on them. Private orders are a little more unpredictable.

PP: How do you go about getting private orders?

SC: Well, living in a high-rise building in New York City, it calls for a little ingenuity. First you have some 500 flyers made, telling about your specialty and giving your phone number. You distribute these flyers to shopkeepers in the area and little by little, you start to hear from people. I take their orders and then leave the cakes with my door-man in the building. The people come by, pick up their cakes and leave the money with him at the same time. He turns the money over to me. I make sure, of course, to give him a very nice tip at Christmas time.

PP: It seems to work out pretty well. Selling private-ly gives the biggest return to you.

SC: Yes, it does. But as I said before, selling privately is a bit more fickle than the steady orders you get every week from stores. But also, once you build up a steady list of private customers who order each week, you'll do well go-ing with that approach. The whole idea is to give yourself as many opportunities as possible. In going into this busi-ness, a woman must take into consideration the area where she lives and what type of customer is available to her *in* that area. The best situation is to have all three sales opportunities available to you: (1) restaurants, (2) gourmet food shops, and (3) private customers. And al-ways you have to consider how much it costs you to reach the people who would buy your product. The cost of do-ing business is a very important consideration.

PP: Talking about costs, we'd like to know about how you go about doing your shopping. Obvious-ly, it's important to keep your costs down, and that's not so easy today. What's your approach?

SC: Well, I'm always going from one store to another and see-ing where I get my best buys. Supermarkets are always having "specials" and that's what you have to keep look-ing for. Also, I believe in buying what's called "no-name" brands. For example, I'm always buying chocolate for my chocolate cakes. Well, I've found that the difference in buying a brand name like Baker's as opposed to the "no-name" brand at the A&P is a dollar—that's a big difference on just one item. Then there's something else I do to keep costs down. I have a *barter* arrangement with some local stores.

PP: **That sounds interesting. How does that work?**

SC: I shop at a local fruit and vegetable store run by these real nice Korean people. They have eggs and milk as well as fruits and vegetables. Well, they give me their wholesale prices—just what it costs them—on the eggs and carrots I buy for my carrot cakes. In turn, because the family there enjoys eating my carrot cakes, I sell my cakes to them at just what it costs me to bake them. I make no profit on the sale to them. So it's like "bartering" with just a little cash thrown in. A good barter is when both people are satisfied with the deal. Also, one of the restaurants I sell my cakes to sells me nuts and cinnamon at the price *he* pays for them from *his* wholesaler. So, all in all, you have to look for all the different opportunities that are around in order to keep your costs down.

PP: **What are your ideas about making your business grow? Do you expect to expand beyond working from your own kitchen? Please tell our readers your feelings on this subject.**

SC: Well, if I wanted to go into this business on a larger scale, then I would need to have a partner. I would enter into what I would call a business marriage. I have seen it in business and it works beautifully. Frankly, I've yet to *meet* that person and therefore I've kept on the small scale that I am because you can lose if you try to expand and you're not sure of your partner. Money isn't my problem because I've had two different people offer to set me up in business. They met me, spoke to me, and afterwards offered to back me to open a store. But I don't want to do it *alone*. You really *can't* do it alone; you need someone to share the responsibility. And I haven't yet found that person.

PP: If you did find the right person to work with, and you had the financial backing you needed, what type of store would you open? Would this be a complete gourmet food shop, one with all the fancy specialties?

SC: Yes, that would be correct. It would have to be a first-rate gourmet shop or you don't even bother to start it. You and your partner *both* have to have excellent cooking and baking skills, and even besides that, you have to know excellent people to hire when you get real busy.

PP: It sounds like a big responsibility, all right.

SC: It is, but mind you, I don't want to put off any of your readers. It can be a *very* lucrative business. Despite the talk of tight money these days, there are a lot of people earning excellent salaries and it's nothing for them to walk into a gourmet food store and spend $25–$35 on just a few items that will only take them through one dinner that evening. And that's just for *one couple!* In New York City today, you find husbands and wives *both* working, and during the week when they're often too tired to go out for dinner, she'll stop by a nice store and pick up dinner. It's usually delicious and always ready to eat. So, there's a lot of money to be made in this business.

PP: What are some of the things you have to be careful of when you're looking around for a store to open?

SC: *Rent* is usually your biggest headache when it comes to figuring out your overhead. Here in New York City, it's nothing to have to pay $2,000 a month, or about $25,000 a year, in rent alone. And that would be for a small store and not in a particularly fancy location. Just for a store in one of the older neighborhoods. And then you have to worry if the landlord is going to *double* your rent when your lease comes up for renewal. You have to think about these things.

PP: It sounds really frightening.

SC: No. . . . I just want to point out these facts. You can *still* come out way ahead in the business. Some gourmet food stores easily make several hundred thousand dollars a year. The business takes in that much. You just have to look at both sides of the picture. For your readers who might consider going into the gourmet food shop business, the most *important* fact to consider is: is the area *affluent* enough to afford what you make and is it affluent enough to afford several gourmet shops—because if you'll do well, you can expect competition!

PP: How does someone check up on these things?

SC: There are many ways. One way is simply looking around the area and seeing the quality of the homes and apartments that people live in. The more upper-scale the community, the better chance you have to succeed. People have to have the purchasing power to be able to buy the fancy dishes you're going to make. That's the first thing to consider. Another thing to do is to check your local Chamber of Commerce. What types of businesses and people have been coming into your area, and what types have been going out? Just get a good picture of the future of your community before going into this business.

PP: We've heard that you've also catered dinner parties. Could you tell us about the catering business? It seems that some of our readers might consider that business instead of opening up a retail food shop. What are some of the pluses and minuses of the catering business?

SC: Well, a big plus is that you're not saddled with the responsibility of a store. The big minus is—it sure is *hard work!* A gourmet shop is hard work, I don't mean to imply differently. But at least, after the customers make their purchase in your store, that's it. But in catering, here's the way it's done. At least it's the way *I* do it. I usually work with two delightful friends of mine—Harry and Ken. We all met when we studied at New York Community College in Brooklyn. When we cater, we call ourselves "The Broccoli Bunch!"

PP: We happen to love broccoli *ourselves!*

SC: Good, so do we! (Laughs.) Anyway, first we would visit the home or apartment of the people we'd be catering to. Is their stove working okay? Do they have chafing dishes? A food processor? Microwave oven? You must know what you would have to bring. Then you'd discuss a menu with them—and I'll get back to that in a moment to talk about prices—and then Harry, Ken, and I would combine our kitchens in order to prepare what we needed, then get everything over to them. We'd serve the hors d'oeuvre, I'd act as hostess, then we'd clean up everything *after* dinner—even stack the dishes in the dishwasher, take 'em out, and leave the place *spotless* before we left for home. And, taking everything with us that we brought. No hostess likes anyone coming back the next day to clean up or pick up! So, all that takes *work!*

PP: It sounds it. How do you make it all worthwhile? What do you charge to cater these dinner parties?

SC: Not enough! (Laughs.) Seriously, we have been guilty of not charging enough. Sometimes I think that's a drawback of mine. I—along with Ken and Harry—have such a *good* time at these parties, that sometimes we do them because we just enjoy being around people who are enjoying our food. Maybe that doesn't sound too business-like, but it's the truth.

PP: We can understand that. Making money is the most important reason for going into this business, but you can't beat that extra bit of satisfaction you get when you see people enjoying what it takes so long to prepare. We sympathize with you fully. But now let's get back to money!

SC: (Laughs.) Okay, we should, because your readers should know about it. First, arrive at a *menu* to propose to a host or hostess. Have a few entrées in mind that you and your partner are equipped to prepare. For example, a dinner featuring a chicken dish as the main entrée would come to about $20 to $25 a person; a beef or lobster entrée would go up to $35 per person.

PP: Could you give us the details of a dinner? Let's say the hostess ordered beef as the entrée. What would the entire dinner consist of?

SC: We might feature a Beef Wellington. Of course we'd have vegetables with it plus a salad. Depending on the time of year, some might want to have a soup before the entrée. Then I'd also prepare at least two desserts and also serve a very satisfying coffee at the end. Mind you, before all this, we'd be serving hors d'oeuvre: raw vegetables with a delicious dip; little bourbon meatballs; phyllo dough with ham filling; tiny individual quiche pies—we'd have 8 to 10 different hors d'oeuvre, all before dinner.

PP: It's quite a production.

SC: It really is, but it has to be done right. Everything has to be prepared beautifully and served the same way. We got more business by "word-of-mouth." People would meet us at parties and when *they* would give a party, they'd call us.

PP: At about $35 or so per person, is it still a good buy for the host or hostess?

SC: Sure it is, figure it out for yourself. We can't speak for the rest of the country, but here in New York, if you'd want to throw a fine dinner party and went to a really good restaurant, you'd pay $50 a person at least. And your guests have to worry about parking their car and all that. Doing it in your own home has a special quality that can't be matched by any restaurant. I don't care how fancy a restaurant is, if your waiter decides he's going to be mean that night, you're going to have a miserable time of it. I, along with Ken and Harry, really have such a good time catering a party, the guests seem to enjoy themselves right along with us.

PP: Would you recommend the catering business to our readers?

SC: Yes, I would, but with these reservations: (1) As I said before, *don't* try to do it alone, you'll need help. (2) You and those with you really need to have fine cooking and baking skills. Remember, you're competing against *restaurants* so you must prepare first-rate dishes. And (3) be prepared to work hard. All in all, I feel that a woman should be in business for a year or two, first selling one or two of her specialties, before she goes into the catering business. When you're in the catering business, you're really running a business, so first, get your feet wet by starting off small.

PP: But it also seems that you can profit from your kitchen without ever getting into the catering business. Does that still hold true?

SC: Of course it does. With just baking one or two "specialty" cakes, you can do very well. What I mean is very rich and luxurious cakes. Later in the chapter I'm giving your readers the recipe to my "Chocolate Whiskey" cake. It's a very good seller and very profitable. I sell that to gourmet shops for $9.50, and I've sold it to private customers for

$12.50. Now I'll tell you a little secret: I've seen a rich, dense chocolate cake—just 8″ around and only an inch high—sell in a gourmet shop for *$30!* It wasn't one of my cakes, but I've seen it.

PP: People would buy a small chocolate cake like that for $30?

SC: I know it sounds crazy but I've seen it happen. And more than once. I could see paying $30 for a *wedding* cake but not a small chocolate cake.

PP: Then how could a store charge that much money and get it?

SC: Because some gourmet food stores go after a very rich clientele. These stores manage to get a write-up in the local paper; they start to get a very fancy image and they see to it that their prices are pushed up over other stores. Believe it or not, there are lots of people who *prefer* paying more. It makes them feel that they're really buying something *special!* A store gets a certain "snob" appeal and some people enjoy shopping there. I tell this to your readers so they can be aware of certain things. And one thing is: DON'T BE SHY! Don't be shy about asking *good prices* for what you make. It's all up to you. If you sell yourself cheaply, nobody is going to tell you to charge more. They're delighted. Only *you* can get the price you're worth. I'm not suggesting that you *rip off* your customers, but you're in this business to make a *profit!* The first step is to make the finest product you can, whether it's a cookie or a full course dinner. Then take the attitude: *"I'm good and I'm worth a lot!"* Sure, you always have to judge what the traffic will bear, but instead of starting out *cheap,* start out *expensive.* It's always easier to come down than to go up!

PP: We get the impression that with the baking and catering you do you haven't been charging enough. Would that be correct to say?

SC: Yes, it would, I admit it. But I guess it has to do with my background. I was always so shy about money; after all, we had so little of it when we were growing up. And I'd see my mother in the catering business work so *hard* for it. I guess a lot of it rubbed off on me.

PP: **Your mother sounds like a remarkable woman.**

SC: Oh, she was very special. You know, I want to pass along a certain trick she taught me. When I started in this business I'd run across a new recipe that I found fascinating but which threw me because it seemed so complicated. The first time that happened to me, I called home frantic, and she said, "Sylvia, you must read a recipe *three* times before you can make it. Read it the first time, just to *read* it. Now read it a second time because now you're going to go out to *buy* what you see on the recipe. When you come home, line up all the ingredients in front of you and now read the recipe—line by line—for the *third* time. It's with the third reading that you're into making that recipe. To use her words, she'd say, "The first is for readin,' the second is for buyin', and the third is for doin'."

PP: **What seems to come through with your mother's advice is "We're better than we think we are."**

SC: Of course. A woman who is going into this business should realize she's *not* exactly coming in as a *stranger!* Depending on her age, a woman has spent a good part of her life in the kitchen *already!* She has a lot of experience there. She doesn't have to be shy about anything. She should be proud of her past, and now make it pay off for the future! Today, to make ends meet, there are a whole lot of women going back to work in an office. *They* have a right to be shy; after all, it's been *years* since they've had to do that kind of work. I think if your readers would pause and think about that, they'd feel very confident about their future as "Kitchen Ladies."

PP: You've been kind enough to tell our readers about how they might earn money selling to gourmet shops and restaurants and catering meals, too. Could we impose on you just to talk about one more possible way to make money in this business? We're talking about a woman eventually opening up a little cooking school and taking in students.

SC: Oh sure, that could be a wonderful business! I'm glad that earlier on in this book, you've provided women with a list of cooking schools all over the country. Because, if a woman is *serious* about starting cooking classes for students, she should first become a student *herself*. It's an expensive investment all right, but a necessary one. Find the very best school you can afford and go there. Many of these schools expect many of their students to eventually go out and open their *own* schools. It's just passing on a tradition. And it's a very proud tradition.

PP: **If a woman wanted to open her own school, what could she charge?**

SC: Well, there are various arrangements. Some classes run for a few weeks, others are one-day classes—they're all different.

PP: **But give us an idea of say, a single day, and having a class that went on for 3 or 4 hours.**

SC: You could charge $25 per student, and depending on the size of your kitchen, have up to 10 students for the day. You earn $250 for the day. I myself enjoy the classes that let the students participate in the making of the foods. Wine is usually served and at the end of the day, everyone sits down together to enjoy what they've made. Cooking classes have a special feeling about them. People come together to learn, share, and enjoy. Food has that special quality to do that. And there's a lot of laughs in a class. When you're working with food, you're having *fun!* You really are. You're meeting people who have the same interests as you, and it creates a special kind of atmosphere. Most people who go to cooking classes don't intend to open up a school, they're just there because they love good food and they want to learn how to prepare it better. But if one of your readers wants to make a business out of it, then go right ahead. As I've said, others have done it so why not *you!*

PP: We happen to know that you're especially good in teaching *children* how to cook. Would you tell us something about that?

SC: Well, that's a special joy of mine. It all goes back to the feelings I had watching my mother in the kitchen. I really want to urge women today to encourage their kids to get into the kitchen with them. And not just girls, boys as well. After all, the top chefs are men. Food is so basic and honest that when you get young people involved in the preparation of meals, they get a certain *perspective* on life that they wouldn't get ordinarily. I'm talking about giving children an understanding about fowl, about fish, about beef, and breads, fruits, vegetables. Together with your child, take something from *scratch*—a dish that requires some skills—and *share* in making it. All of this teaches young people *patience;* it teaches them *discipline, measurement, care,* and *concern.* All of this comes out of the working experience in the kitchen. And then beyond that, they get a sense of *accomplishment!* They helped create something, and they did it with their own hands. When I've done this with children, you should see the smile that comes over their faces.

PP: Well, Sylvia, as you can see, there's a smile on our faces. And just from talking with you. It's been such a positive experience for us, and we sure hope it's been that way for our readers. Ev-

erything you've said has been from your heart—
we know it, we feel it. I'm sure our readers will
profit from what you've been telling us. We want
to thank you for sharing your experiences with
us.

SC: Well, it's been my pleasure. And it's also going to be my
pleasure to now give your readers my recipes. They've
been successful and profitable for me and I hope they'll
prove the same to anyone who wants to go ahead and use
them. They now become yours to use. I do want to give a
few words of caution, and that regards the *costs* of ingredients I have listed. Everyone should understand that
there's *no way* these costs will *stay* that way. Prices are
only going to go one way—*up!* The prices I list are what I
pay here in New York City, and this is mid-April, 1981.
As prices increase, I urge women to *pass along* those increases to her customers. After all, that's been happening
to us every day of our lives. I just wanted to make that
point so there's no misunderstanding later on.

PP: **It just goes to prove that in addition to being a
very sweet and sincere woman, you're also very
*concerned.***

SC: I'm just trying to help as much as I can.

PP: **And that's been a whole lot. Thank you.**

Sylvia Caudell's Recipes

Carrot Cake

A spicy, moist, and delicious cake. You'll need an electric mixer.

    2 cups plain flour
    1 teaspoon baking powder
    1 teaspoon baking soda

    1 teaspoon salt
    2 teaspoons ground cinnamon
    2 cups ground or grated carrots (3 large carrots)
    4 eggs
    1 cup white sugar & 1 cup brown sugar
 1⅓ cups vegetable oil (not olive oil)
    1 cup chopped walnuts or pecans

Adjust oven rack halfway from the bottom of oven. Preheat oven to 350 degrees. Butter an 8- to 10-cup capacity tube pan. Dust it very lightly with flour, shaking off excess. Sift together flour, baking powder, baking soda, salt, and cinnamon and set aside.

Wash the carrots thoroughly—it is not necessary to peel them. If you have a food processor, do use it. If you don't, grate the carrots finely on a grater. Pack down into a measuring cup until you have 2 cups.

Beat eggs lightly just to mix. Add both white and brown sugars. Slowly beat in the oil. Stir in the grated carrots. Add sifted dry ingredients and mix until thoroughly blended. Scrape the sides of the bowl with a rubber spatula. Stir in the nuts.

Pour into prepared pan. Shake gently to level. Bake for 45 minutes or until a cake tester comes out dry. Remove from oven. Cool in pan on a rack for 10 minutes.

Cost of this recipe: $2.50–$3.00

YIELD: *1 tube cake (10 inches)*
            or
      4 small cakes (6" x 3")
            or
      2 loaf pans (8" x 4")

Selling Price: 3 times your cost (to private customers)*
                 2 times your cost (to stores/restaurants)*
* Adjust (higher or lower) depending on what the traffic will bear.

Banana Walnut Cake

- 2 cups flour
- 1 teaspoon baking powder
- 1 teaspoon baking soda
- ½ teaspoon salt
- 1 pound (3 small) ripe bananas, peeled and mashed
- 1 stick (¼ pound) butter (at room temperature)
- 1½ cups sugar
- 2 eggs
- ½ cup milk
- 1 teaspoon vanilla
- 1 cup walnuts

Preheat oven to 350 degrees. Grease or line with parchment paper a 10-inch cake pan or 4 small (6 x 3-inch) pans.

Measure flour, baking powder, soda, and salt—set aside. Peel and mash bananas.

Cream butter and add sugar. Add one egg at a time. Slowly pour in flour mixture and milk. Stop and scrape bowl. Add mashed bananas and beat 20 seconds. Fold in vanilla and ½ cup nuts.

Pour mixture into prepared pans and sprinkle ½ cup nuts on top of batter. Bake about 40 minutes for small pans and longer for large pan.

Remove the golden cakes to rack for cooling.

Package cakes and wrap in plastic film.

Cost of this recipe: about $2.25

YIELD: *1 large cake (10 inches)*
            or
      4 small cakes (6" x 3")

Selling Price: 3 times your cost (to private customers)*
                  2 times your cost (to stores/restaurants)*
* Adjust (higher or lower) depending on what the traffic will bear.

Brownies

  1 cup butter (room temperature)
  4 ounces (4 squares) unsweetened chocolate
1¾ cups sugar
  3 eggs
¾ cup flour
¼ teaspoon salt
  1 teaspoon vanilla
  1 cup walnuts

Preheat oven to 350 degrees. If you have parchment paper, cut a piece to fit a 13 x 9 x 2 inch pan or grease the pan if no paper is available.

Melt ½ cup of butter with chocolate in top of double boiler; cool. Add remaining butter and sugar to mixing bowl and cream for 2 minutes. Stop and scrape bowl. Add eggs, one at a time, beating 20 seconds after each one. Add flour and salt and mix until well blended.

Add melted butter-chocolate mixture, and beat for 30 seconds. Add vanilla.

Pour mixture into pan. Sprinkle nuts on top.

Bake for 30 minutes. Remove pan from oven and cool on rack for an hour.

Cost of this recipe: $2.00

YIELD: *1 dozen large brownies*
        or
   2 dozen small brownies

Selling Price: 4 times your cost. Sell 13 x 9 x 2 inch piece to stores and/or restaurants. (They cut the brownies into small or large pieces as they see fit.)

Orange Liqueur Cake

3½ cups cake flour
 2 teaspoons baking soda
 ½ teaspoon salt
 2 teaspoons of fresh grated orange rind
 1 stick butter (soft)
 ½ cup Crisco
1½ cups sugar
 4 eggs
1½ cups buttermilk
 1 cup chopped walnuts
 ¾ cup raisins (Pour warm water over raisins for 10
     minutes, drain. Dry on paper towel.)

Topping

 ½ cup fresh orange juice
 3 tablespoons of Triple Sec (cheaper than Grand
     Marnier)

Adjust oven rack halfway from the bottom of oven. Preheat
oven to 350 degrees. Grease an 8-inch tube pan.

Measure flour, soda, and salt and set aside.

Grate the rind of one orange. Any left over can be kept in a
small glass jar in the refrigerator for several days.

Cream butter and Crisco. Add sugar.

Add one egg at a time until well mixed. Scrape the sides of the
bowl with a rubber spatula. Add flour mixture and buttermilk
slowly, but at the same time. Stir in walnuts and raisins. Add
grated orange rind.

Pour mixture into prepared pan. Shake gently to level pan.
Bake about 50 minutes or until the cake tester comes out dry.

After cake has been removed from oven, cool for 10 minutes
before pouring the topping over the cake. Remove cake from
pan.

Cost of this recipe: $2.50–$3.00

YIELD: *5 small loaves (6" x 3")*

Selling Price: 3 times your cost (to private customers)*

2 times your cost (to stores/restaurants)*

*Adjust (higher or lower) depending on what the traffic will bear.

Sylvia's Chocolate Whiskey Cake

2 ounces whiskey
2 ounces raisins
¼ pound butter or margarine
6 ounces sweetened chocolate
3 eggs (room temperature)
⅔ cup sugar
¾ cup ground or finely chopped almonds or walnuts
3 tablespoons of self-rising flour

Pour whiskey over raisins and set aside for an hour or longer.

Melt butter and chocolate in top of a small double boiler over moderate heat. After melting, remove top of double boiler from heat and set aside to cool (½ hour).

Adjust rack ⅓ from the bottom of the oven. Preheat oven to 360 degrees. Butter an 8 x 2 inch round pan.

Separate the yolks from the whites.

With a mixer, beat egg yolks. Add sugar. Pour in melted chocolate mixture and mix for 1 minute. Add ground nuts and flour and mix for a minute. Remove from mixer. Scrape sides of bowl with rubber spatula. Blend in the raisin-whiskey mixture and set aside while you beat the egg whites.

Egg whites may be beaten with an electric mixer, a rotary egg beater, or a 4 inch balloon-type wire whisk. Both the bowl and beater must be perfectly clean and dry. Use a shallow mixing bowl to beat 3 egg whites. Beat the whites until you get a peak. Immediately fold whites into chocolate mixture. Pour batter into prepared pan.

Bake 25 minutes.

Remove cake from oven and cool in pan for 2 hours. Remove cake from pan onto a cake plate.

You may serve with or without an icing.

Icing

2 ounces sweetened chocolate
3 tablespoons butter

Melt butter and chocolate in the top of a double boiler over moderate heat. Remove top of double boiler from heat and cool. Pour chocolate over cake. Place in refrigerator for 3 hours before cutting.

Cost of this recipe: $3.00–$3.25

YIELD: *1 chocolate cake (8 inches round by 2 inches deep)*

Selling Price: 4 times your cost (to private customers)*
                     3 times your cost (to stores/restaurants)*
* Adjust (higher or lower) depending on what the traffic will bear.

Chapter 20
There's No Telling How Far You Can Go— Famous True-Life Success Stories

Never Believe
a Dream Can't Come True

America is *still* the land of opportunity! It doesn't matter that prices keep rising and that people seem pessimistic about the future. These are things we cannot change, only hope that they will improve. All we can do is to be morally correct and fair to all those we come in contact with. Then, as far as we are personally concerned, we have to *use* ourselves. You get out of this life what you put into it. This nation is filled with a countless number of people who started out with nothing, but who developed and concentrated on a single particular skill. From that they grew to fame, fortune and, even more importantly, a tremendous sense of accomplishment: "I did it; by God, I did it!" All you need is an idea, that's the *1%* inspiration. Then you have to have the follow-through to be successful—that's the *99%* perspiration! We want to tell you about a few people who, like yourself, started in a kitchen. Today, they are known throughout the nation. We've seen them on TV or read about them in newspapers or magazines. We thought we'd pass along a brief story about each of them.

The Story of McDonald's

Maurice and Richard McDonald thought that if cheap but wholesome food could be cooked fast with a no-frills service, customers would visit their small hamburger shop in northern California more often. They took the basic hamburger, and added some frills to *it* instead of the decor and service. Soon they had more customers than they could handle. A paper-cup salesman named Ray Kroc saw the operation and bought the rights to franchise the hamburger shop. The result is *McDonald's,* and the rest is history. Spread all across the nation, McDonald's became the start of the fast-food industry in America. They gross over *$1 billion a year in sales.* But let's examine the ingredients of their success. There are two reasons: (1) They didn't sell a hamburger, they sold a *"production."* Anyone can make a hamburger, and slap it on a bun, but McDonald's added things that were *unique.* (2) The McDonald brothers felt that, when it came to eating out, most folks really didn't like the *uncertainty* of what to choose from a menu. People wanted to eat something delicious and be able to *count* on it every time they went into the restaurant. They also wanted to be able to "get in and get out." Were the McDonald brothers ever right!

The Story of Julia Child

Look at the case of Julia Child. You see her on TV all over the country. She's a pleasant-looking woman, but by no means a great beauty. But she radiates a terrific confidence that can only come from being sure of oneself. This woman, after World War II, went to a cooking school in Paris and she learned the art of French cooking. She eventually started on a small TV station to demonstrate her skill, and she went on to national fame. Could that happen to *you*? Of course it could! Don't say it's impossible. What if you also have a great skill in the kitchen? So you didn't go to a fancy French cooking school; it doesn't matter. You might get written up in a local newspaper; you might get a call from a TV station in your area. Who knows? *All things are possible!*

The Story of Kentucky Fried Chicken

Some people say, "I'm too old to start anything now." Well, we saw a man on a TV talk show who said, "I was 65 years old, and we were living on our Social Security check of $105 when I got started!" This man was running a small restaurant in Corbin, Kentucky, when, at the age of 60, he learned that the highway that led drivers to his restaurant would soon become obsolete. A new interstate highway was being built seven miles from his location. Business soon dwindled to next to nothing. He struggled on for five years, but knew he couldn't go on.

He did have tremendous belief in the appeal of his fried chicken. His recipe had a special seasoning blend to it that resulted in a crunchy, lip-smacking taste that people really loved. So, this 65-year-old man piled his chicken-frying equipment and samples of his seasoning blend into his beat-up car. Then he went to restaurant after restaurant, signing franchise contracts with those owners who felt his fried chicken was really special. The man's name? Harland Sanders: you knew him as Colonel Sanders! He sold his company in 1971 for millions of dollars.

He's gone now, but he lived past 90 years of age. And, to his great satisfaction, he lived to see his restaurants achieve enormous fame. So much for any person who feels he or she is too old to start to earn a fortune! If you have a specialty that's different and delicious, age makes no difference. You're never too old to get rich!

The Unusual Story of Pizza Hut

We'll tell you a little story we read in a national magazine. It started in Kansas, but got its inspiration in Italy. That was in 1958. In 1977, the three men who were the original partners sold the business for *$7 million!* They started with *$600!* Their stores are called *Pizza Hut.* Of course you've heard of them. But they started, as one of the owners admitted, "with more guts than brains!"

Dan and Frank Carney borrowed $600 from their mother to open their first pizza store in Wichita, Kansas—and they had never seen or tasted pizza! They opened the store because the woman who owned the building where the store was located *read* an article about this Italian treat in the *Saturday Evening Post.* She suggested to the brothers, "Why not open a pizza store in my building?"

The Carney brothers thought they'd give it a try. Maybe it would catch on. By chance, a fellow happened to come into their store, curious because he had experience as a pizza chef and he wondered if he could work there part-time. The Carney brothers were delighted and the three of them joined together. They called their store *Pizza Hut,* and theirs is a story of being in the right place at the right time with the right product.

Pizza parlors were found on the east and west coasts, but none in mid-America. Most of the other pizza restaurants in existence at that time were single stores with no thought of *franchising.* But the fellows in *Pizza Hut* had the wisdom to see that the formula in *their* pizza parlor could be duplicated, based on their equipment, their ingredients, and their management techniques. They knew that the great appeal of pizza would exist everywhere. Pizza is tasty, filling, and inexpensive! That's an ideal trio for a successful fast-food franchise. The Carney brothers have the bank account to prove it!

Special Contest Offer

Take advantage of our offer and enter the "Buy My Recipe" contest. YOU'LL WIN $25 FOR ONE RECIPE—$50 FOR TWO! Just write out your name and address, using the coupon on the back flap of the book jacket. (You're also free to use a separate piece of paper for your name and address.) In addition, on a *separate* sheet of paper (or two), clearly write out the details of the recipe(s) you want to submit for the contest.

We're looking for any "specialty" that you've created and are particularly proud of. It could be a HIGH CALORIE or LOW CALORIE winner: an appetizer or soup; a salad or entree; a side dish or dessert. Beverages, too. *Anything* from A to Z!

We're doing this because we're convinced that the best recipes are *yet* to be found. Just send us one or two of your own. If we decide to print either or both of them in any future publication, we'll notify you by mail and include a check for $25 or $50. (All recipes not used cannot be returned, and the decision of our judges will be final.) So why not try to pick up some ready cash? It'll only cost you a stamp!

Pantry Press
Centerville, Cape Cod
Massachusetts 02632

Extra Pages for Your Recipes

My Recipe

My Recipe

My Recipe